How to Be Useful

How to
Be Useful

»» **A Beginner's Guide to Not Hating Work**

Megan Hustad

Houghton Mifflin Company

BOSTON • NEW YORK • 2008

For information about permission to reproduce selections from
this book, write to Permissions, Houghton Mifflin Company,
215 Park Avenue South, New York, New York 10003.

www.houghtonmifflinbooks.com

Library of Congress Cataloging-in-Publication Data
Hustad, Megan.
   How to be useful : a beginner's guide to not hating work
/ Megan Hustad.
      p. cm.
   Includes bibliographical references and index.
   ISBN-13: 978-0-618-71350-9
   ISBN-10: 0-618-71350-6
   1. Success in business. 2. Career development. 3. Job satisfaction.
4. Success. I. Title.
   HF5386.H97 2008
   650.1—dc22   2007038413

Book design by Melissa Lotfy

Printed in the United States of America

MP 10 9 8 7 6 5 4 3 2 1

Selections from *Sex and the Single Girl* and *Sex and the Office* appear
courtesy of Helen Gurley Brown.

Excerpt from *The Office*, series 1, episode 3, written by Ricky Gervais
and Stephen Merchant. The author gratefully acknowledges permission
to reprint.

AUTHOR'S NOTE
This book includes many anecdotes from people kind enough to share
their impressions and experiences with me. Names of individuals, some
job descriptions, genders, most places of residence, and occasionally
company names have been changed to disguise those who violated non-
disclosure agreements and/or their better judgment.

for Amy

When the individual does move into a new position in society and obtains a new part to perform, he is not likely to be told in full detail how to conduct himself.

—ERVING GOFFMAN,
The Presentation of Self in Everyday Life

The unvarnished truth is almost all of the people you meet feel themselves superior to you in some way, and a sure way to their hearts is to let them realize in some subtle way that you recognize their importance, and recognize it sincerely.

—DALE CARNEGIE,
How to Win Friends and Influence People

There's just no point in behaving like a shit.

—KEIRA KNIGHTLEY,
as quoted in *Elle* magazine

Contents

Introduction

WHAT'S IT LIKE to work in an office? It's difficult to get excited about, for one. The prospect of cubicles, giving your day over to a corporation, having to tell some coworker named Dan that he's got cream cheese on his chin—none of this sounds appealing. The benefits of working 9 to 5 also seem more meager than they have in the past. That is, meager compared to the poolside cocktails bonanza some people are enjoying. Somewhere between your morning shower and sinking into your IKEA chair, you're bound to be reminded—by a magazine cover, or a reference to *Filthy Rich: Cattle Drive*—of the hordes of celebutards getting paid to do nothing, or to DJ, or to just be mildly clever.

Then there's the problem that job descriptions often fail to communicate the many nuances of being a corporate underling, so your expectations get skewed. Ben, a trainee architect at a Washington, D.C., commercial real estate firm, had an illuminating episode his first week on the job. Day three, his boss asked him to get rid of some empty cardboard boxes from an Amazon.com shipment. These boxes had been cluttering up the hallway for the better half of two weeks and she just wanted them gone. So Ben called the downstairs switchboard because his boss had given no instructions and he had no idea whom to talk to about this. He got nowhere. Later that afternoon, with the problem still unsolved, Ben poked his head into his boss's office to say that he'd been as yet unsuccessful in finding someone to come collect them. She examined him for a few seconds before speaking. "You," she said slowly. "The person who throws away boxes here is *you.*"

No one had informed Ben that in addition to drafting and designing, he was responsible for minor housekeeping duties. Nor had he given much thought to office hierarchies, a superior's moods and attitudes, organizational politics, strategy, positioning, or how to cope with the fact that this boss character —practically a stranger—suddenly had all this power over you, and who now—maybe, hard to tell—didn't even like you. That young people aren't prepared for workplace realities is something a number of commentators have picked up on lately, and the list of reasons they haul out to explain this unpreparedness has become fairly familiar: indulgent '80s and '90s parenting practices, MySpace, a culture that prizes self-expression *über alles*, and an educational system that hasn't kept pace with global standards. Fewer kids get jobs in high school and college now, too. Teen labor-force participation rates are falling, and some companies are even reporting that they'd rather hire a senior citizen than a younger worker, because older folks are doing the same jobs better.* Then there's the inconvenient truth that four years of college actually breeds many habits that are completely at odds with the demands of most offices. The more expensive your education, the more time you've spent luxuriating in the highbrow, chasing idiosyncratic intellectual fascinations down rabbit holes, and watching subtitled films. You've made your own schedule and surrounded yourself with people who dressed, acted, and thought very much like you. All this has

---

* Milt Freudenheim, "More Help Wanted: Older Workers Please Apply," *New York Times* (March 23, 2005).

led the author Mel Levine (*Ready or Not, Here Life Comes*) to claim that recent graduates generally "fail to identify at all with the world of adults." One television executive I spoke to had this to say about the entry-level assistants that swung through her firm's revolving doors: "They either get it, or they just don't get it. And increasingly, they just don't get it."

From what I've seen, it's not that young people enter the office empty-headed. Far from it. It's that once they get over the initial shock of stooping to round up cardboard boxes, they sincerely believe their hard work and sparkling intellect will be sufficient ballast to weather any storms and succeed. They think only lazy or incompetent people get bypassed for promotion, neglected, or called into the corner office and told to *please have a seat for the "It's not working out, is it?"* talk. Though I've personally witnessed this faith in pure diligence, though I embraced it myself when I got out of college (and for too long afterwards), I didn't know — couldn't have known — how prevalent it is. But according to a recent survey published by the Network on Transitions to Adulthood, more young people in 1997 believed that "hard work" was the ticket to success than did in 1985, even in 1973.* In other words, my generation has clung more tightly to the notion of big rewards through hard work than our parents ever did.

This is pretty amazing. How is it that young people today, people who aren't naive about *anything else,* can be so naive about making a living? Anyone who has spent any time at all in the corporate arena can tell you that diligence does not write the checks. I'm going to have to take a guess here — because how you'd study the fine shadings of this particular attitude I don't know — but I think the problem is that this naiveté is cou-

---

* Tom Smith, "Generation Gaps in Attitudes and Values from the 1970s to the 1990s." Compiled from the General Social Surveys of the National Opinion Research Center, University of Chicago. Published in *On the Frontier of Adulthood,* eds. Richard A. Settersten Jr., Frank F. Furstenberg Jr., and Rubén G. Rumbaut (Chicago: The University of Chicago Press, 2005).

pled with a potent cynicism about careers and careerism. Of course, looking askance at eager go-getters is nothing new. This generation's cynicism is different from earlier strains of job en-nui, however, because as one twenty-eight-year-old told me, it infects you "before you even walk in the front door." For the 1950s Organization Man, cynical is what you became when you realized that the boss's suck-up son-in-law was going to get that promotion instead of you. It's what happened to you *after* big dreams got kicked down the sidewalk. Now you get spoon-fed cranked-up sardonic posturing every time you turn on the tele-vision. My generation, perhaps duly exhausted by being so ag-gressively marketed to our entire lives, has learned to follow any earnest expression of enthusiasm with "*Nooo,* I'm being sincere" because it will usually automatically be assumed other-wise. I could use numerous cultural references to illustrate this point, but here's one that might do nicely: Gawker.com recently suggested *Ironic Detachment Is the New Giving a Shit* as a T-shirt slogan.

What this means for the office is that a chill creeps into the air whenever the subject of ambition comes up. Not long ago, Sarah, a former colleague of mine, landed a new job and was given the traditional perimeter tour of her new office. This meant fifteen minutes of stopping at every door and cubicle, and the requisite trading names, preliminaries, and *nice to meet you*'s. Later, over lunch with her tour guide, Sarah brought up one woman she couldn't get a good read on. "So . . . Heidi, the blonde? Tall? What's her story?" Her tour guide winced. "Heidi? Yeah, she's good, smart. Real ambitious, though." In the next month, four more people weighed in with the same assessment of Heidi, and every time, "She's ambitious" was inflected the way you might whisper, "She has hepatitis B." Hard to recall the par-ticulars of how it's transmitted, maybe, or what it does, exactly. You just know you should avoid intimate contact.

Earnest job ambition has indeed become unfashionable. "You just can't seem to want the things you want," Steven, a writing instructor, confessed to me. "It's not smiled upon." Steven's assessment was partly a function of where he'd previously worked—the hyper-snotty halls of glossy magazine publisher Condé Nast—and the arty leanings of the crowd he ran with. But with that phrase—*can't seem to want the things you want*—he put his finger on something significant, which is that this ironic detachment doesn't run deep. Of course young people want to do well. Of course they don't want their life choices to be severely constrained by lack of funds. Of course they'd like to see Rome. But they get pushed toward a mindset that privileges being cute and clever, plugging away, and uh, yeah, that's about it.

Which just reinforces ignorance about the office. The idea of studying the art of working was lost on us. My first career-track job was at Random House, and I distinctly remember how we editorial assistants stood clutching manuscripts in the lobby, waiting for the elevator, and proudly professing to anyone who asked that we were mostly interested in "literary fiction."* We had no time for business books or leadership development books and happily left them to those without style, imagination, or the critical skills we thought made us, history and English majors, so fascinating. We didn't work on Wall Street, or wear ties, so we didn't think of ourselves as being, as they say, "in business." After all, what could go wrong as long as we worked hard? How was it possible we didn't know everything we needed to know? It wasn't possible—we were quite sure of this.

Right under our noses, though, was about a century's worth of books that plainly and convincingly argued otherwise. There was a great deal we needed to know—about hierarchies, organizational politics, and how to deal with the fact that your boss maybe didn't even like you. There are shelves and shelves of books on how to channel ambition justly, how to speak distinctly, how to think more strategically, and how to pay closer attention

---

* Some of us would say "literary nonfiction," too, though to this day I'm not sure what that means.

so the world and its opportunities don't pass you by. Thousands of chapters that tell readers how to secure a financial future and perhaps grow wiser while they're at it. Millions of pages that tell us that hard work isn't going to cut it. Most of these books have perfectly straightforward titles — *How to Win Friends and Influence People,* for example — so they're not hard to spot. But we weren't moved to pick them up. Not only did we not have much interest in "success literature" (as some critics call it), but we studiously avoided it.

How this blasé posturing hurts people who have to work for a living has fascinated me for a while now. When I started my research for this book, and began polling friends and acquaintances on whether they'd read *How to Win Friends* or any similar book, the most common response was "Oh gosh, I'd be embarrassed to be seen in public with it." They regarded success literature as the exclusive reserve of ultraconservatives and finance majors, in other words. A handful *had* read these books, but only secretly. One guy I talked to recalled that as an awkward teenager, he had procured a copy of Larry King's *How to Talk to Anyone, Anytime, Anywhere,* hoping it might alleviate his silent suffering in social situations. He was so embarrassed by the book — even worried what his dad might think — that he handled it like porn and kept it under his bed.

Most people I drilled on this subject avoided success literature — which I'll continue to call it because I can't think of anything better — for "the obvious reasons." This phrase became a refrain; I kept hearing it in conversation after conversation. The "obvious reasons" for sidestepping these books were essentially threefold: They didn't have anything to say that anybody with a scrap of common sense didn't already know ("Have a firm handshake, or be more aggressive — who doesn't get that?"); they preyed on people's insecurities and were therefore exploitative ("Like diet pills"); and last but not least, these books were avoided because they were, so very often, so very poorly written. They were universally perceived to have a rah-rah, up-with-middle-management, dumbed-down huckster sensibility. Then there was the sheer boredom factor. Horatio Alger, rags to riches, up-by-your-bootstraps, you've come a long way, baby!, blah, blah, blah — it's the white noise of American culture and it registers on our consciousness like brushing our teeth registers on our consciousness. That is to say, it doesn't. Ironic detachment *is* the new giving a shit.

All these objections to reading these books I had anticipated, because they weren't that different from how I used to think myself. But I never expected to hear what a Los Angeles screenwriter told me: "I don't go there because every person's situation is so unique, and the context for the problems they're facing is so unique, that I just think . . . general prescriptions are basically bogus." I paused for a second when I heard this, over the phone. Had he read any of these books? No, he hadn't. ("The obvious reasons.") Remembering how I struggled mightily to understand what made bosses tick, and having seen so many friends and even competitors fret about making rent and staying late and coworkers named Dan and feeling trapped, all without turning into one of those "Me, bitter? I'm not bitter!" caricatures, I became more firmly convinced that sidestepping the Careers/Self-Improvement shelf was perhaps not a sign of our superior intellect.

Our cynicism really did make us more naive. The truth is that employees in Internet start-ups, the offices of *Vogue,* law firms, nonprofits, Kmart — pretty much any place where you trade a portion of your day for money — all face similar problems, and they're the problems people have been wrestling with for decades. The look, sound, and texture of these problems may be different, but human nature just doesn't change all that quickly. I've now had dozens of conversations with people about their experiences at work, hopes and plans for work, even their fears and misgivings about work, and I can assure you that *no one*'s experience is unique. And ignorance about organizational dynamics doesn't just result in funny-ha-ha slip-ups and blooper outtakes—though those are common enough. It leads to intelligent, well-educated, sometimes quite worldly individuals hitting their twenty-eighth, twenty-ninth, and thirtieth birthdays wondering why they don't have professional lives they're proud of.

It's difficult for me to summarize the fallout because it invariably devolves into glib snippets: So you get stuck in a cubicle for eight years? Gee, that's tough. Failing at the office sounds flaccid and beige; more YouTube skit, less Greek tragedy. The lived reality, though, is plenty heartbreaking.

"So are you one of those people who defines themselves by their job?" someone once asked me. The right answer was clearly no. No, I wasn't that boring, that lacking in compassion, that blind to the rich tapestry of human experience. But, I wondered, surely what you do for half your waking hours has some bearing on your life.* And then I wondered: Is it possible that middle-class young people have been suckered into adopting a cynical detachment that they can't afford? I mean *literally* cannot afford? The tenderhearted and creatively inclined most of all, because they tend to gravitate to industries where "people skills" make the most difference. Social mobility in the United States is on the decline, middle-class incomes are stagnant, and you can only lunge at the occasional zero percent introductory APR offer stuffed in your mailbox so often.

The book you hold in your hands aims to be a corrective

---

* Mind you, this same person was pretty conversant in stereotypes about certain occupations—most of us are. Wall Street Guy. Lawyer. Academic. Construction Worker. Graduate Student in English. Night Manager at Wendy's. Blogger. Express fashion stores even based a clothing line and marketing push on the idea that the "Editor" holds enduring fascination for mall-goers everywhere. (Full disclosure: I have three pairs of these pants.) At the same time, the contempt with which a roomful of creative types will speak of Bankers is something to behold; it is roundly assumed, *though none of the assembled has ever had a conversation with anyone in the financial sector that lasted longer than two minutes,* that Bankers are Assholes. The only thing that can reasonably be concluded from all this back and forth is that people are reluctant to be defined by their job when they feel their work doesn't represent their passions and capabilities—but are happy to define others by their job whenever it makes the world easier to understand.

to this strange, counterproductive loop of naiveté and cynicism. It's a crash course in success literature designed to help the tenderhearted and creative people I like so much to avoid these existential potholes. While it's fair to say I read *The 7 Habits of Highly Effective People* so you don't have to, I was also interested in finding a way to reclaim professional climbing for the smart and sensitive. I'd like my friends to stop scowling when they hear "She's ambitious." I'd like *everyone* to be more aware of what was being written back when working for a living was actually a source of genuine inspiration to people.

To get this started, I've taken the most compelling American success books from the last hundred-plus years—some of them still selling by the truckload and some left undisturbed and unopened for decades—and turned them upside down and shaken out every last bit of wisdom that might be useful to those low on the office totem pole today. This is a short tour of a section of literary history—and what genre of letters is more screamingly American than this one?—but it's also a critical guide to one's first few years of salaried labor. For example, Andrew Carnegie had some things to say about those minor housekeeping duties. Before history forgot him completely, author and publisher Orison Swett Marden taught millions in the early decades of the twentieth century how to dodge psychic bullets. Etiquette maven Emily Post was full of interesting notions about the socioeconomic role of curiosity. The banalities of networking are addressed by Napoleon Hill, author of 1937's *Think and Grow Rich*. Helen Gurley Brown's 1962 *Sex and the Single Girl* shows you how to suffer strategically. And even Donald Trump—not as useless as you might have imagined.

For those still unconvinced this exercise is worthwhile, I'll play the Paris Hilton card. If you read her great-grandfather Conrad Hilton's memoir—*Be My Guest*, it's called, and he's the one who built the Hilton hotel chain, from scratch—you find a lot of advice like this: Get up early. Develop intellectual crushes on people who fascinate and inspire you. (He was partial to Helen Keller. No joke.) Understand sacrifice and delayed gratification. (He served in World War I, and in the New Mexico state legislature.) Really understand what makes you tick. (Still young and kicking around in a dust-bowl Texas town, he came across a photograph of New York City's Waldorf Hotel. He carefully clipped the picture out, slipped it under the glass top of his desk, and told himself that someday, someday . . .) Flash-forward forty-seven years to Paris's bestseller, *Confessions of an Heiress: A Tongue-in-Chic Peek Behind the Pose:* "Trust me, people act differently toward you when you've got jewelry on your head."

To those who argue that Paris's book was never meant to be taken seriously, I'd say, sure, fine, but that's a lot of trees for a joke that goes on way too long. What I found as I paged through older, mustier books is that after a while, the authors' enthusiasm for work, for the possibilities it affords, for the mundane and sometimes maddening ways human underlings adapt to their surroundings—and in some cases change them for the better—is completely contagious. And lest anyone think I'm treating the corporate system a little too reverently, I'd argue that dismissing it wholesale doesn't pay off either. You can learn skills without being co-opted. Even those who seek new and progressive alternatives are better off knowing more about the way things are done and have been done—if only because most of us can't live our entire lives outside the system. (And even solar-powered NGOs have bosses and protocols.)

The advice of these Old Masters is surprisingly fresh, and they're fascinating characters in their own right. I wish I'd heard of some of them much earlier, as it might have saved me some long nights. Success literature is altogether not quite what I expected. The ideal it describes is far from the go-getting, amoral, self-indulgent loudmouth of popular imagination, but instead a thoughtful character, determined to find life as it's lived endlessly engaging. That still leaves one nagging question, however:

Can successful habits be successfully learned through books? As central as the self-made, self-schooled man is to the American story, it's a question that always pops up. I put it to a PR man and political consultant in his early thirties, and his answer did his profession proud: "Well, that's a question *you're* going to have to wrestle with, isn't it?" He smiled as he said this, naturally. He'd been raised by smart, nurturing parents, had an extended family that stretched from Manhattan's Upper East Side to Mumbai, went to private schools, and graduated from Princeton. He seemed to doubt that "a certain polish," as he put it, could be achieved through a stack of advice books. He did not hesitate to say that he'd been born lucky, and that what had been made available to him was not available everywhere. He didn't specify, but I could guess what he was talking about: suburban Milwaukee, say, or working the grocery checkout line.

Well, as Dale Carnegie would say, "One way to get air out of a glass is to pour in water." Worth a shot, right? Cracking open a book is certainly preferable to resigning yourself to subordinate status and hating yourself for it. Some good career ideas and some profoundly stupid ones have been issued over the past hundred-odd years. I hope these pages will help you tell the difference.

How to Be Useful

1

On Being a Poseur

Early Capitalists on Why Writing
Business Letters Takes Longer
Than Reading Them Does

> Never write a long letter. A business man has
> not time to read it. —CYRUS WEST FIELD

ONE OF THE WORST pieces of advice is "Just be yourself."
You hear it a lot. Oh, you're nervous about your new
job? *Don't worry. Just be yourself.* It comes from online career sites. ("The best preparation is really to be
yourself.") It comes from well-meaning mothers. ("Just be your
own sweet self.") It is so prevalent you can almost hear it in
the breeze. Unfortunate, then, that it's ill-suited to any number
of life situations, but at no time and in no place is it more useless, more beside the point, more potentially destructive than
the very moment when you're starting a new job.

Why it's so awful takes some explaining. It certainly seems
to be solid, all-American wisdom: Don't put on some phony act
and try to convince people you're something you're not. Don't
get yourself all worked up trying to impress, instead just be "natural," and then you'll probably be more relaxed, and because
you're relaxed you'll perform better, and best of all, because

you've been being yourself the whole time, you'll never have to explain, later on, why you're not quite the same person you seemed to be before. It promises this, too: That any red-blooded individual who values forthrightness and honesty—who really knows quality when he or she sees it—will recognize your sincerity and appreciate you all the more for it.

One of the first clues that being yourself might not be the answer came to me when I started asking people who'd been working full-time for a while to describe what their first post-college jobs were like, and got dead air. Sometimes I got wounded stares, looks of near incomprehension. People squinted, as if trying to glimpse something through a dense, coastal fog. Their mouths opened but nothing came out while they waited for the right words to surface. Finally they would spit out a strangled cross between "Hah!" and "Huh!," mumble a few words about it being "interesting," grin, and quickly change the subject. Trying to attach adjectives to these dim memories, one interviewee told me, felt like coming across poetry you wrote at sixteen. How you thought then and how you think now is very, very different. But I soon discovered that if you simply ask people what kinds of *tasks* they handled at their first jobs, the words came more easily: They made photocopies. They stood next to the photocopier so they'd be ready for action when the 11" x 14" paper jammed. They pored over Excel spreadsheets until their eyes ached. They answered phones. They forced big smiles while they cried a little on the inside.

They were not themselves, in other words.

Part of the problem with being yourself is that *you* could be anyone. You could dress badly. You could be a shy daydreamer, or you could be a bubblehead. *You* might be the only person who thinks your comic stylings rival Will Ferrell's. *You* might think your story about that lesbian bar in Amsterdam was a winner but your senior colleagues might not. So I started to wonder if this particular piece of nonwisdom was really as all-American as it sounds. Have we always been sending inexperienced young people into the capitalist lion's den with the flimsy instructions to *just be themselves?*

We haven't. In the early days of the American office, it turns out, the advice was different. Flip through the first texts written to help the novice through entry-level employment, and you'll find they were pretty much all agreed on one thing: Act a certain way, and you'd be going places. Behave in other ways, and your corporate overlords would lose interest in you, and very quickly. The steel tycoon Andrew Carnegie, for one, was quite clear about what he wanted to see in young recruits, and in a speech called "A Road to Business Success: A Talk to Young Men," he offered up an interesting warning: Forget yourself, he essentially said, and maybe try being somebody else a few hours a day. Maybe somebody better than you.

I was familiar with Carnegie's track record—that he'd started the company that became U.S. Steel, that he'd made millions of dollars on the backs of thousands of coal miners, and that he was a short, pushy firecracker of a man who later felt somehow guilty about his piles of money. But I hadn't expected to find him articulating a strong case for being, in essence, a total poseur—and for feeling no shame about it either. Looking at the train wrecks narrowly avoided by people feeling a little too at home on the job, I have to say that Carnegie was onto something. Striking a pose may be the best route for anyone hoping to emerge from corporate underlinghood with their dignity —and even, strangely, their sense of self—intact.

These very early job advice books started appearing in the mid-1800s, and they took a dim view of "you." Most begin with the basics of public life; they reminded readers of the importance of discipline, self-control, accepting criticism without getting into fistfights, and covering your mouth when you yawned. More than one mentions the need to keep one's fingers out of one's ears and nose. Some authors tried to push the young office clerk toward physical robustness as well, like C.B.C. Amicus did

in *Hints on Life: And How to Rise in Society* when he recommended a regimen of swimming and gymnastics.* *The American Chesterfield, or Way to Wealth, Honour, and Distinction . . .
Suited to the Youth of the United States* stressed the importance
of social graces. Others recommended Sunday school. Horatio
Alger's novels, which appeared with relentless regularity beginning in 1868, made it clear that smoking, petty theft, ripped
clothing, and hanging around with juvenile delinquents were
not OK by most employers' standards. As for Carnegie, when
he delivered his "Business Success" talk to the graduating class
of Pittsburgh's Curry Commercial College in 1885, he quickly
reassured the crowd that he wasn't going to dwell on moral issues. "You all know that there is no genuine, praiseworthy success in life if you are not honest, truthful, fair-dealing. I assume
you are and will remain all these," he said. And that's as far as
he went in the "be yourself" vein.

What was really pressing on Carnegie's mind was the subject of janitors. He thought janitors were a bad idea. The people
who should be cleaning up around the office, he felt, were the
junior associates. "Many of the leading business men of Pittsburgh had a serious responsibility thrust upon them at the very
threshold of their career," he said. "They were introduced to the
broom, and spent the first hours of their business lives sweep-
ing out the office." It made little sense from a budget perspective—division of labor and janitors being cheaper by the hour
and all that—but somehow the sight of company underlings
pushing industrial-sized brooms around warmed the cockles of
Carnegie's heart. He wanted everyone to start at the bottom, or
as he put it, to "begin at the beginning," just like he had.†

---

* A quick historical aside: "Clerk" was a job title that encompassed everything
from secretarial work to basic accounting to minding the store. Being an administrative assistant was not regarded as the dead-end proposition it is now, but rather
as the first step in white-collar professions.
† As a poor Scottish kid, fresh off the boat, he found work as a bobbin boy in a
Pennsylvania cotton factory for $1.20 a week. While still a teenager, he became a
telegraph operator, got a job with the railroads, and worked his way up from there

This willingness to grab a broom, or do any kind of poser grunt work, was necessary because bosses had a jaundiced way of looking at underlings. The view from the boardroom, Carnegie went on to suggest, looked something like this: a teeming pool of talented young people, undifferentiated, difficult to tell apart, and vaguely pathetic. And it was hard, in those early days, to predict who in this pool was destined for bigger and better things. But Carnegie knew, and any boss worth his salt knew, that some of them wouldn't amount to much. It had nothing to do with how special they were. These young people would do good work, sure, and were probably even overqualified for the mundane entry-level work they were being asked to do. But when the boss took a break from expanding his empire and looked over at them, clustered at the end of the hallway, and imagined a scene twenty years into the future, he saw Bob Cratchits, stooped over their desks at age forty-two and still answering to The Man. Good bosses might like to do right by everyone they employed, but eventually all that humanity started to blur before their eyes and they resigned themselves to leaving some underlings bobbing in the talent pool, undiscovered and unrescued. They could only do so much for so many.

So if you didn't want to get tagged as a Bob Cratchit, you had to adopt a certain ready-for-anything posture. You had to ATTRACT ATTENTION on the job. (This portion of the speech transcript is actually set in all caps, as if Carnegie—5'3" in socks—stood on tiptoe and shouted.) Carnegie's list of what you could do to ATTRACT ATTENTION is shockingly banal, however. Shipping clerks could double-check invoices for errors. Weighing clerks would make sure the scales were accurate. Messenger boys wouldn't just fling deliveries through door-

---

to dominate the steel industry and become the second richest man in the world (second to John D. Rockefeller of Standard Oil). By the time Carnegie died, in 1919, he'd given most of his fortune away to various philanthropic causes. It was a stranger, more romantic story than anything in *The Arabian Nights*, swooned the editor of his autobiography.

ways, but wait around to make sure those letters and packages got into the right hands. The boss didn't just want you to be willing to do menial dirty stuff, he wanted you to be meticulous, thorough, and attentive to small responsibilities.

This is a modest list of character traits—by no means an exhaustive catalog of any bright young thing's capabilities. But it was the foundation of the office pose, and basically all that the boss cared to know at this point. So if you were tempted to show off the many intricacies of your personality in full flower, the advice was simple: Don't. Other business philosophers agreed. "No doubt there are a few men who can look beyond the husk or shell of a human being—his angularities, awkwardness, or eccentricity—to the hidden qualities within; who can discern the diamond, however encrusted," wrote William Mathews in his 1874 *Getting On in the World.* "But the majority are neither so sharp-eyed nor so tolerant."

To be yourself, in other words, was to gamble on your boss being an unusually tolerant, perceptive soul. Being yourself was essentially leaving it up to your boss to decide for himself which parts of your personality were the most reliable indicators of your potential. And that, not to put too fine a point on it, was ceding a lot more power to the boss than was wise.

Aleksey Vayner, a Yale undergrad, achieved brief notoriety in 2006 for precisely this misplaced faith in a future employer's perceptive abilities. He made a résumé video that was leaked through e-mail onto the Internet after he'd submitted it to UBS, a major international bank, in hopes of landing a job. New York newspaper the *Sun* summed up the video this way: "Mr. Vayner identifies himself on his résumé as a multi-sport professional athlete, the CEO of two companies, and an investment adviser. The video depicts him lifting a 495-pound weight, serving a tennis ball at 140 miles an hour, and ballroom dancing with a scantily clad female. Finally, Mr. Vayner emerges enrobed in a white karate suit and breaks six bricks in one fell swoop. Between athletic bits, Mr. Vayner takes the opportunity to opine on success.

After being described in the opening lines of the video as 'a model of personal success and development to everybody,' Mr. Vayner says, 'Failure cannot be considered an option.'"

It ended badly; Vayner didn't get the job, and started looking into potential legal action against UBS (as the source of the leak) instead. Right, you think—obviously too much information, no sane person would mount such a production. But I've heard many examples of smaller moments that had career-crippling effects. There's the assistant who always wanted to discuss the novels he'd read in college—the ones that moved him profoundly sophomore year. The new kid who was overheard laughing about Jell-O shots four times in one week. Or the go-getter who felt his intelligence was being insulted by all that photocopying he had to do, "so he'd come by, lean against the doorframe, take a seat, and delve into his unified theory of Grand Theft Auto while I'm sitting there trying to get some work done," as one former colleague complained. Or the Wellesley grad so worried that her pitch-perfect résumé made her seem a little too color-within-the-lines that she let it slip to her new boss that she's constantly wearing clothes with the tags on and then returning them. Or the young woman who gave "diamondthong@aol.com" as her home e-mail address. Or the guy who asked, six months into the job, when he was going to get promoted, because, as he told his boss, he thought things had been going pretty well.

Even more common, though, is being what early success books plainly called "dull." I was a dull underling. I was at times so soft-spoken that a person sitting five feet away might not realize I'd just "contributed" to the conversation. I didn't want to be too aggressive, because I thought that looked rather tacky. (That's probably how I would have phrased it, too: *rather tacky.*") It's not worth dwelling on the particulars of what I thought came across as reserved elegance because it wasn't registering—at all.

I barely escaped from being classified as a Bob Cratchit, in other words. I didn't discover this, however, until after I'd been at this job for a full year. One evening the editor in chief had to fill out some forms for human resources (nothing he'd trouble with normally, but his assistant was out sick), and as everyone else had left for the day, he was forced to come over himself and ask me personally *what my last name was.* It wasn't that he couldn't remember — he had never known. This was in a department of only twelve people. From his office door to my cubicle was only ten steps. So I told him my last name, he thanked me kindly, and that was that.*

Of course, Carnegie might say. In the opening remarks of his janitor speech, he took a quick swipe at young women who thought all they had to do was show up and people would be impressed. But the surprising angle of Carnegie's formulation is that the too-aggressive, happily volunteering-too-much-information crowd would probably end up Bob Cratchits too. Sure, they had energy to spare in the beginning, but over time it would leach out of them because they were clearly somewhat oblivious, and the effects of making gaffe after gaffe would chip away at their confidence until there was none left. The best approach, business advisors concluded, wasn't a happy medium between too hard and too soft, but something more precise. The best way to get a corporate overlord to rescue you from the talent pool was to master a very particular persona. So the question becomes: Besides being willing to sweep up; besides meticulous, thorough, and attentive to small responsibilities; what else? If we can't be ourselves on the job, who should we be?

Their suggestions were highly specific. *The American Chesterfield* recommended: "well-bred, without ceremony; easy, without negligence; steady and intrepid, with modesty; genteel, without affectation; insinuating, without meanness; cheerful, without being nosy; frank, without indiscretion, and secret,

---

* I realize now that he had probably been waiting for me to leave — because he couldn't very well discreetly check the nameplate on my cubicle as long as I was still parked there.

without mysteriousness; to know the proper time and place for whatever you say or do." Which all sounds great but difficult to implement while standing next to the photocopier. Carnegie's right-hand man Charles M. Schwab was more succinct. In a tract called *Succeeding with What You Have,* he wrote: "The man who attracts attention is the man who is thinking all the time, and expressing himself in little ways . . . It is not the man who tries to dazzle his employer by doing the theatrical, the spectacular."

Schwab also felt a solid contender wouldn't strive for genius—he felt genius was entirely overrated. Carnegie seconded that; the only time he used the word *genius* is when he stated that any clerk who had "the genius of the future partner in him" would take over cleaning duties on days the janitor happened to be absent. Eugene Brewster, in *Success Secrets,* said genius was important but then defined genius downward as a "mastery of details," and a habit of tending to "the little things," much as Schwab advocated.

The correct pose was not too terrifically intellectual, either. One of the first tenets of this business philosophy was that the law of diminishing returns pertained to intelligence; being smart was great, but after a certain point, smarter wasn't going to get you much farther. Some business theorists even remarked that J. P. Morgan—another very rich man of the time—was relatively slow to make his millions because he was so well educated. (He'd gone to college in Germany.) James W. Alexander, author of 1856's *The Merchant's Clerk Cheered and Counselled,* had noticed that some young men had problems with work—they grew resentful, and would go to bars at night to drink themselves into oblivion—and he felt this had a lot to do with misplaced intellect. His solution? They needed to stop expecting their entry-level jobs to deliver intellectual excitement. There just wasn't any to be had.*

---

* Alexander, for his part, was so worried about the effect wrong expectations might have on new office boys that he called them the Endangered Classes. Swarms of them in the city, he fretted, many miles away from their homes and families—anything could happen to them.

For Horace Greeley, speaking in 1867 to the graduating class of Packard's Bryant & Stratton Business College, in New York, the correct pose boiled down to exhibiting "many-sidedness," which he haltingly defined as being capable and adaptable. "Now, that is what we want," he said. "Men who do one thing, it may be, today, but who are prepared to do something else tomorrow, if something else is needed and that which they are doing is not."

By which he meant, I believe, that the poser would never say, "But that's not my job." Nor would he say, "This is retarded," while stomping away from the janitor's closet, mumbling something to the effect that all those years and all that tuition money were clearly wasted. The clerk who did grunt work while at the same time making sure everyone within earshot understood that he was generally above this sort of thing, or capable of so much more, well, such a clerk was a snob, and snobs were also not OK by most employers' standards.

The ideal office clerk also kept his feelings largely to himself. Which meant that if he didn't actually feel it in his bones, he pretended to be happy to be there. One of Carnegie's early jobs had him stoking coal fires in a factory basement boiler room, so just working above ground, at a desk, with "newspapers, pens, pencils, and sunshine about" was once enough to make him smugly satisfied. (In his autobiography, Carnegie recalled walking into his first day of work at an actual office and thinking, "Paradise, yes, heaven.") Now that he was the big boss, he was drawn to a similar cheerfulness in underlings. Upbeat was more polite, and more pleasant to be around.

And that's the sum total of what was wanted from *you*. It's also a decent explanation for why stupid incidents that don't seem to mean much at the time turn out to have an unexpected — and lasting — power. Lauren, for instance, was once informed by a senior colleague that she owed her promotion to apple juice. She thought he was kidding, but he wasn't. What happened is that an author — an older, fatter man — came to their office for a meeting one day, and as he squeezed himself into his seat at the conference table, Lauren asked him if he'd like any coffee, tea, or water. The author said, yes, apple juice would be fine. Now, Lauren had never met this man before, and apple juice was not something her office kept on hand. But she found herself nodding, and saying sure, no problem. Then she backed out of the room, returned to her desk, grabbed her wallet, climbed down two floors to the nearest vending machine, fed it a dollar, hit the apple juice button, and out came a bottle of orange juice. She smoothed out another dollar bill and tried again: orange juice. She called the elevator, descended ten more floors, and ran to the corner Walgreens. There she stood in line with two 15.2-ounce bottles of Minute Maid apple juice because she had a premonition that her man was a two-bottle kind of man. Back upstairs, she deposited the apple juice in front of him—along with a glass to pour it into—found a seat, and tucked her hair back, while everyone else at the table watched the author empty the first bottle into the glass, drink it, and immediately repeat with the second. All apple juice was gone within minutes.

In the midst of entry-level fog, it might not be clear how all this running around and playing fetch could be seen by your superiors as genius, bordering on heroic. "I thought I was being too servile," Lauren remarked later. "And that maybe, if I wanted to be taken seriously, I shouldn't designate myself refreshment committee."

But volunteering for refreshment committee, grabbing the broom—this was all very American, according to this first generation of career counselors. And by "American" they meant a new kind of personality, and a better one than anything Europeans had come up with. "A Briton might be stolid, a Spaniard suspicious," one business author chimed in, but an American would do business with *anybody*. A European might ask too many questions. The American office worker, on the other hand, would clap his hands, rub them together, and ask if there were any packages that needed delivering.* The American clerk was easygoing, energetic, alert, smart — not *too* smart — and quick with a smile. Perhaps he smiled so much because he firmly believed he was destined to run the whole show someday. And oddly enough, so did his boss. (Said Carnegie: "I would not give a fig for the young man who does not already see himself the partner or the head of an important firm.")

Which is perhaps the best reason not to be yourself. If you think you owe perfect sincerity to a large capitalist concern, or you need to be actively representing the essence of your being at all times, you're not likely to stay optimistic on the job for long. You could get too self-conscious, thinking that everything you did had to communicate something about you. You might get so self-conscious that you didn't pay enough attention to other people and their little quirks. You might say, "No, sorry, we don't have apple juice," because you thought it was important to draw a line around who you were, and what greater feats you were capable of, and let everybody else deal with the consequences of a cranky old man's low blood sugar. Or instead, you could forget about yourself for a while; you could stifle the urge to say what you really wanted to say and demonstrate something else, namely, that here was that once-in-a-long-while underling who was thinking all the time, who had an uncanny sixth sense for when two bottles of Minute Maid plus a glass were called for. Who knew what else you'd pick up on?

Still, if the posing proves too much, keep in mind these are just the opening moves. Until things get more interesting, here are some other ways to ATTRACT ATTENTION:

Do realize you don't have much time. Early business thinkers took the idea that first impressions were important and ran with it. Carn-

---

* Packages are a recurring motif. Horatio Alger's young heroes were perpetually scrambling to return lost packages to gentlemen who had dropped them in the street, while his antiheroes — rich boys, snobs, and cigarette-smoking delinquents — always tried to avoid the carrying of packages.

egie claimed that evaluations of an underling started "from the day he begins work." Alexander, champion of merchant's clerks, agreed—verdicts on career prospects were reached "before the first week is out." This premium on speed extended to how you communicated. Cyrus West Field, the man whose company laid the first telegraph cable across the Atlantic (and presumably someone with a vested commercial interest in long-windedness), advised employees: "Never write a long letter. A business man has not time to read it." It was better to give a man the compliment of assuming he had more vital things to do than pore over your prose, and get right to your point.

Do know how you are going to characterize aspects of your life well in advance of being asked to characterize them. Needless to say, limited time meant you had to have answers to many basic, introductory questions at the ready, so you were never caught off-guard, rambling extemporaneously or pointlessly—or worse, too self-conscious for words. This sounds so simple as to be self-evident, but many people appear slightly stunned when asked about where they're from, what part of the city they live in, where they went to college, or what they studied. They'll mutter that they studied "psychology" and leave it at that—as if that piece of information alone were enough to captivate people—or they'll delve into their senior thesis topic, their elective courses, what the dorm food was like, and try to leave everyone with a solid understanding of their overall undergraduate experience, hangovers and all.

Having a *brief* biographical summary prepared is important because if you hesitate before speaking, people may wonder why you hesitated, and that wondering can and does lead their imagination down some dark paths. The ideal, as one journalist who once visited with Schwab put it, was "frank self-confidence"—which is to say, reasonably sobered by experience but optimistic about what's to come. This is why it's also wise to avoid describing anything as "horrible," or, alternatively, "totally,

totally fantastic, just amazing" in an interview. Gushing can trigger an employer to doubt your ability to see the world clearly.

One last note on this score: Be prepared, also, to respond gracefully to comments that indulge stereotypes about your part of the country. A West Virginian I know has long had to endure smirks when he—now a New Yorker—tells people where he's from. It is assumed he doesn't read, or that he's into Civil War reenactments. As a native Minnesotan, I get asked whether I've ever seen Prince perform live about once a month—roughly the same frequency I'm asked for my thoughts on Garrison Keillor. There is little one can do about this clumsy cultural shorthand—which invariably arises whenever people riff off limited information—at the outset of making someone's acquaintance. Smile through the stereotypes as best you can, and pass along new information when possible. Whatever you do, don't get defensive, and start insisting people are crazy to think Detroit's a tough town.

Do wear your learning lightly. In jobs and in life, people who try hard to show how very smart they are often get passed over for someone who's equally bright but easier to get along with. The guy who feels entry-level work insults his intelligence is everywhere. In creative industries, this is the person who drops the name of a 1970s German art rock band into water-cooler conversation and then looks surprised/embarrassed/worried for you when you say you're not real familiar with them. In financial services, it's the guy who tosses around EBITDA/EBITA amongst people he *knows* won't know what he's talking about. Having a conversation with this person feels like being dragged onto a quiz show, or being lectured by a manic TA. You don't want to be this person. (Or, if you do, maybe the office is not the place for you.)

Don't be so taken with "authenticity" that you can't bring yourself to read from a script from time to time. You may be expected to say things that sound nothing like you. My friend Josh once assisted a documentary film producer, and this job at times required him to double as office receptionist. Sometimes the person on the line was his boss, calling from his second home in London. Josh's boss usually started the conversation by thanking Josh just for being there, being there in the office, and then immediately launching into a lament that nobody, absolutely nobody, loved him. After several awkward conversations, Josh eventually learned he was expected to come back with something like, "Oh, but *I* do. *I* love you!" Which usually got an audible sigh from the boss before he'd go on to say, "But nobody *understands* me," and then Josh would have to clear his throat and cough up reassurance that, in fact, his boss was understood by many people, many important people, too—but not *that* many, of course, because as a filmmaker he was wrestling with some really deep, complex issues that not everyone could appreciate.

Don't assume people know you've got designs on moving up. Your bosses might have you pegged as someone who prefers clocking in and clocking out and doesn't want or expect anything more than a steady paycheck. If you were such a person, no robber baron was going to do much for you. Said Carnegie: "We make . . . Book-keepers, Treasurers, Bank Tellers of this class, and there they remain to the end of the chapter." This is not to say you should inquire as to when you're getting a promotion. Simply that you can't assume your boss is aware of, and sensitive to, your ambitions. Some are, some aren't.

Don't walk in the door with wet hair. If you come in shirt-untucked, or looking in any way like you're not completely prepared for the day from the moment the boss sees you in the morning, you're being yourself too much. Another unspoken truth about the first days of entry-level employment, and most significant from a practical standpoint: You need to be at your desk *before* your boss arrives. After a few months, show up a little later and see what happens.

Do tell yourself small lies about the glory in drudgery. Alexander suggested that if you started to feel sorry for yourself—he used the example of a clerk walking down Broadway in the bitter cold to deliver a package—remember ancient Sparta. The kids there had it rougher. Alexander also had issues with using the word *menial,* and thought it triggered bad thought patterns. "To consider any thing menial, which belongs to the career of training, is to be a fool. The greatest philosophers and the greatest commanders have passed through toil as humble and as galling." Best to endure the worst first, he concluded.

Having galling experiences early on also comes in handy later in your career, when you'll be expected to trot out hard-luck stories. (More on that in chapter 8.)

Do have a firm handshake. The authors of 1971's *How to Read a Person Like a Book* said a flaccid handshake suggested weakness but also "something vaguely un-American." All I know is that the dead-fish handshake gives people the impression your mind is elsewhere. It's usually accompanied by a glance over the shoulder, or off to the side, to see who else is in the room. It borders on offensive, in other words.

»»

Knowing how much rests on getting the pose right, meanwhile, might allow you to forgive yourself for taking absurd amounts of time doing very simple tasks that one might think, on first hearing the assignment, shouldn't take long at all. There's the day I spent an entire morning composing a three-line cover letter to Martin Amis, for example. All the letter needed to convey was please-read-the-following-page-and-sign-it-and-send-it-back-to-me-thanks. That's it—four sentences at most. I was a twenty-four-year-old editorial assistant whose previous experience with Martin Amis consisted of gazing longingly at his books on a shelf, and had been on the job two days. Amis was—is—a pedigreed, world-renowned author. In the photo that appears on the jacket of his first novel, he bears a striking resemblance to a young Mick Jagger. I was writing to obtain permission to reprint an excerpt from his novel *Money* in an upcoming anthology my boss was compiling. Whether or not Amis said no—thereby disappointing my boss and everyone else involved with the project—was a matter of some importance. What kept me from knocking the letter out was fear that his answer depended entirely on how well I phrased the question. "Dear Mr. Amis: I am happy to enclose herewith a permissions form requesting . . ." I stopped. Am I really "happy"? Maybe skip "herewith"? Then again, I thought, Amis is English. He'll like that word. But he also, I thought, probably has little tolerance for sniveling editorial assistants unable to cough up even a simple sentence without drooling. "Dear Mr. Amis: Enclosed please find a form requesting permission to use your . . . as described on the attached . . ." No, too brusque, I decided. Martin Amis was funny. I should try to make him laugh. A little. Just elicit a wry, salty smile.

This went on for hours. Meanwhile, nothing else got done. I can't recall how the letter ended up, but weeks later, I received the desired release form with a scribble in the place where Amis was asked to sign. There was no accompanying note, but I had the signature, or something like it, in hand. Paradise, yes, heaven. You take what you can get in the early days.

2

Dodging the
Great Failure Army

Orison Swett Marden on the Strange Power
of Finding Something Nice to Say

> . . . to all who believe that there is a better life
> than dollar-chasing, and that everybody ought
> to be happier than the happiest now are.
>
> —from the dedication to *Everybody Ahead*

THE BRITISH AUTHOR Toby Young once described how his American colleagues—he worked briefly for *Vanity Fair* in the late 1990s—would refer to anyone who called the office twice a day as a "stalker." Meaning it was very uncool to call the magazine twice, as it suggested you were too emotionally needy. *Vanity Fair* is not the only workplace that encourages such sly dismissals; in fact, they're increasingly common. As an editor friend said of the atmosphere around his office's conference room table, if you happened upon any piece of damaging gossip, or heard any disappointing news, the correct reaction was somewhere between a blank nod and a grin—not exactly pleased, more a look of serene acceptance. Just enough to communicate that you expected something like that to happen. "It's not that nothing surprises you, exactly," is how he described the correct look. "It's that nothing *bad* surprises you."

Exactly the way it should be, I thought, when I found myself amongst colleagues who, like me, knew that a little slapdash bitchery was a good way to make it through a trying workday. There were several junior staffers in our office—many of us twenty-two, twenty-four, twenty-five years old. And if every last cubicle wasn't inhabited by someone very clever, there were plenty of us who had mastered snark. The ones you knew from the get-go would be able to keep up were the mumbling young men in thick black-framed glasses. But even some of the women in pink J. Crew twinsets—they too were usually able to articulate what, precisely, was wrong with Gwyneth Paltrow. We were addicted to Gawker.com and other snark-infested websites. A typical Tuesday in this office would begin with a gripe about the gross inefficiencies of public transportation, and by 11:30 at least one person would have questioned, in a subtle, multilayered way, the integrity of the CFO's family life. In the evening, over drinks, we could speak even more freely—and phrases like "black stirrup pants" could take on enormous meaning. One midlevel publicist who was not terrifically popular with us junior employees wore black stirrup pants—last in style when Janet Jackson was promoting *Control*—to the office about once a week. A male coworker made a little speech about these pants one night, and the ways in which black stirrups stood for all this woman's habits—her voice, her hair, her peerless ability to condescend to us. From then on all he had to do was drop the words *black stirrup pants* into a conversation—any conversation—to make us all convulse in giggles. It felt like a needed release.

If your job is less than gratifying intellectually, of course you also try to exercise critical muscles wherever you can. It's small compensation for the fact that you're low on the totem pole. And in some sense it seems like the only means of deflecting the power some people have over you. (Our superiors might have been able to tell us what to do, but they sure couldn't tell us what to *think*.)

But how well does this knack for new and inventive put-downs correlate with getting ahead? More exactly, how does zeroing in on humanity's weak spots help you climb, socially or professionally?* I found an answer in *How to Get What You Want,* a little red book published in 1917 that I discovered quite by accident. That is to say, I didn't discover it through meticulous research so much as by opening my mailbox one day. Someone had sent it to me, unsolicited. (This is significant. Remember it.)

How to Get What You Want was operating on an entirely different frequency than we were on. It was written by Orison Swett Marden, a man who clearly appreciated titles that got right to the point. He's now as good as lost to history, but at one point in time, he could count on his name being recognized across the United States and a few places beyond. He was an inexhaustible writer and publisher and his entire career was devoted to a very simple proposition: Criticism was for losers. Criticism that was crisply and originally phrased was no better. Too many bright young things, he claimed, believed that being hypercritical was a path to distinction. (No one in a competitive economic environment wanted to be seen as a dupe, after all.) But this was entirely mistaken, he suspected. Making negative assessments—didn't matter much what you were talking about—could do harm, and in unexpected ways.

Why and how this was so remained mysterious. Beginning in the 1890s, it took Marden fifty-four books, a handful of pamphlets, thirty years, and two incarnations of a magazine he called *Success* to explain how it all worked.† His audience

---

* The question, I'll be honest, didn't occur to me until the stage described in chapter 7.

† Among Marden's other titles: *Cheerfulness as a Life Power* (1899); *Prosperity: How to Attract It* (1922); *Everybody Ahead* (1916); *Pushing to the Front* (1897); *Self-Discovery: or, Why Remain a Dwarf* (1922); *Do It to a Finish* (1909); *Talks with Great Workers* (1901); *Every Man a King: or, Might in Mind-mastery* (1906); *The Victorious Attitude* (1916); *Architects of Fate* (1895); and my favorite, judged on title alone, *You Can, but Will You?* (1920).

was the average person who didn't necessarily aspire to be any kind of tycoon, but who could clearly see that the pace of work and life was ramping up. Companies were getting bigger. *Success* assured people they weren't going to be left behind by these changes. So the initial step to engaging Marden's philosophy was simply looking around the room. Marden had noticed that some personalities had a dampening effect, and he had trouble even being around them. "Their presence depresses. One feels cold perspiration while in their company," he wrote in a 1907 tract called *The Optimistic Life.* "Everything about them is chilly and forbidding. They dry up thought. One cannot think to be natural when with them. Their sarcasm, irony, detractions, and pessimism repel, and one shrinks from them." He coined a term for these sarcastic types: "mental paupers." In another book he called them "calamity howlers." But Marden's preferred coinage, judging from how often he used it, was "The Great Failure Army." He imagined it'd be difficult, but he was determined that the ranks of the Great Failure Army be kept to a minimum.

The best way to do this, Marden claimed, was to alter a culture's prevailing thought patterns. The gist of the idea belonged to a very loosely affiliated group known as the New Thought movement, and though Marden was one of New Thought's loudest advocates, he was by no means its only disciple. All New Thoughters agreed that criticism was for losers, but they went one further: Training yourself to dwell on kind, positive, and hopeful words should be central to your life strategy. In fact, it might be all the strategy you need. New Thought practitioners believed that happy dispositions had the potential to transform lives and careers because *everything under the sun obeyed the Law of Attraction.* To understand how the Law of Attraction worked, you had to first come to grips with the notion that the air itself was teeming with possibilities—possibilities that could be conjured into hard fact and material existence if only you thought the right thoughts. There was a giant, universal Mind, and you could tap into it with your own mind—small *m*—to

draw down the results you wanted.* Which was not to say that
you didn't have to work for the things you wanted. But basically,
the universe was generous and held enough wealth for everyone. The Law of Attraction got results—you didn't even have
to be aware of how the law operated for it to be working in your
life. If you spent your days thinking about poverty, you'd continue to just scrape by. If you focused on joy and money, then
joy and money is what you'd get. And if you didn't "scatter the
flowers of kindness," as Marden put it, everywhere you went,
then you could never expect sweetness and sunshine to radi-
ate in your direction either. For New Thought devotees this
was a natural, ironclad law of the universe, as nonnegotiable as
gravity.

Avoiding conscription into the Great Failure Army was first
and foremost a matter of letting all thoughts of how irritating
humanity could be end with you. ("We blame everything but the
right thing. The trouble is in ourselves," Marden quipped.) Instead of rehashing how people disappointed you, you needed to
think generously, and then take the time to say, out loud, those
nice things you were thinking. Once you accepted the premise
of the Law of Attraction, it made no sense to fixate on somebody's shortcomings. In fact, it was wholly counterproductive.
Snark would come right back at you, like a karmic boomerang.

In other words, most everything my colleagues and I were
doing was very risky. Rather than communicating our rare wit,

---

* If you're even passingly acquainted with Rhonda Byrne's *The Secret* (2006), the
Law of Attraction should sound familiar. Here are two things you need to know
about *The Secret* in relation to Marden. (Incidentally, Byrne makes no mention
of Marden or New Thought in either her book or the DVD. Instead she pretends
the "secret" was handed down by the sexier likes of Newton, Beethoven, Shake-
speare, and Einstein.) First, in contrast to the tone of Byrne's production, Marden
never claimed marshaling the Law of Attraction was easy. He paints it more as a
strenuous spiritual and ethical struggle. Second, Marden wasn't really interested
in consumer goods, and didn't promise his readers an unlimited flow of products
the way *The Secret* does. As for "unlimited freedom"—another phrase from the
DVD—his early twentieth-century audience would have found the concept too
strange to contemplate.

we were, in fact, flirting with being seen as precisely as lame as the lame-asses we saw all around us. But even if someone had told us this at the time—and no one did—there were several immediate and substantive obstacles to putting this mystical, wide-eyed hoo-hah into practice. For one, Marden's prescription for relentless cheerfulness sounded simply like putting blinders on. Two, this was not how we had learned to demonstrate intelligence. Our ability to locate wrongdoing, failure, and the loose threads in any argument—and then yank on those loose threads until the whole thing unraveled—was highly prized. Three, there was a glaring logistical concern: What to make of the fact that the office's higher-ups seemed to have reached their cozy positions and inflated salaries by displaying *their* critical chops? Our bosses—and this is true in most industries—were perpetually saying yea or nay to projects, making (what looked like) snap judgments, and one would naturally assume that the path to power was to demonstrate that we were capable of same. Four, there was "the lingering suspicion that everyone above you was just ridiculously untalented," as Samantha, a graphic designer, remarked to me. Perhaps the people in those coveted spots got there because, well, someone even higher up wasn't really paying attention, and promotions came about through nepotism, or logic-defying happenstance, or some other injustice. When we considered the organization chart, and then our to-do list, the thought of throwing metaphorical rose petals in the direction of anyone more enviably placed struck us as insane. *That* was sucking-up—and it was unheard of.

Once I discovered Orison Swett Marden, I asked around to see if my office had been exceptional in this regard. It hadn't. Dave, who worked in the relatively staid field of compliance, had a boss who, at the end of Monday morning meetings, meetings that began at 7:30 sharp, would put down his latte, smack the nearest available surface, clear his throat, and try to rally the troops. "Let's go kick some fucking ass, *Dave!*" he'd say, always emphasizing *Dave*. As Dave told this story, his voice trailed off and he stared out the window, shaking his head at the memory. Not only had he worked for a man he didn't admire and knew to be untalented, all conversation amongst the firm's employees dwelled on this idiocy. As for sucking-up? "It would come across as too transparent, too blatantly calculated," said Adam, a copywriter at a branding agency. He could not recall a single instance in which anyone at the office had engaged in what Marden termed "the silent power of love." The prevailing wisdom was that it was always better to risk sounding a little snotty —and opinionated—than approving and thereby unknowing. Adam was able to come up with several terms for someone who might—ass-kisser, apple-polisher, bootlicker, brownnoser, gladhander, and toady—but to him it sounded like something left over from the days of *Leave It to Beaver,* both quaint and oddly stylized by today's standards.

Of course, our approach had its antecedents, too. In *This Side of Paradise,* F. Scott Fitzgerald encapsulates 1920s-style snark by having one character brag about how he'd write reviews calling the latest serious, big-idea book "a welcome addition to our light summer reading." Or Dorothy Parker, who is reputed to have shot off lines like "If you can't think of anything nice to say, come sit next to me" at dinner parties. Snark is not only nothing new, it has a time-honored, predictable style. It's both vaguely nihilistic and excellent at suggesting that the object, person, or topic under discussion is not only not that good, but doesn't even deserve to be taken seriously. And all our joking aside, at our office we liked things that demanded they be taken seriously. So in addition to pointing out wardrobe mistakes, we were also skilled at calling out all the things we did not want to see any more of on our desks, down the hall, in the world: anything that could be described as half-baked, sloppy, uninspired, or clichéd.

But if we'd been more alert, we would have noticed something happening. What began as a way to demonstrate our high standards in front of colleagues became an end in itself. Which is exactly what Marden predicted: The contents of your head other may suggest the 'United States Steel Corporation' ... Buṭ my answer to the question is different, as I believe that the biggest thing in the world is the *law of action and reaction,* namely, *for every action there is an equal and opposite reaction.*" Still, this fervent belief in the power that would be unleashed if only you fully appreciated the interconnected psychic nature of all input and output raised an interesting question: Why so many poor people still kicking around, hanging out on street corners? The answer they came up with was that living by the Law of Attraction was demanding, and thinking lovingly required a considerable amount of sheer will.

What were you supposed to do if you couldn't muster the energy to try it? Besides taking a long hard look in the mirror—and realizing how flawed a specimen you yourself were—Marden suggested a few more pragmatic techniques. Like checking your facial expressions. (He cited approvingly one man who had "one corner of his mouth always curved up as though he had received some good news and was just dying to tell you about it.") He also suggested you squelch the urge to put labels on people—that is, any label beyond a rudimentary, judgment-free HERE'S MY BOSS, WHO TELLS ME TO KICK ASS. (Because one of the epitaphs in Marden's Cemetery of Failure read "He was too sensitive," and another, "He clung to his prejudices.") The important thing was not to "pinch your own supply" of universal goodwill by fussing about other people's habits.

Third, Marden wanted everyone to find and study people with a knack for warding off pessimism and nastiness—people like Benjamin Disraeli.* A popular novelist and prime minister under Queen Victoria, Disraeli demonstrated the truth of the Law of Attraction to an unusual degree, Marden felt; he was widely considered an unparalleled expert in laying it on thick. One of his oft-quoted quips was "Talk to people about them-

---

* At various times Marden also suggested Thomas Edison, Charles M. Schwab, the apostle Paul, the Buddha, John Wanamaker (the department-store magnate), and Jane Addams.

selves and they will listen for hours."* When the queen published *Leaves from the Journal of Our Life in the Highlands,* a
vanity book of no particular literary importance, Disraeli would
consistently use the phrase "we authors, ma'am" when talking to
her (he himself had published some fifteen novels by this time).
"You have heard me called a flatterer," Disraeli is reported to
have remarked to Matthew Arnold, "and it is true. Everyone
likes flattery; and when you come to royalty you should lay it on
with a trowel."

Marden didn't advocate scattering kindness flowers only in
the path of high-placed people — your garden-variety brown-
nosing. He wanted you to be an equal opportunity flatterer, and
send those kind and encouraging words both up and down the
societal ladder. Marden left the matter of what to say largely
open but singled these people out for particular attention: "a
newsboy, a waiter in a restaurant or a hotel, a conductor on a
car, an elevator boy, a toiler in your home or your office, a poor
unfortunate man or woman in a wretched home, or on a seat in
the park."

A noble goal, to be sure, but it still begs the question of how
it advances one's career, in any practical sense, to be friendly
to homeless ladies. Well, the Law of Attraction was difficult to
marshal but it didn't really discriminate; good or bad, high or
low, it could be used to procure just about anything. (One New
Thought practitioner went around Greenwich Village telling
women she could get them diamond necklaces — "Anything you
want!" — if they only *thought* about diamond necklaces in the
right way. Marden himself might say that the sudden appearance of *How to Get What You Want* in my mailbox showed that
the universal Mind was aware of my needs.) The Law of Attraction could also bring about personal transformation. While
Marden was busy scribbling, a Frenchman named Émile Coué

---

* Many American success-lit authors have had crushes on British prime ministers.
Disraeli comes up often in the early works — but was unceremoniously dumped in
favor of Winston Churchill after World War II.

made a splash on both sides of the Atlantic by touting something he called autosuggestion, a New Thought practice that revolved around repeating the phrase "Every day in every way, I'm getting better and better" every night, twenty times, before bed. But as Hugh MacNaghton, the author of a book on Coué, wanted to know, how could repeating a false statement over and over again possibly help you? What if you weren't, in fact, getting any better? When he got the chance to observe Coué in person, however, he felt forced to concede that perhaps success lay in the doing. Sure it sounded childlike; you had to admit that if you were at all intelligent. But masters of autosuggestion seemed to glide through the streets with the greatest of ease. And since it was obvious that talking about pain, incompetence, and grossness rarely prevented those things, perhaps it was also true that being highly critical of others did *you* more harm than it did them. And so it might also be true that a little positive feedback, on whomever it was bestowed, could lift you up in the eyes of the whole world. Or at least in the eyes of your boss.

I know at least one strict, if inadvertent, follower of the Marden philosophy. I once worked with an editor who was incessantly proclaiming, "Oh, I'm so happy!" She kept her office door open nearly all the time, and she talked loudly, and you could hear this phrase trilling down the hallway. Sometimes it made phone conversations for people in nearby cubicles challenging. When the art director presented her with cover designs that she liked: "Oh, I'm so happy!" When a literary agent finally got her on the line: "Oh, I'm so happy you called!" When anything went particularly well: "Oh, I'm so happy!" When she asked a fellow editor to read a manuscript to get his support for Thursday's editorial meeting, and he returned with a glowing report: "Oh, I'm so happy you liked it!" I thought she was an idiot. That her delivery was usually breathless and excited, like a cheerleader after a handstand routine, didn't help.

It was only later that I recognized her particular brilliance.

If making someone happy is a pleasurable activity (and it generally is), and we can see that some people are relatively easy to please while others are impossible to please, the natural human impulse is to lean toward the easy-to-please.* So is it possible that by making her joy so very obvious, she was nudging people toward choosing her as the person they wanted to please most?

"Oh, I'm so happy" is, of course, also an indirect form of flattery. (Saying you're happy with something the art director has produced is pretty close to saying you're happy with the art director, period.) It can change someone's opinion of you as well. Edward E. Jones, a sociologist who spent a lot of time studying this dynamic—he called his book *Ingratiation*—claimed that the effectiveness of pleasantries and compliments "seems to derive from the premise that people find it hard not to like those who think highly of them." If we perceive that someone likes or respects us, we're likely to shift our opinion of that person— if it's negative to begin with, or just neutral—closer to a match. Cheerleading, in other words, is a diplomatic masterstroke.

Taking Marden's ideas to their logical conclusion suggests you may not even have to be within earshot for it to work. Actual sucking-up isn't strictly necessary—simply zapping generous assessments into the ether could have much the same effect. Which is why Marden and all other New Thought preachers were constantly encouraging young workers to carry on like they had just won the lottery. Or as the author David Bush succinctly put it in his 1924 pamphlet: "Smile, you rascal, smile. Think pleasant."†

That Marden spent so much time touting kindness suggests he must have actually believed this. He rambled on far too long and passionately to be dismissed as an opportunistic hack (several of his fifty-four books run on to five hundred pages).

---

* Unless you're a certified masochist.
† New Thought spurred a lot of independent publishing. Bush's *Spunk: How to Lick Fear* was one of many self-published pamphlets sold primarily by mail order.

In 1895, Houghton Mifflin published Marden's *Pushing to Front*. It went through twelve printings in twelve months, and soon it had been translated into twenty-five languages. One million copies were sold in Japan alone. "Didn't you know it was that book which gave us the courage to resist the Russian encroachments?" a Japanese visitor reportedly told his American host. "Among ourselves we often call it the Japanese Bible." In 1926, the critic H. L. Mencken grumbled about having seen Marden's books propped up on newsstands as far away as Spain, Poland, and Czechoslovakia.

"You know, at the end of the day, snark is a problem because there's a certain amount of self-referentialism to it," concluded Gabriel, the screenwriter. "You could be at lunch, talking about what an anorexic headcase your last boss was, or how the production company you last worked for had a ridiculous reporting structure that stifled initiative, blah, blah, blah, and . . . there's always the risk that your conversation partner will be sitting there, taking small sips from her water glass, and thinking, well, maybe so, or maybe the problem was *you*." Gabriel said he'd eventually discovered it was wiser in many situations to keep the sullen wanderings of his mind to himself—even amongst people who slapped their cell phones shut like they'd just walked off the set of *Entourage*.

This again is not easy. "It's much more difficult to write an arresting piece 'In Praise of' something," remarked a former colleague who pens reviews from time to time. "It's easier to be interesting when you're taking something down. The real challenge is to swoon and still sound sharp." As Dale Carnegie would later point out in *How to Win Friends and Influence People,* Disraeli was such a successful flatterer because wherever he went, he could count on being one of the smartest men in the room. But it seems he dodged the Great Failure Army by meditating on something other than, say, Queen Victoria's resemblance to a stalker.

It's a lesson worth remembering whenever you're tempted

to let bitchy typecasting punctuate your workday. Why risk the undertow when your ultimate goal is to raise others' opinion of you? Should you decide to explore Marden's "Cheering-Up Business" instead, you might want to bear these other things in mind as well:

Don't be "nice." Express gratitude and say nice things, sure, but don't strive to be "nice." Marden doesn't use the word himself. He writes about being generous, optimistic, fun-loving, warm, encouraging, healthy, and joyous, but *nice* doesn't make the list. There's a tepid and watered-down quality to "nice," and it seems to me that most everyone who uses it to describe somebody else isn't really talking contours of character, but rather surface gestures and keeping up appearances.

Not being "nice" also means an end to "Thanks!"—or worse, "Thx!"—e-mails. "Thx!" is "nice," and therefore a big waste of time. (E-mails need to be opened, read, and deleted, after all—altogether too much effort for "Thx!") It's better to add *something* distinctive and personal that makes the thank-you message both more memorable and more gratifying for the recipient.

Don't affix labels to people you don't get along with. Fixating on a so-called difficult person just long enough to imagine a label on her forehead—COMPLAINER, DICTATOR, DOUCHEBAG—is a strategic blunder. Some books suggest carving humanity up into types is useful when you're trying to cope and communicate with said difficult person, and that once you understand and can categorize his MO, you can work on altering his objectionable behavior. (See "Interlude.") To that I'd say: Good luck trying to manage another adult's behavior. Trying to *improve* your boss—or anyone who outranks you, for that matter—is rarely an enriching exercise.

All this said, if you must scratch the itch, reserve your arrows for those who are well paid, pampered, and take themselves a little too seriously. Spare the office receptionist. (So Gwyneth Paltrow is probably fair game, come to think of it.)

Do be careful whom you compliment. Scattering compliments willy-nilly is tricky for people lower on the group's totem pole—because tossing one up to those ranked higher suggests that you imagine yourself in a position to judge their performance. And while you might think you're capable of judging their performance, they might not. (This is why it sounds bizarre to say, "You did a terrific job today" to your boss.) Flattery, Jones said, was always difficult to take at face value, and the wrong context for your comment could reduce the credibility of your statement to zero. Timing was also important. If you gave a compliment to someone seconds before asking for a favor, you rendered that compliment null and void. If you gave the exact same compliment to two or more different people, especially two people stationed just down the hall from each other, then you also sounded less than reliable. If you were really sophisticated and smart, you would flatter someone behind their back, and on occasions that didn't call for you to be saying anything sweet. (And then trust that it would get back around to the intended audience. It usually does.)

Complimenting attributes besides the obvious is another time-honored technique. In *This Side of Paradise,* Fitzgerald had one of his ingénues say this to one of her suitors: "Please don't fall in love with my mouth—hair, eyes, shoulders, slippers—but *not* my mouth. Everybody falls in love with my mouth." Even more effective is complimenting someone on a quality you know her to be proud of, but also a little unsure as to whether anyone else can see or appreciate it. This is what Disraeli supposedly did—ad nauseum—with Her Majesty. Assuaging people's self-doubt is a sure way to endear yourself to them.

Do be sure you're being asked to display your devastating wit and intelligence before you whip it out. John, a creative director, described

how once, midmeeting, a colleague popped up to grab something back at his desk, and as he was headed out, was asked if
he could, by the way, please bring back a stapler while he was
at it. This prompted a pause at the door and a monologue about
"errand boys" and how Lyndon B. Johnson might have handled
a similar situation. Which only led John, his senior colleague, to
think, if not actually say out loud: "Now is not the time for you
to perform. Now is the time for you to fetch a stapler."

Don't worry about sounding phony. Which is not to say that you
should lie, only that you shouldn't stop yourself from saying
something affirming just because you think your motives might
fall under suspicion. All the above warnings about complimenting aside, studies show that confident, high-ranked individuals
appreciate and will gladly take all the praise they can get—even
if they *know* they're being buttered up. Their ability to "see
through it" doesn't affect their enjoyment of it.

Ingratiation also floated the suggestion that as "a person
tends to bring his private feelings in line with his public actions,"
speaking affirmative words, even if they sounded phony at first,
might actually prompt a transformation in how you perceived
your job.

Do criticize artfully. Sometimes you're asked to give an opinion on
an idea or project that—can't be helped, no matter how hard
you try—plainly disgusts or bores you. Conveying that disgust
without offending (unnecessarily) or making yourself look bad
is a challenge. It's an art that thrives on repeated practice, however. Marden often referred to saying affirmative words as a
habit—something that got easier, and came more naturally, over
time.

Meanwhile, try something in the vaguely constructive vein
of "I liked _____. I would have liked it even more if she had
done more of _____ toward the middle." You remain upbeat,
and still show off your analytical skills. If you have to reject a
proposal, try any variation of "Thanks, but it's not quite right

for me/now's not the ideal time/it's not quite what I'm looking for at the moment. But best of luck with it."

Do, if you're going to deploy snark, be so very skilled at it that you'll be able to dine out on your pithy commentary for a long time. Some people have been able to translate their knack at sarcastic asides into lucrative careers writing blogs, op-ed columns, and books. If you think you might be equally gifted, maybe ask around to determine whether you really are. No need for me to pile on with the names of those who've tried and failed to make snark, backstabbing, or publishing nasty tell-alls pay the bills, but they're greater in number than those who succeeded. (Marden, of course, would say that even their flush of early success will be short-lived.)

»»

In 1914 another New Thought author added that he believed most wealthy Americans had not been reincarnated that many times, and that this explained a lot about the economy. Americans were predominantly young souls, and so had "not had the opportunity to create very much negative energy with their Intellect"; thus they excelled at manipulating the Law of Attraction to their advantage.

As for Orison Swett Marden, he simply felt that the average person—young soul or old—wasn't inclined to get much work done wallowing in an atmosphere of cynicism. (From *The Optimistic Life,* again: "Nobody does good work when discouraged. There is no spontaneity in it, no resourcefulness, no inventiveness, no originality, no enthusiasm. It is mechanical, lifeless. . . . Give! give!! give!!! It is the only way to keep from drying up, from becoming like a sucked orange,—juiceless, insipid.")

The point of dwelling on the good parts, in other words, was that it led to gains in productivity. Seen in this light, the Law of Attraction, far from a load of pseudoscientific hoo-hah, is pure pragmatism.

3

Party Tips for the Nouveau Riche

Etiquette and the Importance
of Asking Questions

> People, particularly Americans, like to know Why
> and What and How. They want to know the rules
> of the game, whether they observe them or not.
>
> —FRANK CROWNINSHIELD, on Emily Post's brilliant career

MILY POST CARED less about which fork you shoved in
your mouth and when than she did what came out of your
mouth. On that point, the godmother of etiquette was a
fanatic. She was obsessed with dinner-party conversation,
and what she witnessed during the 1910s and 1920s was that
people needed a brush-up course. All those rubes from midwestern backwaters who had taken Andrew Carnegie's example to heart, who'd made a killing in railroads, lumber, oil, or
all of the above, and who then moved to glittering East Coast
cities and bought their wives and daughters long, lacy dresses,
wishing, hoping, and otherwise straining hard to break into
"society"—they would sit at the table with their lobster bisque

and dinner rolls, and chatter their blundering way through the meal. Post felt that their poor conversational skills were squandering their best chances. But she had a real soft spot for them, even though most of her fellow blue bloods would sooner they had stayed down on the farm. Her 692-page *Etiquette: In Society, In Business, In Politics, and at Home* was a smash-hit—the number one nonfiction bestseller of 1922—largely because it sought to make life easier for the yahoo nouveaux riches.

American new money has always been subject to very unflattering stereotypes, which is peculiar, really, given how this country was founded by people who had no time for inherited privilege.* In movies, on television, in novels, people who've recently come into money are depicted as clumsy, cloying braggarts, always bumping into sofas and up against the establishment. They buy too many trinkets, and barge into rooms and situations without knowing exactly what's going on. There's a line in *Breakfast at Tiffany's*—the Truman Capote novella, not the movie—where aspiring socialite from the sticks Holly Golightly (she's from somewhere in small-town Texas) says something like "Anybody with their nose pressed against a glass is liable to look stupid." By which she means, basically, that a new arrival shouldn't let on that she's been standing outside, peering through the window and waiting to get in, because God forbid someone think she hasn't been an insider the whole time. Unfortunately this strategy doesn't work out so well for her, and she ends up leaving New York, possessionless and on the run from the law in Argentina with a shifty (and married) father of seven.

Golightly's blaze-ahead approach doesn't work well for aspiring professionals either. The director of a major fashion magazine's online division recently told me this story: One day he stepped into the elevator at Four Times Square, a fabled office

---

* Witness *The Beverly Hillbillies,* George Jefferson (of *The Jeffersons*), and *The Anna Nicole Show.*

tower in midtown Manhattan. Already inside were three young women. He imagined they were just out of college, perhaps interns or assistants—he hadn't yet met them. Nor did they take much notice of him, because they were deeply absorbed in the glossy magazine they were sharing among them. "That's the one I want. I want her job," the tallest one said, pointing at the masthead. The other two agreed it sounded great, though a few other job titles were mentioned as pleasant alternatives. Beauty editor, for instance. A few hair flips later, the elevator dinged and they walked out. At no point did it occur to them that (a) the man who had gotten in on the third floor might be an industry bigwig; (b) the woman whose job they'd selected was a good friend of his; or (c) they might have gained in their quest for professional advancement by, say, acknowledging his presence.

When he recounted this story, he was laughing, but it clearly annoyed him. It wasn't that they'd treated the elevator like a bar —and seemed to believe it their duty as impossibly attractive young women to be aloof and standoffish. It wasn't their ambitious daydreaming—nothing wrong with that, though something in their tone suggested they thought getting a plummy job required the same strategic process they'd use to get something off a high shelf. (Rather than climb a ladder, they'd point from the floor and ask someone to get it down for them.) Time would take care of that attitude soon enough, the executive thought, but then added, "Call me old-fashioned, but I wasn't like that growing up. That way of thinking, talking . . . it's completely foreign to me." As he saw it, the whole exchange amounted to piss-poor manners.

Hearing about incidents like this makes me think Post's *Etiquette* is worth revisiting. Not only would Post's ears have pricked up at the obvious faux pas, but she could have patiently explained to the elevator girls why they should consider not saying anything beyond "Hello" in those situations. The problem—1922 and now—is that people don't always *realize* they're being obnoxious. Then they suffer the effects of their

and every question asked of you. Someone asks you how you're doing, you express interest in how she's doing. Someone asks you what you're working on, you inquire as to what he's working on. This give-and-take was polite, sure, but it also allowed a savvy newcomer to gather information. Asking questions was important because it both buoyed conversation and let you do some basic fact gathering. Here Post again gave a quick nod to the rare conversational wizard—"but the ordinary rest of us, if we would be thought sympathetic, intelligent, or agreeable, 'go fishing.'"

So how would Post rate the following exchange? Anne, a curator, described to me a typical evening at an industry party. She spots William, an old friend she could reliably expect to see at these functions, across the room. "I go up to him, I'm happy to see him, and standing next to him is the new kid in his office. Maybe twenty-two, but he had the air of someone who graduated a year early." William introduces the two ("Anne, this is Matt, he's our new . . .") and promptly excuses himself to locate the restroom. To jumpstart the conversation, Anne asks, "So, how long have you been there?" Just two weeks, Matt mumbles. "Liking it so far?" Well, he was just getting his feet wet, you know, but on the whole, he was liking it. "Great. I know William is very happy there." Silence. Matt says nothing more. So Anne continues, glances around, makes a remark about the room's bordello-like red velvet wallpaper, and when that lands with a thud, she asks what kinds of things he's been working on lately. Matt goes on at some length, comes to the end of his narration, bites his lip, and smiles wanly. Silence again. Anne nods, keeps nodding for a while, then says it was nice to meet him and makes her excuse to get away, because, as she later said, "He made me feel like one of those parents in *The Graduate*. As if . . . if he gave me the slightest opening, I'd start lecturing him on plastics."

It might not seem like a make-or-break moment—conversations that take place with a plastic cup of Pinot Grigio in

hand rarely do. And it's possible Matt truly wasn't interested in
Anne's storied career. Post, however, would put a stop to that
line of thought straightaway by stating, matter-of-factly, that
Matt's boredom was of no consequence. It was only Old Money's evaluation of the conversation that mattered—that is to say,
not his, not New Money's. If you were a bore firmly entrenched
in the power structure, then it mattered less that you kept missing your cue, or couldn't run with a joke. You could drive listeners to hot tears of frustrated boredom and someone would
still ask you round if your name ended in "III." But if you were
new to the scene, no one felt obligated to keep sending you invi-
tations.

The fishing approach touches on one of the potentially
seedier elements of working your way into insider status. New-
comers may be unsettling, but they don't have any of the shared
knowledge that keeps a system humming, and that's always reassuring to anyone threatened by their presence. All closed systems run not just on shared operational knowledge (how things
are done, or where stuff is kept), but also on collective memory
of all the characters who've ever passed through. Every organization is haunted, Post is saying. This means you'll hear coworkers refer to Mr. Fascinating, who left the company four years
ago, and as they do they'll see him before them, as if it were
yesterday, and remember how he clutched his vodka tonics, how
he chuckled at the CEO's jokes, and how he and the sales director dated for months, thinking no one noticed, before finally going public. They'll recall how he'd lean far over the conference
table while waiting to make a point, and that there was something aggressive and territorial about it, and come to think of it,
some things you do remind them of him. These capsule histories
of past employees become a form of currency—totally worth-
less in any other context, but extremely valuable within the four
walls of the office building. I was once haunted by constant reference to "Rebecca," my immediate predecessor at a job. *Rebecca did this,* my boss would say, or *Rebecca would usually that.*
I feared I was losing to the memory of Rebecca until I flat-out

asked the woman at the next desk how wonderful, truly, this Rebecca person was. Turns out Rebecca had quit in tears after three months and informed everyone she was applying to graduate school. Perhaps, my informant suggested, the boss simply kept mentioning Rebecca because she was his first direct report and only reference point.

Of course, whenever you're trying to gain a foothold in a group, details of a member's life are worth knowing for their own sake. In another instance, I innocently typed up a dismissive reader's report for a manuscript, stating something to the effect that I had a hard time caring about the troubles of a privileged Connecticut boarding school girl—and promptly handed it in to a boss who, lo and behold, had been a Connecticut boarding school girl.*

Ignorance, unfortunately, doesn't get you a free pass on that kind of obnoxiousness. (This is what Post would have said to my dismissive report: "She who says, 'That does not interest me,' or 'That bores me,' defines her own limitations.") Going fishing beforehand might have worked better, and I might not even have needed to ask my boss about her background; someone else could have easily filled me in. But very few new arrivals —supposing they should avoid looking like they've had their nose pressed against the glass—express *any* curiosity about people ranked above them. It's worth repeating because it's so pervasive and yet so fundamentally limiting: few junior staffers express the necessary curiosity about more senior staff members. It's almost as if they think they know the answers, so they don't even bother asking. When I asked a reporter, someone I assumed was comfortable with asking questions, why this might be so, he suggested that it was probably just awkward shyness. He went on to say this was the main problem with shyness, at least shyness in adults: it's very easily mistaken for lack of interest. In fact, the line between not reciprocating when someone asks you a question and saying outright that you aren't in-

---

* The title—almost too ironic to be true. *The Hazards of Good Breeding.*

terested in them is a line so fine as to be effectively negligible.

Here's where it might be helpful to divulge something from Post's personal life, because if all you know is her clipped phrasing and finger wagging, you might get the wrong idea about *Etiquette*. Post began to write—fiction, mainly—when she found herself feeling stifled by her sheltered existence. (Think of Michelle Pfeiffer looking like she's about to pass out all throughout Martin Scorsese's adaptation of *The Age of Innocence*, and you've some idea why.) Her writing didn't make her tremendously popular with the people she grew up with, however. "Whenever any of the Tuxedoites who had known Emily from girlhood remembered that she was now an author," her son Edwin wrote decades later, "they were prone to inquire with a touch a whimsy, 'Darling, how are you getting on with your writing?' and not pause for a reply." But Post carried on writing, and more urgently when her 1905 divorce left her with bills to pay. The senior Edwin Post had turned out to be an indifferent husband at best, and one day, over lunch, Emily was informed he'd been keeping a mistress—a showgirl—in an apartment across town. The person who told her this was a scandal sheet publisher trying to extort $500, assuming the family would want to keep the story out of the papers. They didn't play along, and Post was publicly humiliated. The divorce made her a single, working mother—uncommon for her time, and all but unheard of in her social set. It's a detail that adds unexpected resonance to lines like this, in a chapter of *Etiquette* she titled "One's Position in the Community":

> Life, whether social or business, is a bank in which you deposit certain funds of character, intellect and heart; or other funds of egotism, hard-heartedness and unconcern; or deposit—nothing! And the bank honors your deposit, and no more. In other words, you can draw nothing out but what you have put in. If your community is to give you admiration and honor, it is merely necessary to be admirable and honorable. The more you put in, the more will be paid out to you.

And with this we are far from silverware and wrist-corsage territory. This led me to wonder if there was any way to recover from an initial failure to grasp curiosity's importance. Could you bounce back from a beauty-editor-in-the-elevator moment, in other words? Not sway the bigwig toward forgetting your spasm of obnoxiousness—because that's beyond your control—but prompt him to take you seriously? The advice from Andrew Carnegie's era suggested no; one strike and your corporate overlords would move on to the next contestant. Post seems to be saying otherwise. For one, good manners on Old Money's part meant they were obligated to try hard to keep an open mind about you. Second, if the point of etiquette was "instinctive consideration for the feelings of others," it made no sense to impose a time limit on that open-mindedness. You can start expressing more curiosity about people at any moment, and people wouldn't think you'd changed so much as grown up. "Most of us go through life mentally wrapped in the cotton wool of our own affairs," Post ventured wistfully. Any exceptions to that general rule were bound to get favorably noticed.

This marks the first point in American success literature where the naturally shy—and constitutionally feminine—are actually accorded an advantage. What better way to overcome shyness than to shift the burden of speech to the other person? What better way to do that than by asking the kinds of questions that keep that person talking? Shyness disappears, and in its place comes the gentle, breezy deference that Old Money feels they deserve. You get the information you need, *and* you make your presence felt.

I did notice this once in another former colleague. It was not that Analena was physically prepossessing. (She was undeniably pretty, but in some industries, pretty twenty-four-year-olds materialize in cubicles overnight.) One day I commented on her ability to keep people's eyes riveted to her face. She responded quite seriously. Well, Analena said, she only asked questions—one after another after another. An hour of conversation would pass, and though she had revealed next to nothing about her background (half-Danish, half-American), accomplishments (nothing especially trailblazing yet), or predilections (having affairs), her partner would walk away completely gratified. They would be happy merely for the opportunity to tell their own stories. And when she wasn't in the room, and came up in conversation, they'd go out of their way to mention what an interesting person Analena was.

Which perhaps explains why Post's rhetoric became so heated. It was really very simple, you see. Very, very simple. Curiosity about others is what made you appear to be an interesting person yourself, what saved you from obnoxiousness, and what allowed you to appear passionate and engaged without having to express any passion outright—always a sticky proposition at the dinner table.

It's a subtle process that begins with asking deeper and timelier questions. The following guidelines might help, whether you're nouveau riche or just nouveau:

Don't skip a question because you're pretty sure you already understand what's going on. Occasionally, you get an answer that's not what you'd assumed it would be. In those cases, you've benefited by being reminded (privately) how much people's readings of situations can differ. For example, you might assume someone is angry because of X, but it turns out it's Y and also Z that has them riled. This tells you some things about the angry person that are probably useful to know. But even when political calculations are the furthest thing from your mind, answers to questions you nearly didn't ask in the first place are often the most rewarding. There's no law at work here—just the fact that people can be pleasantly surprising.

Do pick your moments. The newcomer who runs to the boss every time the fax machine isn't working is quickly going to exhaust his boss's patience. To a certain extent, you want to consider the organizational status of the person you're posing the question to.

(As will be discussed later on, most higher-ups don't even kn[ ]
where the fax machine is, let alone how it works—but executive
assistants and mailroom guys generally do.) On the other hand,
you should never assume someone low on the totem pole isn't
qualified to answer substantive queries. Many outside callers, for
instance, annoy both company VIPs and their staff by insisting,
per Donald Trump, that "they only deal with the boss," when in
fact the boss employs many people capable of fielding any question related to his business—indeed, who are employed for just
that purpose.

Last note on this front: Try to distinguish between an invitation to "sit in on" and an invitation to actively participate.

Do fashion some sort of all-purpose three-question primer. How did you
come to work here? How long have you been here? What are
you working on right now? Not asked all in one breath, but following the general flow of conversation. The answers will invariably provide a sense of the lay of the land, of who has seniority
in the organization, and the amount of pride someone takes in
his or her job. This last proves very significant the longer you
work somewhere, and the more entwined you get in the politics
and emotional rhythms of the office.

Do have one signature question you can resort to whenever you can't think
of anything to say. It shouldn't be a test of knowledge, tied to current events, or of the "what's your favorite color?" variety. Ideally it's a question that can be used on people you've known for
five minutes as well as those you've been running around with for
five years: What are you reading these days? Any travel plans?
Anything was better, Post specified, than feeble stabs at seeming
exciting, like dropping *Au revoir* or other foreign phrases into
your conversation.

"What was your first job?" works well too. In her 1970 crack
at the self-improvement shelf, *How to Talk with Practically Anybody About Practically Anything,* Barbara Walters relates how
she once had a particularly difficult time getting Aristotle Onas-

sis to open up to her. They were at lunch, he was yammering about high-seas finance, and she found herself wondering how this short man with a mouth full of gold fillings could be considered a world-class charmer. She found him uncooperative and intimidating. When she finally found an opening in the conversation, she decided to plow ahead with this: "Tell me, Mr. Onassis, you're so successful—not just in shipping and airlines, but in other industries too—I wonder, how did you begin? What was your very first job?" He opened up like a flower. (His first job was washing dishes, it turns out.)

Do be aware of regional differences. In some parts of the country, a long, leisurely introduction to a professional conversation or phone call is expected. In others—New York and Los Angeles come to mind—any small talk beyond a certain point is seen as a gross imposition. Fortunately, it's not difficult to tell when you're starting to wear down someone's patience. Hearing "uh-huh, uh-huh" while you're pausing midsentence is a clear sign you need to wind up and get to the point. The rude party in these exchanges is *not* the one in a hurry, because to take your time is to assume the person you called is not busy—and that's an insult in her book. In the South and Midwest, be prepared to stick with pleasantries for six, seven minutes.

Don't talk to a cripple about the joys of dancing. *The American Chesterfield* counseled, when starting a conversation, "never to speak of ropes, in the house of one who has been hung." Nor, Post said, should you veer into the advantages of "bloodline" to a self-made man. It's reasonable enough to expect adults to be able to stand hurt feelings, but the point is to be aware (and to realize that the person who might suffer the most from someone's hurt feelings—if you're New Money—is you).

Don't ask people you don't know well to opine. "How about those Sox?" is not a useful question because it asks people to express an opinion apropos of nothing. People can freeze up when you ask them to make judgments on the spot—even when fudging an answer wouldn't be all that difficult for them.

»»

Etiquette sparked a trend, and many copycat titles were published throughout the 1920s and 1930s. Most of them lacked Post's way with words—and nearly all abandoned her overarching goal of paying more attention to other people's feelings than one's own, at least as long as one was in public. The editors of 1929's *Vogue's Book of Etiquette* tried—particularly in their section on the office—but missed the mark, presuming as they did that anyone who'd be reading their book was a limp snob: "Don't ever be too grand to disentangle difficulties or misunderstandings for anyone who, either at the telephone or in person, appeals for help . . . Behave politely. Speak distinctly. Hear discreetly. Dress demurely. Be indispensable, and see some fun in work." In their *Guide to Effective Living,* a grab bag of lifestyle advice that came out in 1957, husband and wife team N. H. and S. K. Mager delivered their rules for conversation in another list: Do be pleasant. Do ask people with expertise in a particular area for advice. Don't exaggerate. Don't ask people if they have any children (you'd hear about it if they did). Do read newspapers (so you'll be able to talk about something other than yourself). Try carrying on a conversation without making personal references. Do be kind. Don't be a crusader. Don't complain, "especially around males." Do tell jokes about yourself. "Don't admit you are self-conscious, have an inferiority complex, or are sensitive." Pause. Vary the tempo of your speech.

All decent advice, but you can imagine Post stifling a yawn. *Vogue's* halfhearted "fun in work" aside, there's a certain joyless, carpet-gazing quality to these prescriptions. Conversation was not about close, checked observance of the words coming out of your mouth, Post felt, but intense interest in what people had to say for themselves. A few years after the success of *Etiquette,* she joined the pantheon of authors who get to write pretty much anything they please and get it published. Her son Edwin likened the book to both *Uncle Tom's Cabin* and *Gone With the Wind,* the first because it shaped popular opinion, the second because its publication changed the life of the author. And for all her gentility, Post was not above cashing in. She was sought for countless commercial endorsements, and once pocketed $3,000 for scribbling a note to the effect that ginger ale was a refreshing drink to serve at parties—she didn't even have to specify the brand.

As the success-literature canon expanded, more and more pages would be devoted to the connection between a real democratic curiosity in people—whoever they might be, whatever they might do—and realizing one's own earning potential. Indeed it was Post's doggedness in fact gathering that made her career. Edwin estimated that about seven-eighths of *Etiquette* was not drawn from his mother's personal recollections of life amongst the silver-spoon set but from patiently mining other sources. What qualified Post as an authority on etiquette was not blue blood but her "inveterate thoroughness in assembling all the available information on any subject." She'd simply been extraordinarily adept at asking questions, and better than most at recording the answers.

4

On Near Universal
Self-Absorption

How to Win Friends and Influence People
by Recognizing What Navel-Gazers People Are

> The truth is that we can only sell
> what people are willing to buy.
>
> —LEE IACOCCA, former car manufacturer
> and Dale Carnegie devotee

BESTSELLER LISTS have a self-generating property. At some point people start wanting to read a book because they get the uneasy feeling that everyone else already has. This phenomenon is partly responsible for the astounding success of Dale Carnegie's *How to Win Friends and Influence People.* First published in November 1936, *How to Win Friends* reached the top of the *New York Times* nonfiction bestseller list by the end of the year. By April 1937, it had gone through thirty printings. Some twenty million copies later, it has become one of twentieth-century America's most recognizable literary exports. Years before John Lennon ventured a similar comparison, Carnegie's publisher declared that sales of *How to Win Friends* were second only to those of the Bible.*

---

* Dale is no relation to Andrew Carnegie. At least, not that anyone's aware of. Dale was born "Dale Carnagey" in rural Missouri, and though his father, James, claimed some dim, distant connection to Andrew, Dale himself never did. He did,

Carnegie has been blamed for all kinds of social frustrations since. The fact that some grinning stranger greets you with a "Hi, how ya doing today!" every time you stumble into The Gap. That waitresses draw smiley faces and write "THANKS!" on your dinner check. The expectation that, in a well-functioning world, we would all just get along. My home state has a concept it likes to call "Minnesota Nice," which as far as I can tell means you never know whether someone is being honest with you, or simply trying to avoid saying anything that might be controversial. The first Dale Carnegie parody—it was called *How to Lose Friends and Alienate People* and was released within months of the original—blamed him for the "I'm-Going-to-Make-You-Like-Me Movement," and for the fact that everyone was now expected to suffer through wheezy, overly polite chit-chat.

The few highbrow critics that have bothered to study *How to Win Friends* put Carnegie at the forefront of hiring policies that place a premium on personality—never mind actual merit. In the late 1980s, even Stephen Covey, the author of *The 7 Habits of Highly Effective People* (and not someone you'd expect to turn his nose up at anyone else's self-improvement efforts), strongly hinted that Carnegie's book marked a sad shift in American thinking on success. Covey suggested that where once upward mobility ethics were about "fidelity, temperance, courage, justice, patience, industry, simplicity, modesty, and the Golden Rule," we now had a nation of ever-ebullient, smarmy, amateur PR people running around.

The book appeared at an unusual cultural moment, and this is worth keeping in mind. Emily Post's readers could worry about charm and conversation because they had handfuls of cash—the only thing they lacked was social status. Carnegie's readers had neither. *How to Win Friends* was written when the country was still wriggling out from under the Depression, when nobody could believe that hard work would ensure financial security.

---

however, change the spelling of his last name upon moving to New York City and going into business. Any confusion could only be to his benefit, he reasoned.

When the economy's in full swing, it's easy to talk about happiness and the universal storehouse of goodwill, as Orison Swett Marden did, or to celebrate young genius à la Scott and Zelda. Free markets always give advantages to those blessed with big brains because they can use their smarts, if they want, to finagle a larger piece of the pie for themselves. No one's getting less than his or her share, and we can all breathe easy, knowing that with just a little extra effort, we too can put on cocktail attire and traipse champagne-drunk through fountains. But when the economy tanks, as it did so spectacularly after the Wall Street crash of 1929, and the national money spigot is turned off, one of the first casualties is admiration for precociousness. It quickly becomes a nagging reminder that talent is not—and never will be—distributed evenly across the population.

This is a sobering idea. It is far more sobering if you aren't one of the gifted ones, because now you've got a much more daunting problem than your cleverer neighbor does. Unless, unless, unless . . . the key to success is *not* a function of distinguishing yourself. The strangely uplifting message of *How to Win Friends and Influence People* is that people are endlessly fascinated by themselves—by you, and what you can or can't do, not so much. Carnegie's outlook is similar to his success-literature predecessors, but he states the implications a little more baldly. "When we are not engaged in thinking about some definite problem," Carnegie wrote, "we usually spend about ninety-five percent of our time thinking about ourselves." The Big Secret of Dealing with People was that everyone wanted to feel important, and that whether you reached them or not had everything to do with whether you confirmed that feeling of importance.

This sounds like Emily Post: Success is wrapped up in being considerate—or at the very least *aware*—of other people's feelings. But Carnegie believed attentiveness to others' needs wouldn't just help get you accepted, it could actually put money in your pockets. He claimed that all the trouble salesmen were having could not solely be blamed on hard economic times. Some of them, he said, were simply too focused on what *they* wanted out of every transaction—in other words, big commissions. These salesmen needed to shift their focus to helping customers solve problems, and if they did that, they never had to worry about where their next check was coming from. The same was true for butchers, bakers, auto mechanics, and elder statesmen—*How to Win Friends* is a riot of democracy. Carnegie wanted you to get better service at your local diner using the same methods Abraham Lincoln used to break into politics. He mentioned past presidents of Harvard in the same breath as part-time piano teachers from Tulsa. When he invoked Ralph Waldo Emerson, it was not to wrestle with transcendentalism, but to pass on Emerson's surefire method for getting a stubborn cow to go where you wanted it to go.

This we're-all-in-it-together impulse can make the Carnegie philosophy somewhat difficult to implement on the job. He doesn't take pecking orders into account, and he seems defiantly, willfully ignorant of class. We learn from him that Theodore Roosevelt's valet considered the former roughrider a real hero, and we learn why—Teddy was a nice boss, and remembered all his servants' names, and the names of their spouses, too. But how the president's position in life was fundamentally different from the man paid to wait on him hand and foot didn't seem to interest Carnegie. He was not really concerned with who had power in the exchange and who didn't.

I started to wonder how one might translate the advice in *How to Win Friends and Influence People* for those at the bottom of the ladder. In other words, how do you influence people on the job if you can't assume that people are even thinking about you? "A person's toothache means more to that person than a famine in China which kills a million people. A boil on one's neck interests one more than forty earthquakes in Africa," Carnegie cautioned his readers. "Think of that next time you start a conversation." If navel-gazing is the name of the game, what does that mean for someone who's dependent on the navel-gazer for promotion? It takes some maneuvering of Carnegie's original principles, but I found at least three big repercussions bubbling up from beneath the surface. In all instances it demands an outlook that seems, at first glance, totally wrong.

The first principle of the 95 percent self-absorption standard is that people only listen to what you have to say if you take the time to talk about what's on their minds first. Carnegie put it rather brusquely: "Why talk about what we want? That is childish. Absurd. Of course, you are interested in what you want. You are eternally interested in it. But no one else is." Humans weren't even unique in this regard. (The way Emerson got that calf into the barn was by putting his finger in its mouth and letting it suck.) You could get someone to do something, but ultimately they would only do it for their own reasons—not yours.

Carnegie wasn't alone in this line of thinking—the idea that people were fundamentally apathetic and self-serving was already changing advertising. In a 1929 book called *How to Turn People into Gold* (unfortunate timing, considering that Wall Street crash), the adman Kenneth M. Goode claimed that the old way of advertising was useless now that audiences were more sophisticated. Ads used to tell you why a product was good—the quality of the craftsmanship, or the purity of the ingredients. The first shift in technique came when ads started plugging a product's effectiveness—how quickly you'd be finished with the floors using this new soap. On the horizon now was copy that sold the effect of the effect—with all the time you saved washing floors, you'd have more time to do your hair. This was necessary, Goode said, because John Q. Public couldn't be expected to care about the merits of your product. He devised the following list to sum up the psychological profile of the American man-in-the-street as he saw it. Such a man, he said:

1. Won't look far beyond his own self-interest.
2. Resents change and dislikes newness.
3. Forgets past and remembers inaccurately.

4. Won't fight *for* things when he can find something to fight *against*.
5. Dares not differ from the crowd unless certain his difference will be recognized as superiority.
6. Except in high emotion, won't exert himself beyond the lines of least resistance.
7. Won't act, even in important matters, unless properly followed up.

Carnegie was less cynical, but not by much. "So the only way on earth to influence other people is to talk about what *they* want and show them how to get it."

The translation for today's underling would look something like this: The most direct route to reaching your professional goals is to help others meet their goals first. This becomes very clear when you realize that your boss also has a boss — and in the early stages, your job is fundamentally to help your boss look good in front of his or hers. You need to help your boss get promoted. As discussed, this can involve mind-numbing, tedious work, the purpose of which may not be clear, but which seems somehow designed to build trust and suss out the depths of your loyalties.

It also means ascertaining what those bosses' needs are so you can effectively fill them. Here's a short list, ripped from actual experiences, of what people gradually learned their superiors really wanted:

1. Not to feel short. (A 5'10" woman employed by a 5'4" woman figured out she got along better with her boss when she took care to always be seated in her presence. Sometimes this meant crouching on the floor.)
2. Coffee. (One young analyst assisted a man who, walking out of his office, would pause midstride at the assistant's cubicle and say, "Coffee" — that's it, just "Coffee" — and walk on with the full expectation that a fresh mug would be on his desk upon his return.)
3. To not feel like he is disappointing anyone. (A young

take on a mind of their own. (So to speak.) I myself came to realize—after about a year and a half—that I'd sent enough poison darts flying through the air that some of my superiors were reflexively starting to limit my opportunities. Imagine, if you would, the following scenes:

Boss emerges from her office, is about to put a manuscript box on your desk, then when the box is inches from impact with your inbox, she suddenly halts, pauses, and brings it back to her chest. "Nah. You won't like this," she says.

Or this one: Standing at the microwave, a colleague asks, "So what *do* you like?"

Marden was very worried about how "smart boys" would fare in the office. Because they *were* actually better equipped to pinpoint cracks in the china, they might get a little carried away. They'd do well in academic settings, but because they were so irritable, "squeamish," and so "scornful of men's dullness," they'd eventually "drop back into nothingness [while] their plodding schoolmates rise slowly but surely."

That being so smart can lead to a certain impatience, a kind of squeamishness, around more average intellects is something some masters of snark readily confess to. "Everywhere I've worked, I've been generally liked. I get along with people," said Gabriel, an aspiring screenwriter in Los Angeles who paid his dues in the William Morris mailroom and various small production companies. "Except at Paramount, where I acted like I was smarter than everyone else. I *was* smarter. Much smarter. And I had a real hard time pretending that, uh, we were all equally . . . gifted." This attitude was common, he'd found, amongst people paid to give their impressions of other people's creations, but who weren't required to cough up any product themselves—he cited Hollywood "development" staffers in particular.* It wasn't

---

* The race to jump on colleagues' ideas is not unique to creative industries. A *Harvard Business Review* article on "The Smart Talk Trap" described a phenomenon similar to snark this way: "At a global financial institution we studied, junior executives made a point—especially in meetings with their bosses present—of

that they were miserable people eager to rain on others' parades, and in fact, many felt that every time they dismissed a pitch as "legless" they were scoring a point for good taste—or even stemming the dumbing-down of America. But Gabriel had also found that this stance of his wasn't sustainable for long.

Marden might say it wasn't sustainable because it sent vibrations of impatience into the air that would ricochet off the atmosphere and return to earth to make Gabriel himself appear uninspired. Then there was the fact that saying no to projects—be they movies, books, deals—didn't help the bottom line. Marden believed the universe made its preference for people who said "yes" known by giving these intrepid characters more money. So if you were a young American in 1904, a little threatened by looming socioeconomic changes, you could find some solace in these words, from Marden's chapter on the "Cheering-Up Business": "The love of cheerfulness can be cultivated like any other faculty, and in practical life it will be worth more to you than a college education without it." And also: "The pessimist repels trade and new business. The cheerful man, on the other hand, attracts it. There is a great drawing power in optimism." (There's the Law of Attraction again.) And as he restates it later: "The habit of feeling kindly towards everybody, of carrying about a helpful manner, an expression of love, of kindness, in one's very face, and a desire to help and cheer, is worth a fortune to a young man or young woman trying to get on."

By "worth a fortune," Marden meant "worth a fortune." In the late 1920s, the industrialist and New Thought disciple Roger Babson was no less convinced. "What is the biggest thing in the world?" he asked. "Some may suggest 'The World War.' An-

---

trashing the ideas of their peers. Every time someone dared to offer an idea, everyone around the table would leap in with reasons why it was nothing short of idiotic. Senior executives didn't try to stop the verbal fray. Sometimes they even nodded approvingly as smart-sounding faultfinders critiqued ideas to death." The smart talk, claimed authors Jeffrey Pfeffer and Robert I. Sutton, was something managers should worry about because it got in the way of solving problems—people all too easily substituted clever discourse for action.

thoughts, when an unfamiliar voice from the corner of the conference room made a suggestion about a book that was about to
be published: Maybe the package wasn't working? Maybe they
should consider changing the title? The boss had no idea who
this young woman was—or so I gathered from the "Who *was*
that?" she hissed at me as everyone filed out of the room another hour later. The girl's title suggestion hadn't been ignored,
but it was shot down without a terrific amount of regard for her
feelings.

Even if the marketing assistant's idea had been a flash of
raw genius (it wasn't, unfortunately), I don't think it would have
received much more consideration. If she had given the situation a few minutes of thought, she might have realized these
people had collectively devoted dozens of years to deliberating
book titles, so perhaps her four-day-old insights weren't quite as
valuable as theirs. Post would have had her show some deference, because Old Money liked deference, and not speaking until spoken to was an easy way to show it. In any event, the scene
left everyone feeling ill at ease. Not least, I suspect, the young
woman herself.* Two weeks later, she was spotted stuffing enve-
lopes in the mailroom without her shoes on. The strange thing
is, no one was surprised—it was as if she'd already signaled her
intent to walk around on that nasty carpet barefoot.

"The faults of commission are far more serious than those
of omission," Post tut-tutted. "Regrets are seldom for what you
left unsaid." So many dangers associated with opening your
mouth, but you can't keep it shut forever. You have to speak
because you're no Bob Cratchit. Post felt the only way New
Money could do so and avoid obnoxiousness was by adhering to
what she called "the need for reciprocity." In theory, this meant
mere curiosity. In practice, it meant asking a question for each

---

* It occurred to me later that she had essentially attempted something like those
thirty-second TV spots, where the new guy suggests something radical like changing the long-distance calling plan, or using FedEx, or Burger King for lunch, and
everyone is just blown away by his vision. This does not happen in real life.

physically fit in Mrs. Astor's ballroom. But that wasn't true — imposing a cap was the whole point. "If you go outside that number," socialite henchman Ward McAllister said, "you strike people who are either not at ease in a ballroom or else make others not at ease." Finding reasons to exclude people, in other words, is what some people do for fun.*

I've never met anyone who, *Mean Girls*-style, openly begrudged new hires, but I do know that every arrival changes the mood of the office a little. Even an underling has the ability to momentarily raise the temperature of an organization, if only because (like New Money to Old Money) he or she's a vivid reminder that time marches on, and things change, and change is unpredictable. For those who have been working in a place for a while, it can be unsettling. This new person could be a force for good, could make no difference whatsoever — or this person could cause hitherto unknown suffering.

Whatever their suspicions, most longtime employees do prefer that new arrivals put in some time before they start serving up opinions. This was made abundantly clear the time a marketing assistant, on just her fourth day in the office, was invited to sit in on a major meeting at the publishing company where I used to work. This meeting was held only twice a year, and was attended by about fifty people, half of whom flew in from far-flung parts of the country. Her invitation to join was a rarity — a privilege, really, to the extent that sitting in day-long meetings can be considered a privilege. Two hours into the proceedings, the boss was wrapping up one discussion and preparing to move on to the next, and glancing around, asked for any last

---

* Edith Wharton, Post's favorite novelist, wrote almost exclusively about this phenomenon. Ms. Undine Spragg, the relentless social climber at the center of *The Custom of the Country,* newly arrived in New York, frets constantly because she knows she's surrounded by people who regard her and her family as "Invaders." In this light, entry into society was partly a matter of overcoming the fear that you weren't really wanted: "They all had their friends, their ties, their delightful crowding obligations: why should they make room for an intruder in a circle so packed with the initiated?"

know better, people who are perfectly capable of intelligent understanding if they didn't let their brains remain asleep or locked tight, go night after night to dinner parties, day after day to other social gatherings, and absent-mindedly prate about this or that without ever taking the trouble to *think* what they are saying and to whom they are saying it!

It was clearly a subject that riled her, but perhaps she felt keenly how much was at stake for New Money. She herself was about as firmly entrenched in the power elite as a girl born in 1873 Baltimore could be. Her parents raised her in Tuxedo Park (the country's second country club and first gated community), and she went to *the* finishing school (Miss Graham's). This all helped her snag a husband—at nineteen—who came from even older money, and a tony address in New York.* Post knew precisely how stodgy Old Money was, and how loath they were to welcome outsiders. And perhaps most important for New Money to understand, she knew that Old Money had its unwritten codes, and standards were high: "Once in a while—a very long while—one meets a brilliant person whose talk is a delight; or still more rarely a wit who manipulates every ordinary topic with the agility of a sleight-of-hand performer, to the ever increasing rapture of his listeners," but this was rare. The people who think they're amusing always outnumber the people who truly are.

Ever increasing rapture? Realistically, the most foolproof way to avoid obnoxiousness when you found yourself in the same reception room with Old Money was to say nothing. You'd hang back and just observe the proceedings for a while, otherwise you'd remind them why they didn't like new people. Mrs. William Backhouse Astor Jr.—the woman who ran New York society in the Gilded Age—kept a list known by anyone who read the society pages as "the 400." It was widely rumored that the number was chosen because only four hundred souls could

---

* The Posts had stepped onto American shores as early as the mid-1700s, so it was considered an ideal match.

obnoxiousness without ever knowing they were the cause. It's a particular problem in the "extraordinary modern world which is half-social, half-professional," as *The New Yorker* described Post's milieu. Ours is much the same. Your fate depends in a small but crucial way on whether someone wouldn't mind having to sit next to you at lunch.

After seeing more than a few fresh faces blunder—badly—through attempts to endear themselves to their new colleagues, it also occurred to me that imagining oneself nouveau riche might be a good way to approach conversation while new on the job. You = New Money. *Everybody else who was hired before you* = Old Money. (I mean everybody, from chief operations officer to the mailroom supervisor.) There is no other way to know you're sharing an elevator with the only man in the company who has the authority—and after hearing you natter on for a while, the sincere desire—to fire you on the spot.

The first way New Money got a foothold in society, according to Post, was to demonstrate familiarity with basic procedure. There were correct and incorrect ways of doing things, she believed, and which was which had been determined over generations of trial and error. She starts the 692 pages of *Etiquette* with fourteen pages on Introductions. ("Mrs. Jones, may I present Mr. Smith?") She flatters her audience by reminding them—as if it's an issue in their day-to-day lives—of how to respond when introduced to the president of the United States, a king, a cardinal, and visiting foreign ambassadors.* She moves on to acceptable Greetings. When she comes around to Conversation, Post gets more strident:

> Nearly all the faults or mistakes in conversation are caused by not thinking. For instance, a first rule for behavior in society is: "Try to do and say those things only which will be agreeable to others." Yet how many people, who really

---

* But not the pope, notably. Catholics were still a little suspect in her world.

woman who thought she had a joking, gentle-ribbing rapport with her male boss eventually realized he and his long-term girlfriend had a rocky relationship that left him perpetually on the defensive. Those "friendly insults" on the job just wore him down.)

4. To have someone cute to look at. (See chapter 7.)

5. To have someone around who has no life outside the job. (Rare but true. One woman overheard her boss, an editor, express a wish for an assistant "who's in the office until nine, then goes home and reads manuscripts.")

6. To be extravagantly obnoxious without suffering any consequences. (According to a former production assistant at a family-friendly network sitcom, story meetings were filled with cracking wise. Not your garden-variety trash-talk. More like things you'd expect to hear in a prison yard, or unfriendly suggestions about your mother's sexual health. "How about I do you against the wall? Like, right now?" was a particular Tuesday morning favorite.)

7. To watch someone suffer the way she suffered when she was young. (This person is often heard saying things like "You think things are bad here? Now? Well, let me tell you about . . ." This person tends to reserve the term "honey" for people she doesn't actually like, and often has significant life regrets.)

All of which provide yet another reason to observe, restlessly, those around you. But bullying, insecure, paranoid ones aside, some ambitious bosses truly would like to pull their assistants up with them once they get promoted. It would, after all, be further affirmation of their power.

Carnegie's life provides a perfect homespun illustration of the edict that gratification sometimes only comes when you start ministering to someone else's needs. He floundered for years trying to assert himself before finally hitting his stride — by helping other people get their own professional footing.

His beginnings were nothing if not Norman Rockwell–style

picturesque. Jimmy Stewart might have played him in the movies — a photo taken in the '50s shows him smiling outdoors, hair mussed, wire-rimmed glasses, and wearing a hoodie. He remembered his childhood as one of constant, soul-withering anxiety. His family was poor, his pants always too short, and he was shy. Around age eleven, he lost part of his left index finger in a farm accident. But despite his overall awkwardness, he had a knack for oratory and ended up at Warrensburg State Teachers College. When he left school (he failed Latin and never graduated), he grossly disappointed his mother — who wanted him to enter the seminary — and became a traveling salesman. The first company he knocked on doors for was an outfit called International Correspondence Schools. In two years, he sold exactly one course packet. His next job, working for the Armour Company, involved trying to sell meat to South Dakota farmers. (How one convinces South Dakota farmers, who presumably have cattle, pigs, and chickens nearby and at their disposal, to purchase meat is anyone's guess.) He dreamed of acting, and pulled together $500 in savings and went east. He'd been fantasizing about Boston, but a friend tipped him off that New York City might be a better bet if he wanted to get into theater. His only part of note — after enrolling at the American Academy of Dramatic Arts — was a minor turn as a doctor in the touring production of *Polly of the Circus.** Whether out of financial necessity or force of habit, he couldn't leave salesmanship behind. On the road, after performances, he'd haul out his suitcase and try to sell neckties to fellow cast and crew.

When Carnegie finally decided to give up on acting — the year was 1912 — he convinced the director of the YMCA on

---

* The central story line of the play concerns an injured female trapeze artist who gets carried into the home of a small-town pastor. Trapeze artist and pastor then fall in love and get married, thereby completely scandalizing his congregation. *Polly* was made into a feature film in 1917, and produced again in 1932 as a vehicle for Clark Gable and Marion Davies, mistress of newspaper magnate William Randolph Hearst, aka Citizen Kane.

125th Street in Manhattan to let him teach a night class on public speaking. (Then, as now, 125th Street was the center of Harlem, though the neighborhood was then white and heavily Jewish.) The YMCA wasn't Carnegie's first choice; Columbia University and New York University had already turned him down. To Carnegie's ultimate benefit, instead of giving him the standard $2-per-session salary, the YMCA decided he should work on commission instead. Soon the Dale Carnegie Course in Public Speaking and Effective Human Relations was pulling in $30 a night, and he again went on the road, holding seminars at other Y locations and in conference halls across the country. *How to Win Friends and Influence People* began as a supplementary text.

"When dealing with people, let us remember we are not dealing with creatures of logic," Carnegie wrote. "We are dealing with creatures of emotion, creatures bristling with prejudice and motivated by pride and vanity." He often claimed there were more Americans suffering from mental illness than from all other diseases combined. Some authorities, Carnegie said, had been looking into it and had concluded that 50 percent of the time it was a matter of damaged brain cells—from syphilis, alcohol, or lesions. In the other half of mental cases, postmortem examinations revealed brain tissue as healthy as the next person's. Carnegie once put the question to a doctor: "Why do these people go insane?" The doctor had no idea, but he did tell Carnegie a story about one of his patients, a woman who, in order to escape life's sadness (she was childless, her husband hated her, she had no job or standing in the community), started imagining herself divorced and happily remarried into the English aristocracy. Every time the doctor called on her, she would breathlessly report—delighted—that she'd given birth the night before. She had plainly lost her mind.

Maybe this wasn't so tragic, Carnegie suggested. For people whose dreams had been dashed on the sharp rocks of reality, insanity might provide welcome relief. This is the second plank of his self-absorption standard: that people would rather go insane, or behave insanely, than admit that they weren't important. A desire for a feeling of importance is what drove Abraham Lincoln to pick some law books off the floor and start studying. But it was also why, Carnegie claimed, John Dillinger took up bank robbing and cop-killing.*

An office worker today might take this to mean the following: Not everyone, especially not your boss, is looking to be impressed with you. Sometimes, he might want to feel his importance by being able to look down on you. Same goes for colleagues occupying the same lowly station as yourself: they'd prefer not to feel threatened by your brilliance. So those underlings who are very careful to cut an impressive figure, who make sure they're never taken advantage of, who demand they get full credit, or who insist that every professional accomplishment gets a gold star—these people don't do well in hierarchical organizations. Those who fail to see someone else's need for importance often forget to let the other kids have a turn. It's a critical mistake. "If you want to know how to make people shun you and laugh at you behind your back and even despise you, here is the recipe: Never listen to anyone for long," Carnegie wrote. (The "behind your back" part is key, it seems to me—resentment generated by this kind of behavior is rarely expressed to your face.)

Those who ignore another's need to feel important also stumble into what we might call the Dostoyevsky problem, the best illustration of which comes from the original BBC production of *The Office*. It's the day of the seventh-annual quiz night. The office manager David Brent is excited, and gets his staff to throw out some typical practice questions, only to get stuck on the name "Dostoyevsky." Ricky, the new intern, pipes up, "What

---

* As recently as 1934, John Dillinger was public enemy number one. The juxtaposition of his name with Lincoln's seems quaint now, but probably struck a more jarring note to Depression-era ears.

D was a Russian dissident who wrote the novel *Crime and Punishment?*" Brent slinks back to his office. Some time later, he re-emerges:

BRENT: We were talking earlier about Dostoyevsky, weren't we?

RICKY: Oh yeah?

BRENT: Yeah, the usual. Theodore Michaelovich Dostoyevsky, born 1821, died 1881. Just interesting that stuff about him being exiled in Siberia for four years, wasn't it?

RICKY: Oh. I don't know much about that. Didn't cover it really . . .

BRENT: All it is is he was a member of a secret political party and they put him in a Siberian labour camp for four years. So . . . y'know . . .

RICKY: Oh, hang on . . . I read about it in, er . . . He wrote *House of the Dead* and I think he put all his . . . yeah, all his memoirs in that, didn't he?

BRENT: *(quiet as a mouse)* Yep.

Brent slinks off again, humiliated. Later, at the copier:

BRENT: Talking earlier about Dostoyevsky's *House of the Dead?*

RICKY: Yeah, I think we mentioned it, yeah . . .

BRENT: . . . which he wrote in 1862. I was just gonna say that, of course, that wasn't his first major work.

RICKY: Wasn't it?

BRENT: No, his first major work was *Notes from the Underground,* which he wrote when he got back to St. Petersburg in 1859.

RICKY: Really?

BRENT: Yeah, definitely.

Brent is about to leave, having at last displayed his comprehensive knowledge of Dostoyevsky, but Ricky continues.

RICKY: Well, of course, my favourite is *The Raw Youth*.
         It's basically where Dostoyevsky, he goes on to ex-
         plain how science can't really find answers for the
         deeper human need . . .
BRENT: Yeah.

Now it's clear who the boob is in this exchange, but that's not
the point. The point is that while it's tempting to slake your
thirst for competition, sometimes it's to your advantage to let
someone carry on being dumb. This is especially true if your op-
ponent in this battle of wits is your boss, but it's also true for casual conversations with colleagues. Here again the insecure person who feels his genius is getting short shrift is in real danger,
because he has a hard time not flaunting his knowledge. He'll
then tie in an obscure reference that's only marginally related
to the conversation's ostensible subject. "Or," he'll say, laughing, "I could just swap in Wole Soyinka's résumé for mine. *That*
would be funny." Now, the standards of happy-fun conversation
require you to pick up the joke and keep going with it, but if
you're unable to do so—because you have no idea who Wole
Soyinka is—you're not likely to leave the conversation marvel-
ing at this person's intelligence.* You may even wonder if this
person really likes you or not, and if he does like you, why he
wants so much for you to feel stupid. For much the same reason,
Carnegie told his speech class students that it was never wise
for a speaker to make his audience feel inferior in an attempt to
impress them. ("If he thinks well of himself and his knowledge,
let him not make an offensive show of his self-congratulation."
Or, as Tyra Banks recently told *America's Next Top Model* candidates, "If you're a bitch, hide it.")

   Even when working for a boss who knows more about Dostoyevsky than you do (which, trust me, is ideal), it's a good idea
to perform above average but *excel* only sporadically. If you con-

---

* Anecdotal evidence suggests that guys, particularly guys who read Thomas Pyn-
chon, do this type of thing more often.

sistently overperform, your boss may feel you're snapping at his heels. And if you consistently go above and beyond the call of duty, you'll eventually be expected to keep up that pace. Slacking from time to time keeps expectations at a more reasonable level. It also relieves people from having to admire you daily, which gets old pretty fast.

(One more note on importance-seekers behaving insanely: In 1921, when Carnegie was not yet famous, he married a woman named Lolita Baucaire, who claimed to be a long-lost countess from Alsace, the oft-contested French-German border region. For the first couple years of their marriage, Dale and Lolita lived in Europe, settling not far from the palace of Versailles, while Dale worked on a novel. Every day on his walk he'd pass by the palace gardens, and for a former Missouri farm boy, this was all very exotic and gratifying. Lolita, however, was not so impressed with her husband's intractable Americanness. They were divorced by 1931—after "ten years and forty days," Carnegie would later sigh. Lolita had evidently believed Carnegie could be transformed into French aristocracy by sheer osmosis. And his desire for importance led him to believe that some weird woman claiming to be a long-lost countess from Alsace actually was one.)

The third and final principle of the self-absorption standard is that content matters, but not if it fails to get across. This may sound obvious but it's easily forgotten by people who are worried mainly about themselves, and how they're doing according to some internal standard, and so they forget they have an "audience" that matters just as much, if not more. This is how the New School University professor Harry A. Overstreet—one of Carnegie's intellectual heroes—put it in his own book, *Influencing Human Behavior:*

> It is a bit of sentimental nonsense to say that it makes no difference at all if a writer convinces not even a single soul of his

pertinence and value, so be it only that he "expresses" himself. We have a way of being over-generous with so-called
misunderstood geniuses. True, this is a barbarian world; and
the fine soul has its hard innings. But the chances are that
a writer who can convince no single person of the value of
what he writes, probably has nothing of value to write.

The concept is touched on briefly in Carnegie's first book. In
1915, when he was still Dale Carnagey, he coauthored *The Art
of Public Speaking,* a textbook, which runs 512 pages long and is
liberally peppered with quotes from Rudyard Kipling and Vol-
taire.* It is heavily theoretical, pompous and abstruse, and more
than a little sanctimonious—it's little wonder why this wasn't
one of Carnegie's biggest sellers. A typical line from the preface:
"Training in public speaking is not a matter of externals—primarily; it is not a matter of imitation—fundamentally; it is not
a matter of conformity to standards—at all. Public speaking
is public utterance, public issuance, of the man himself; therefore the first thing both in time and in importance is that the
man should be and think and feel things that are worthy of being given forth." Which sounds, to me, like he's recommending
spiritual cleansing before stepping up to the microphone—but
it's hard to tell.

The Art of Public Speaking was quite clear, however, on the
notion that speakers have tremendous obligations to their audience. They were obligated to prepare presentations well, and to
not stammer or stumble over their thoughts. (Ironic, then, that
this should be his least articulate book.) This was not for your
sake, so everyone could marvel at your excellence, but for their
sake. If you were ill-prepared, or found yourself standing at a
podium with nothing much to say, "you ought to be ashamed to
steal the time of your audience." If your audience didn't understand your point, the problem was you. A polished delivery also
simply provided the audience more pleasure. A monotonous,

---

* The book was actually written for use in a correspondence course. How effectively one might learn public speaking in the privacy of one's own home, I'm not
sure.

tone-deaf delivery wasn't just wearisome or maddening, Carnegie and coauthor scolded, like hearing the same key on a piano struck over and over. It was a *sin*.

The thing you had to keep in mind, they continued, was that no audience would simply assume a speaker was competent and had a good heart. The speaker's competence and goodwill had to be demonstrated—demonstrated very clearly—so as to leave no doubt. You had to convince people that what you were saying, doing, or writing was of value, and if you couldn't, well, consider that maybe it wasn't. You got zero points for being "misunderstood."

For today's underling, this is the takeaway: You can't just show up and quietly do your job. Your competence and dedication have to be *performed* in some way. You have to *look* as busy as you actually *are,* because if you aren't reaching people, it's the same—to your audience of colleagues—as if you spent your day making a grocery list. Looking busy is inherently difficult in many office jobs, as doing something and doing bupkis look very much the same (in both instances you're probably seated in front of a computer monitor). If your boss regularly gives new assignments and regularly asks for updates, then your visibility is less of a problem. But if she doesn't, and there are long stretches when you're unsupervised, then what you're doing all day has to be expressed in some deliberate fashion—and unfortunately this generally demands an entirely different skill set than your regular job requires.

It requires more planning, in other words. The sociologist Erving Goffman would later call this "dramatic realization" of a job, and when you press people for their methods, you'll find that many seemingly impromptu acts turn out to have been mulled over, weighed and considered, sometimes even practiced at home.* But often looking busy is just a matter of exploiting

---

* Here's how Goffman explained it (and this particular quote is about as accessible as his prose gets, or he'd be all over this book): "Thus to furnish a house so that it will express simple quiet dignity, the householder may have to race to auction sales, haggle with antiques dealers, and doggedly canvass all the local shops

the fact that the communal printer time-stamps every job and so if you print a document at 8:17 P.M. on a Wednesday night and leave it there until 10:00 A.M. the next day, someone — no telling who — will know you stayed late. An even more common manifestation of this is sending an e-mail at 9:01 P.M. saying, "Here is the _____ you asked for, Mr. Jackson." (Translation: I stayed until nine-freaking-o'clock to do this.) It's a matter of actively taking notes during meetings instead of sitting there with your hands folded. Filing is a controversial subject. Some contend that if you're too meticulous, then it looks like you've got nothing better to do, while others maintain that "people *know* it takes time to keep all that stuff straight," and so files are a relatively easy way to communicate diligence. Sometimes it simply helps to walk briskly down the hall, brow furrowed and papers tucked purposefully under the arm, instead of strolling like it's Sunday in the park. As Overstreet put it, "We influence very largely in ways far more subtle than we suspect." Gestures that sound banal can be surprisingly persuasive.

At the height of his fame, Carnegie held meetings that brought enough success-seekers, sitting on the edge of their folding chairs, to fill up hotel ballrooms. Not many underlings read it now, being largely unable to imagine that *How to Win Friends and Influence People* offers anything that's not already widely known. Carnegie, facing similar criticism in his own day, readily admitted he wasn't an original. "Of course I deal with the obvious," he said. "I present, reiterate, and glorify the obvious — because the obvious is what people need to be told." In that spirit,

---

for proper wallpaper and curtain materials. To give a radio talk that will sound genuinely informal, spontaneous, and relaxed, the speaker may have to design his script with painstaking care, testing one phrase after another, in order to follow the content, language, rhythm, and pace of everyday talk. Similarly, a Vogue model, by her clothing, stance, and facial expression, is able expressively to portray a cultivated understanding of the book she poses in her hand; but those who trouble to express themselves so appropriately will have very little time left over for reading."

here are some other hoary no-brainers for navigating institutional self-absorption:

Do tell the people you like that you like them. Upon receipt of the one-hundred-thousandth copy of his book, Carnegie wrote his Jewish editor, Leon Shimkin, to express his appreciation. "Every morning I arise and face the East and thank Allah that you came into my life," he wrote. Which is thoughtful, but not "nice." If your assurances and thank-yous are too vague and too bland, you'll be indistinguishable from the greeter at The Gap.

Also watch out when people don't give you this same assurance. If they plain don't like you, or simply don't plan to lift a finger in service of your career, it will be clear in these ways:

1. They will have a hard time smiling at you. (Forced American smiles are easy to spot. The lips get pulled back too far or too high, while the eyes stay flat, and the effect is altogether disconcerting. It's been called the Pan American smile, after the stewardesses of the now defunct airline.)
2. They will not enthusiastically share information with you.
3. They will drop comments into conversation that deflate your own sense of importance. An example from *How to Lose Friends and Alienate People:* You mention you discovered a great new restaurant in New Orleans; they say, *oh sure, we ate there just last year,* and *yeah, cute little place.*

Do figure out who the mentors are. A hint: They will not be the going-insane-in-order-to-feel-important types. Jason, a publicist, once worked for a woman who had a habit of announcing, generally during meetings but on other, less formal occasions as well, that she had the largest penis of all assembled. Her exact words: "I've got the biggest dick in this room." Anyone who speaks like this is not likely to be the best advocate for her employees, however they are endowed.

Those who *do* enjoy giving underlings a helping hand generally show it in these ways:

1. They will ask you what you're working on. Not as a challenge, or out of charity (making a feeble attempt to appear interested), but because they're generally curious about what you're going to say.
2. They will bring items to your attention that they think might help you out—connections, articles, job opportunities, and the like.
3. They will be very frank with you. Which is to say, they won't waste your time or their own with too-generous appraisals of your work or future prospects.

Do use people's names. This is one of Carnegie's simplest and most ingenious prescriptions. People just like seeing their name; Carnegie suggested it's why the rich gave money to museums and art galleries—they loved having their name in gold leaf, in capital letters, up on the wall for everyone to see.

The corollary is that failing to recognize somebody can be incredibly, irrationally maddening to him or her. ("You know the type, you've been introduced to her on three previous occasions, you have a couple of mutual friends, and you bump into her, and she extends her hand for a handshake and gives her name, as though for the first time—and the thing is, you *know* what her name is, where she works, and on what occasion you last saw her, and the length of her last romantic relationship. It's infuriating.")

The corollary to the corollary is that if you're guilty of this kind of blanking, you should send an e-mail the next day and express (1) mild embarrassment, and (2) interest in whatever life projects she's got going on at the moment. Even if it seems forced, you've made the effort.

Do close with a snap. Another, often ignored, implication of the self-absorption standard is that people mostly want you to stop

talking. Carnegie was no friend to the windbag, precisely because the windbag neglected the other person's desire to talk.

Overstreet wrote in *Influencing Human Behavior* that any
speaker who kept promising to wrap things up but didn't was
shooting himself in the foot. He also suggested that, if at all possible, you let your audience see the pages you're speaking from
dwindle in number (that is, you wouldn't shuffle the page you'd
just finished to the back of the stack, but instead create a dis-
card pile). This gave people a satisfying way to gauge how much
longer you'd be droning on.

»»

A final note concerning a bizarre coincidence I only discovered
after flipping through *How to Win Friends and Influence People*
for the third time, alone late at night, with a laptop and Internet
connection nearby. I was going through the revised edition that
came out in 1981, which added new material vetted by Dorothy
Carnegie, Dale's widow. (He died in 1955.) The result is a book
that blends stories of the Taft administration with anecdotes
about Stevie Wonder's childhood. One new quote worked into
the text was from a Professor James V. McConnell. It's about
smiling, and McConnell's point is that "there's far more information in a smile than a frown." It so happens that James V.
McConnell was targeted by the Unabomber in 1985. He wasn't
killed in the attack, but he did suffer some hearing loss. The
only meaningful link between McConnell and Ted Kaczynski,
as far as investigators could tell, was the University of Michigan, where McConnell taught and where Kaczynski received his
PhD. There was no clear motive. Several years later, in 1994,
when another of Kaczynski's mail bombs killed an advertising
executive, a letter sent on the occasion tried to justify the mur-
der by saying that the PR industry was guilty of manipulating
people — a very bad thing, in his mind.

Carnegie would undoubtedly have added the Unabomber to
his list of people who'd go insane in order to feel important. He

had no delusions about the extent to which a person could be criminally self-involved. Nor did he have much truck with cowards; when combined revenue from the book and Dale Carnegie Training courses (now franchised in over sixty-five countries) had made him a rich man, he remarked that his making a living from teaching public speaking was incidental: what he had really set out to do was help people develop courage. Not least because, in his mind, "a rabbit-hearted coward invites disaster."

Or, sometimes, less dramatically, rabbit-hearted cowards just wasted a lot of time. Too timid to confront other people's navel-gazing, they ended up sniffing around for recognition in all the wrong places and all the wrong ways. Over time, it led to passivity; they doubted their ability to influence others and so stopped trying. And then not a whole lot got accomplished. Which is, not to put too fine a point on it, a fairly reliable way to make sure no one gets promoted.

5

The Master Mind

Napoleon Hill on the Proper
Use of Friendship

> We flounder about making empty, vapid, pleasing
> remarks and before we know it we have another
> "friend" and have invited him to lunch "some day."
>
> —IRVING TRESSLER,
> *How to Lose Friends and Alienate People*

WHEN I WENT to the vast New York Public Library to read up on Napoleon Hill—the "Billy Sunday of Business Evangelism"—I came up empty. His *How to Raise Your Own Salary*—cataloged as missing. *The Law of Success,* both the 1928 and the 1965 editions—gone. *Think Your Way to Wealth, Success Through a Positive Mental Attitude,* and *How to Sell Your Way Through Life,* ditto. Missing too were *The Master-Key to Riches* and the library's two copies of Hill's signature title, *Think and Grow Rich,* which came out in 1937. This confirmed an initial suspicion I had about Hill and his followers: they're the kind of slick idiots who try to kick-start their fortune hunt by stealing from a public library.

In the canon of success literature, Napoleon Hill stands over to the seedier "motivational products" side. His prose, for one, has a late-night infomercial tone to it.* His life story is marked

---

* His aesthetic isn't impressive either. The Napoleon Hill Foundation website displays his books photographed alongside stacks of shiny gold coins.

by relationships left in tatters and business ventures gone bust. He once sicced the FBI on a former associate who had a German accent, and who was threatening to sue, which led to the man spending much of World War I in a detention center. A native of Blue Ridge Mountains country, Hill practiced such childhood hobbies as rolling boulders down hills and strutting down Main Street with a handgun. He mellowed—a little—when his step-mother persuaded him to trade his six-shooter for a typewriter. Nor was Hill much of a family man; his wife and kids relied on financial assistance from relatives while he traveled around the country in tailored suits and a Rolls-Royce. Of his eventual three marriages, two ended in unmitigated disaster. His son Blair once called him an "unscrupulous, holier-than-thou, two-timing, dou-ble-crossing good-for-nothing." Hill claimed to have coined the phrase "we have nothing to fear but fear itself" during a short stint in Franklin D. Roosevelt's administration, but nobody has confirmed this story. Too busy preaching about business savvy, Hill neglected to make and keep friends.

Which makes it all the more interesting that Hill's advice on how to mix friendship and business is among the best avail-able. Blending companionship and money-making has tradi-tionally been seen as an oil spill in the making, for several valid reasons. One, there's a sense that trading on your connections smacks of retrograde high school cliques and old-boy networks. Then there's the time-honored American preference for going it alone—Thoreau on Walden Pond, the Lone Ranger, being told that *you* can do it, and so on. And if mixing friends and ca-reer advancement weren't already fraught, somebody went and dreamed up the greasy term *networking,* a euphemism that al-lows us to sound like we're not talking about what we're talking about, which is leveraging relationships to make more money. All this has left most of us with the idea that it's only OK to ap-preciate people for who they are, uniquely and specially, deep down inside—and that to take into consideration what they can *do* for you is craven and shallow, possibly evidence of a thor-oughly corrupted soul.

In *Think and Grow Rich,* Hill gently suggests that this purity and high-mindedness is super until you realize how hazardous it is to living well. Using people who like you is nothing to be ashamed of, because, at the end of the day, it's a cold, cold universe, and it can get rough out there. Would you rather rely on those who *don't* like you? Not only should you exploit your friends unapologetically, Hill argued, but you should do it expertly. To this end, he devised a highly specific methodology.

After tossing his ideas around for a while, I began to see how they might help those of us who look up at the ceiling, or pretend we don't hear, when more outgoing colleagues encourage us to mingle. And I started to suspect that our queasiness over using people might just stem from the fact that most of us simply don't do it correctly.

Hill's ideas on friends in business come bundled in a concept he called "the Master Mind." He defined the Master Mind as "coordination of knowledge and effort, in a spirit of harmony, between two or more people, for the attainment of a definite purpose." Basically, your Master Mind is any group of people you can call on for help, or who might know things you don't, or whose imagination travels to places yours doesn't. (His phrasing is confusing, because he referred to it as a singular Master Mind, but he's at all times referring to a collective entity.)

Hill believed that a Master Mind was behind all the name-brand American fortunes, including those of Andrew Carnegie, William Wrigley (chewing gum), Henry Ford (cars), and John Wanamaker (department stores). But it also operated on smaller scales, and in most entrepreneurial ventures. The important thing to remember, *Think and Grow Rich* stressed, was that friends were a determining factor in your financial status. The basic idea Hill got from Andrew Carnegie himself, whose four-story, sixty-four-room Fifth Avenue mansion Hill had been dispatched to as a rookie reporter, on behalf of a small outfit called *Bob Taylor's Magazine,* in 1908. The question that Hill put to then-retired Carnegie—he'd recently cashed out of U.S.

Steel to the tune of $480 million—was simple: How? How had he done it? Carnegie, it turns out, was more interested in young Hill, who reminded him somewhat of his younger self (they also had coal-mining backgrounds in common). Their meeting was supposed to last three hours, but Carnegie kept him at the mansion for three days, and one evening, over after-dinner cigars, a proposal was cooked up. Carnegie wanted Hill to interview all of America's great businessmen, catalog everything they had to say about success, and then come up with some usable theories. Some of these men were in Carnegie's Master Mind—he reckoned about fifty men had at one point or another been in his group. Anyhow, he thought the whole project might take twenty years. He did not offer Hill any compensation—just reimbursement for expenses. At which point Carnegie pulled out a stopwatch to clock Hill's response time. If he had taken any longer than sixty seconds, Carnegie claimed later, the offer would have been withdrawn (because any man worth his salt knew a good offer when he heard one).*

Hill took twenty-nine seconds to decide yes, and then spent the next twenty years, on and off, quizzing self-made millionaires about their personal habits. He found that all of them relied on meetings with advisors—hardly a news flash. The economic principle was pretty straightforward—two or more brains, working together, can generate more activity than one brain churning away in isolation. Politicians exploited the power of the group, too. FDR had his "Brain Trust," a group of academics who helped him chew over domestic policy questions. But the Brain Trust never met in person, and quite possibly didn't even know

---

* It's a dramatic scene, and its premise—that the novice only gets a moment to decide his fate—appears in a lot of make-it-or-break-it tales. In the movie *Wall Street,* Bud Fox is given five minutes to impress Gordon Gekko. In *Mean Girls,* Cady Heron has only seconds to choose which cafeteria table she's going to sit at. *The House of Mirth*'s Lily Bart was expected to answer unexpected marriage proposals from wealthy but otherwise unappealing men while they stood and impatiently waited for her answer.

each other. (The president spoke to them mainly over the phone, one on one.) This is where Hill offers something new, and a little more complex: *Your Master Mind group had to meet in person twice a week, with a specific goal in mind, and always in "a spirit of harmony."* And ideally, if you'd planned things just right, you would be the biggest dimwit in the bunch.

All three elements were vital, but having a clearly defined goal was most important to Hill. He was a stickler for definiteness. "What a different story men would have to tell if only they would adopt a DEFINITE PURPOSE," he ranted, and what an even better story if while fixating on that purpose, they let themselves teeter on the brink of obsession. Part of this thinking was straight-up New Thought (or as Hill writes: "Our brains become magnetized with the dominating thoughts which we hold in our minds"). Hill wanted his readers to lust after *people,* and lust after specific people. Besides meeting twice a week, a fully functional Master Mind required that you be very clear on who was going to be part of it, and why you wanted them in the group. You had to pursue relationships with your professional heroes as zealously as you would any romance.

Hill opens *Think and Grow Rich* with a story about Edwin C. Barnes, a would-be entrepreneur he deemed worth mentioning—repeatedly—because Barnes had a hankering to work with Thomas Edison. And so he hounded Edison. More precisely, he hopped a freight train to East Orange, New Jersey, and showed up on Edison's doorstep, without connections, without a letter of introduction, without even much in the way of qualifications, and he stood there on the stoop until Edison reluctantly gave him a job. This gambit worked, Hill wrote, because Barnes went to East Orange with the intention not of asking meekly for a job of some kind, but of putting Edison "on notice" that they'd be doing business together. For Edison's part, faced with this complete stranger, we're told he thought something like this: ". . . there was something in the expression of his face which conveyed the impression that he was determined to get what he had come after. . . . I gave him the opportunity he asked for, because I saw he had made up his mind to stand by until he succeeded."*

Security guards, reception desks, administrative assistants, human resource departments, and key-card access make this stunt virtually impossible today. Not to mention that if you did try to storm the barriers to reach some high-placed individual, people would start to wonder about your emotional stability. Looking for heroes in the more immediate vicinity of your cubicle rarely brings satisfaction either. It's difficult to find people who qualify for unchecked admiration in any field, in any office, but it's much, much more challenging in offices where people aren't terrifically invested in their jobs. David, an ambivalent New Jersey banker, can walk down J. P. Morgan's cubicle row without glancing at a single nameplate that makes his heart skip. "My colleagues are bums," Deanne, a paralegal, told me when explaining why she hadn't gone to anyone for help with a sticky job quandary. (She'd read through more "actionable" e-mails and IM transcripts than was good for anyone's soul.)

Part of the problem, of course, is that most corporate settings don't allow us to pick our own teams. Whom we report to is determined by many things, but the extent to which we admire and respect their skills is usually not taken into consideration. Nor is the extent to which we share goals with them. Be it snark, be it siloed management, be it misguided competition, the fact is that the setup of most offices actively discourages looking

---

* This affecting doorstep scene may have struck a chord with Hill because he himself had done something similar. Hill's first mentor was former Virginia attorney general Rufus Ayres, a big man and an "active promoter" of the state's coal interests. (What that meant is not entirely clear, and probably for good reason.) In 1901, at age nineteen, Hill sat down and wrote a letter to Ayres that began: "I have just completed a business college course and am well qualified to serve as your secretary, a position I am very anxious to have." He was quick to add that he was pretty green and inexperienced. "I know that at the beginning working for you will be of more value to me than it will be to you. Because of this I am willing to pay for the privilege of working with you." Instead, he got both job and salary.

at your colleagues as sources of inspiration. The result is a slow, steady erosion of desire.

Of course, you can always search beyond your office walls for people to lust after professionally, but that, too, can be demoralizing. Here's how it always seemed to work for me:

One of the more forward-looking among us junior publishing types — this was never me, by the way — would organize an evening for the lower ranks from different publishing houses. It even had a name — "Overtime," it was called. (Because it was like work but yet it wasn't really, like, *work,* y'know?) This orgy of connection-making was held every few months in a downtown bar, the only requirements for the venue being $5 gin and tonics, a black leather couch to throw our ratty coats on, and a sound system that blared Coldplay. Far from hewing closely to Hill's prescriptions for a definite purpose, I, and many of my colleagues, would arrive with only the vaguest notion of "meeting people." When aspiring editors were asked what kinds of titles they hoped to work on, you'd hear murmurs of "narrative nonfiction" or "pop culture." People who might not otherwise have met got to meet, which is a good thing, but the conversation — after "Can I get you another drink?" "I'm sorry, what?" "DRINK! ANOTHER DRINK!" — tended to devolve into venting and gossip. After three hours of making stock footage of twenty-somethings in a bar, I'd take the subway home, alternately vowing to make more of an effort next time, or, on the other hand, never to "network" like that again. No one I've spoken to could recall anything significant developing from these Overtime events.

We had all the building blocks for Hill's Master Mind — people all pretty much the same age, none of us making very much money, all doing something mildly humbling in our jobs and eager for change, wanting sincerely to produce quality books, and all enjoying a surplus of free nights. We were all willing to share information, too. That we failed to meet the first criterion for the Master Mind — meeting twice a week — is obvious. But

could the entire setup have been flawed? The secret to making these putative meetings of the mind work, Hill wrote in his
preface to *Think and Grow Rich,* was to "KNOW WHAT IT IS
THAT YOU WANT." (His caps.) The Master Mind's "definite
purpose" had to be something very particular, something you
could get your hands on. More money wasn't even a legitimate
goal in Hill's eye—you had to pick the exact dollar amount if
you were going to have any luck at all. The purpose could be
stacks of coins worth $200,000, or it could be a nationwide chain
of Betsy Ross Candy Company outlets (one of Hill's many short-
lived entrepreneurial ventures)—but every member of the Master Mind had to come to the table ready and unembarrassed to
articulate exactly what it was he or she was there for. So could
it be that the problem with "networking" is not that it "moves
fast, and comes with a plan, and doesn't really value people for
who they are," as one reluctant schmoozer told me, but that it
isn't specific enough about what that plan might be?

Here's what you can get out of Hill, even if you're unconvinced that his whole Master Mind theory holds water: Do all
the mingling you want, even lean over that folding table, marker
cap in mouth, to fill out a "Hello, My Name Is _____" sticker,
and you might just as well stay home as long as you don't know
precisely why you've come. Or as long as you think that "trying to meet new people" is a precise goal. Trying to stay "open
to the possibilities of the moment," as another, more wide-eyed
partygoer suggested to me, more often than not just means you
stay too late and wake up at 7:30 the next morning bleary-eyed,
anxious, and combating a vague, existential dread.

In other words, maybe when the young man in the tweed
jacket leaned in and asked, "So what kind of stuff are you working on?" I should have plainly told him that I had nothing I was
particularly jazzed about at the moment but was hoping to work
on a book about Alice Paul, or the changing racial politics of
inner-city high schools, or an anthology of artists' writing, or a
book like Paul Fussell's *Class,* but updated—the things I actu-

ally wanted, in other words. And then asked him if he knew anyone working on such projects. But this would have taken some forethought, some preparation, and an ability to keep talking even when the self-irony starts kicking in. More on that later.

Here's another reason why Overtime was unsatisfying, even in an industry that supposedly ran on the fumes of our collective love for literature. Maybe, in addition to not getting together often enough, not being definite about what we wanted, we weren't walking into that bar looking for people who'd completely blow us out of the water.

Hill was adamant on this point: For the Master Mind to do you any good, you had to invite people whose accomplishments outstripped yours, or who were smarter, funnier, quicker on their feet, altogether more sparkling than you. Possibly even better-looking. It almost goes without saying that this is difficult; in fact, it's completely at odds with instinct. Suppose you spot that person who's always at these parties, that guy who stands straight at 6'1", is extremely articulate and frighteningly clever, is fluent in German and Arabic, plays in a band on Saturdays but makes it to services on Sundays, and who works in the same field as you but has a more high-profile job. When you see him across the room, tossing his head back and laughing, showing off very white teeth, your first thought is probably not, "I bet he'd like to be my friend. I should go over and talk to him." You're more likely to turn to the bartender and order another drink. If jealousy doesn't get in the way, insecurity will, because the moment you stand next to this person is the moment you become the shorter, sillier one—the funny friend to his romantic lead (the Janeane Garofalo to her Uma Thurman, and so on).

By Hill's definition, though, every successful person was someone who didn't mind doing this. It came naturally to Hill himself, and he freely admitted that he was susceptible to hero-worship—always eager to learn, ever ready to pick up pointers from people he understood knew better than he. But he couldn't abide being outshone for long, which is probably why so many of his relationships rotted from the inside out. He would start out apprenticeships with a bang (". . . came to the office early, stayed late, and worked tirelessly in between," according to his biographer). He poured himself into partnerships (starting up one magazine, then another) with people who raised his game. Then he'd find something to get upset about and break things off or send the other party screaming in the opposite direction. By the time he wrote *Think and Grow Rich,* Hill seems to have figured out intellectually that anyone who had to be the tallest tree in the forest was not capable of making a Master Mind happen. But actually acting on this intellectual understanding and changing his habits proved impossible for him.

Which is probably why he couldn't illustrate the benefits of having smarter friends with examples from his own life. His favorite story for that purpose was Henry Ford's 1919 libel trial against the *Chicago Tribune.* The newspaper had published an editorial labeling Ford an "ignorant idealist" some time earlier for his efforts in preventing American engagement in World War I. While Ford had never prided himself on his book-learnin', he was not happy with the label, and decided to file a lawsuit against the paper. The case eventually found its way to court in Dearborn, Michigan. If the *Tribune*'s lawyers could prove Ford was an ignoramus, they'd prevail. So they put Ford on the stand and lobbed a series of questions aimed at establishing that while he knew a thing or two about cars, Ford was, generally speaking, dumb as rocks. They asked him who Benedict Arnold was. "I have forgotten just who he is. He is a writer, I think." When did we fight the American Revolution? "1812." According to observers, Ford sat sharpening a pocketknife on the bottom of his shoe until he'd had enough. He leaned in, pointed his finger at his questioner, and as Hill tells it, spewed out the following:

> If I should really want to answer the foolish question you have just asked, or any of the other questions you have been

asking me, let me remind you that I have a row of electric push-buttons on my desk, and by pushing the right button, I can summon to my aid men who can answer any question I desire to ask concerning the business to which I am devoting most of my efforts. *Now, will you kindly tell me why I should clutter up my mind with general knowledge, for the purpose of being able to answer questions, when I have men around me who can supply any knowledge I require?*

Ford won the case but was awarded only six cents in damages. As Hill saw it, there was no shame in Ford's tenuous grasp of history. ("History is bunk," Ford said from the stand.) The point of the story was that you didn't need to worry too much about groping around for knowledge yourself as long as you had a reliable Master Mind at your disposal.

But is that enough to help people over any lingering insecurities about being the sidekick? Probably not quite. It's worth exploring Hill's ground rules a little more deeply, because it brings up some interesting potential complications. Here's part of the schema from *Think and Grow Rich,* one more time, verbatim from page 147:

(a) Ally yourself with a group of as many people as you may need for the creation, and carrying out of your plan. . . . (Compliance with this instruction is *absolutely essential.* Do not neglect it.)

(b) Before forming your Master Mind alliance, decide what advantages, and benefits, *you* may offer the individual members of your group, in return for their cooperation. No one will work indefinitely without some form of compensation. No intelligent person will either request or expect to work without adequate compensation, although this may not always be in the form of money.

Master Minds ran on volunteer labor, in other words. As per his experience with Carnegie, Hill believed that a little willingness to be exploited went a long way. In the ideal world, everything would even out in the end—one person would extend himself for a while without compensation, then some day, don't know where, don't know when, he would reap his reward. But he had to chip in regardless.*

There's risk involved here. Say you do your bit for the Master Mind, and then your "friend" says thank you very much and scampers off without contributing his fair share. Or say your Master Mind group works for a while, and some members start to advance as you all hoped and planned for, but not everyone in lockstep—as is rarely the case—and you're the one lagging behind. Or what if your turn never comes? Or you get duped by someone without a conscience? The Master Mind, looked at this way, sets people up nicely for disappointment and betrayal. (This is certainly the gist of books like *What Makes Sammy Run?* or movies like *The Devil and Daniel Webster,* both of which came out in 1941, around the height of Hill's popularity. Both played on the fear that you cooperated only to be hip-checked and backstabbed by a mean little twerp—that is, if your "friend" and the champion of your ambitions didn't turn out to be Satan himself.)

Speaking of the devil reminds me of an incident at one of my early jobs. There was a much-loved editor who was known to be messy, so messy you couldn't see the carpet of his office for the piles of paper. He was perhaps not the savviest when it came to technology, either, and his friends at work knew he never—ever —shut his computer down. Which made him vulnerable. One night, they slipped into his office and tinkered with his Microsoft Word AutoCorrect feature so that every time he typed in his name it would revert to "Prince of Darkness." When he noticed this—it was at least a day later—he spent several hours trying to figure out what had happened. When the prank was

---

* This sounds, to me, suspiciously like "from each according to his abilities, to each according to his needs." A little bit pinko, in other words, so you can imagine how hard Hill spun it.

revealed, he could laugh along. But it made others uncomfortable, just being witness to it. It was as if he'd been exposed, as if people knew him too well, and were perhaps too comfortable zeroing in on his weaknesses. It almost served as a warning to keep your cards closer to your vest.

Hill knew he was advocating something very difficult, especially for people employed by companies. He even conceded that achieving a functioning Master Mind might be nothing short of miraculous. So miraculous, in fact, that occasionally he resorted to imaginary friends to populate his networks. Every night for years—he unselfconsciously writes in *Think and Grow Rich*—just before bed, he would dream up clandestine round-tables around which were seated not only Andrew Carnegie, Henry Ford, and Thomas Edison, but also Ralph Waldo Emerson, Thomas Paine, Charles Darwin, Abraham Lincoln, Luther Burbank, Napoleon Bonaparte, and himself, Napoleon Hill. "I would shut my eyes, and see, in my imagination, this group of men seated with me around my council table. Here I had not only an opportunity to sit among those whom I considered to be great," he writes, before ruining the effect completely by adding, "but I actually dominated the group, by serving as the chairman." (An astounding sentence that pretty much explains why Hill had so much trouble. Most people would cede the floor to Bonaparte, or failing that, Lincoln.)

The solution to this need to dominate, this fear of being exposed—in fact, to all stumbling blocks to networking—lies in Hill's emphasis on "definiteness." The more precise, the more specific, you can be about what you will do for the group, and what you don't need to do because someone else better qualified will be doing it, the more you can let your guard down. You can relish what might at first seem a subsidiary role, too, and tell yourself it's complementary, cooperative, and necessary in order to achieve that elusive spirit of harmony. When you got right down to it, Hill concluded, the Master Mind was a force far greater than the sum of its parts. "No two minds ever come together without, thereby, creating a third, intangible, invisible force which may be likened to a third mind."* No mere apologist, Hill believed that combining friends and business could actually lift you to a higher plane of human understanding.

I'm not entirely convinced, but I do know that once you've found people with whom you can openly, sincerely discuss what you wish for, you spend less time dwelling on the pedestrian events of the day, or the smell of your cubicle neighbor's tuna sandwiches, and more time talking about things you actually want to bring into existence. "Just one person who, when you tell them you have an idea, or that you'd like to accomplish something, will not only get you but toss another log on the fire," remarked the ambivalent New Jersey banker—that's what he wanted. And when I think about people I admire, I see a number of Hill's principles in effect. They don't conceive of it as such, but they essentially do build small teams. They are constantly referring so-and-so to so-and-so, introducing old acquaintances to newer acquaintances, and matching people who have problems with people who might offer interesting solutions. They know their friends' strengths and talk incessantly —*gleefully*—about their friends' strengths. They know what they themselves are good at as well, and admit to being driven, idealistic, and susceptible to hero-worship—all at once. They write e-mails, they write thank-you notes, they surround themselves with people who will not agree so much as ask the right questions. They are deliberate and precise about their allegiances. But somehow over time their calculations morph into an unusual variety of selflessness, and they're somehow able to celebrate their friends' triumphs as enthusiastically as their own. Which means they get to celebrate a lot.

Still, if the idea of a Master Mind strikes you as too cold, you might want to bear in mind that the alternative is essentially de-

---

* Those familiar with 1980s business books will realize he's talking about "synergy"—before that word was invented to make it even easier to ridicule the whole idea.

ciding to go it entirely alone. That way, you get the satisfaction of knowing that both your triumphs and failures are yours and yours only. Which is, I think, about as elegant a life strategy as stealing from a public library. Should you decide to attempt the Master Mind yourself, some other considerations also apply:

Do be interested. Emily Post and Dale Carnegie already said as much, but Napoleon Hill's take on the matter was different. It had less to do with getting other people interested in you and more to do with simply noting other people's strengths. If you were too focused on yourself, you might not notice that so-and-so had a particular gift—or a cabin in Vermont you could use for annual retreats.

Do keep your mouth shut when you don't have anything to say. Hill himself is said to have been a real chatterbox, although he cautioned against it. Talking too much can hurt your chances of corralling the people you need for your Master Mind, which is to say it's tempting but ultimately counterproductive to form alliances through gossip about a third party. Once, while trying to endear myself to a magazine editor, I wondered aloud why a mutual acquaintance was such a sourpuss; she seemed polite enough, but otherwise pouty and distracted. "What's her problem?" I asked. Cancer, was the answer. Her problem was that she was twenty-four years old and had breast cancer.

If it doesn't backfire immediately, as it did here, it can in time, if only because your audience might assume that a trash-talker is always a trash-talker. By spending time chatting with you, they're only giving you material for trashing them later, once they've left the room.

Don't ask a favor of anyone you haven't yourself helped in a while. Hill didn't think you should be shy about asking people for help. (Not least because it gives you information—if someone hesitates when you ask them to contribute to your project, or says yes but leaves you somehow wishing you hadn't asked, you know he or she isn't Master Mind material.) "But in seeking the help of others, you must be prepared to make an even trade," is another Hill chestnut. "You can't come empty-handed." We can assume he meant "even" in terms of size of contribution, not outcome. (The outcome, again, is completely beyond your control.)

Do understand that someone will take credit for your work. You may function as a shadow member of someone's Master Mind, and not really be aware of it. This happens when higher-ups take your good ideas and run with them, and it happens plenty. There's very little you can do about it. (So enjoy!) Interestingly enough, when Hill was young the fact that employers sometimes poached ideas from employees was seen as a positive, even quite progressive, development. Department-store king Marshall Field—to name just one—got a lot of press and praise for taking the suggestions of hourly-wage employees as seriously as those of his highly paid senior advisors. Some even said his department stores were the best *because* he implemented so many employee ideas. Whether the girls at the perfume counter felt the same way is difficult to say.

Do be completely democratic in outlook. Candace Bushnell has the dumb, doomed, social-climbing blond of her novel *Trading Up* consistently treating "service people" like ugly furniture. Being rude to anyone paid to wait on you, of course, is an unmistakable sign you've got a tacky person on your hands. (Which is why novelists and screenwriters use this device so often.) But you see misguided ideas about how to treat so-called inferiors in the office as well, as when the guy who finally moves from his cubicle into an office tries to distance himself from old friends still on cubicle row, thinking it will help solidify his position on a higher rank. There are some books out there that will tell you this is the smart, strategic thing to do. It's not. The number of people who reach the top of the ladder only to get knocked off and fall back to the bottom, and there get kicked by those they were rude to, neglectful of, or plain impatient with on their way up, are legion. (Michael Ovitz, Judith Regan, Leona Helmsley—just a few who made some mistakes in this regard.)

All that said, don't make it a numbers game. When aspiring rapper Jamal Woodard, from Brooklyn, was scheduled for a promotional segment at radio station Hot 97 (he just signed with Warner Brothers), he showed up three hours early accompanied by a sizable entourage—about forty men, all dressed in extra-large blue T-shirts that read GRAVY on the front. Woodard was told to come back later, and so went and got a sandwich. When he returned, he was shot in the left buttock by someone in the crowd outside. He went ahead with the interview anyhow (as he'd decided that "I was standing downstairs—got shot in the ass" was not a legitimate excuse), and later, sobered by the experience, but still optimistic, he tried to see it as a welcome life lesson: "There's no reason you should be up at Hot 97, thirty or forty deep, with shirts on. You try to show your movement—'Wow, he got a lot of support'—but sometimes, you know what? The movement can hurt you. So many dudes cause problems. My motto now is: Four or five deep, I'm good. Four or five dudes, plus security."* He's absolutely right: four or five deep is a good Master Mind starting point. Any more than that early on in your career, and you'll—at the very least—get branded an innocuous social butterfly.

Do start to worry if you notice that none of your friends ever critique you.
Harry A. Overstreet used to tell his students to look for a companion "who is willing to risk his friendship by telling you just how disagreeable or nonsensical or pathetic you are!" If you had obnoxious habits and no one pointed this out to you, chances are you'd never get rid of those habits. That said, if you find yourself

---

* From "Where Hip-Hop Lives: Hot 97's Turf Wars," by Ben McGrath, *The New Yorker,* July 10 and 17, 2006.

with a friend who likes punishing people for their mistakes a little too much, or is a little too focused on how people perpetually
disappoint, you might want to insert some emotional distance.
(See chapter 2 if you don't understand why.)

»»

I never would have thought that the same kind of Hail Mary
maneuvers that brought Hill to the doorstep of powerful people
still happen. They do. Here's one contemporary example, told
in *Think and Grow Rich*–style. A young San Francisco bookstore clerk wanted a publishing job on the opposite coast but
had no idea how to go about it. One gray day she pored over
the acknowledgments page in the back of a novel she liked—it
was by A. M. Homes—and sat down to write to everyone con-
nected to the publisher, HarperCollins. She didn't realize this
at the time, but one of her correspondents turned out to be the
CEO of HarperCollins. Most improbably, this CEO (not someone with a lot of time on her hands) wrote back to thank her for
her interest and wish her the best of luck. No immediate job offer, but step one. Step two was moving to New York, steps three
through five included using her bookstore experience to land a
job, then a promotion, then another one. Along the way, friend-
ships were formed, phone calls made on her behalf, and she'd
tell this story—about her far-fetched goals when she was working retail, about that improbable note—that made it clear just
how serious and devoted she was.

This former bookstore clerk is now the associate director of
publicity at a major publishing house and making close to six fig-
ures. (Hill liked to include salaries in his roundups.) It's a cold,
cold universe indeed, but sometimes worthy people get what
they have coming, and you sense yourself warm up a bit.

6

Checking Yourself at the Door

What Brooks Brothers and Midcentury
Handwringing over Bland Conformity
Reveal About Personal Style

A good plain look is my favorite look. If I didn't
want to look so "bad," I would want to look "plain."
That would be my next choice. —ANDY WARHOL

WHATEVER SYMPATHY I had for the idea of clothes as
a valuable form of self-expression disappeared one
afternoon late in 1997, when I sat down for a job interview wearing a jacket that cost $14.99. Up to that
instant, I had been an adventurous dresser. If you were to break
into my apartment, you'd find a photograph of me in East Ber-
lin in 1996, wearing black tights, short tweed skirt, chunky black
shoes with big silver buckles, large-collared baby blue men's shirt,
and dark green vintage men's shirt *over* that—a $2.99 jacket
—with granny barrettes in hair that was short, dyed black, and
curled in a way I sincerely believed made me look like silent film
star Gloria Swanson, only indie rock. There were many more
outfits like this, though I toned it way down for the interview.
But as my interviewer scrutinized me while I fielded his ques-

tions that afternoon, staring at my gray synthetic blend much as one watches someone trying to parallel park in a space that's clearly too small, I realized the idea of "being yourself" through distinctive dress was perhaps not so smart.

More recently, when I walk anywhere downtown at 6:30 P.M. on a weekday, amid a sea of men ages twenty-two to forty-five, standing at happy-hour bars and all dressed in blue button-downs and khakis, it strikes me that "business casual" is not the liberating force it was cracked up to be. Men are still in uniform, just as they were in the days when suits were required. Then I imagine Cary Grant in *North by Northwest* dodging crop-dusters in a blue button-down and khakis, and I feel something significant has been lost.

Looking back on that interview outfit now, I see that sacrificing my chance at getting my foot in the door because it was important for my outside to match my inside was not a particularly useful form of integrity. The guy who interviewed me wore a rumpled shirt that looked like he'd slept in it, he smelled of smoke, his whole office smelled of smoke, and there was a cardboard cutout of Austin Powers propped up in the corner. This was not an extravagantly formal workplace, in other words. But after I left he called the placement agency to complain that they'd sent over some kid who couldn't be bothered to put on a suit. My problem wasn't that I was unaware of the strictures of corporate life — my local Laundromat had one piece of decoration on the wall, and it was a sign informing clothes washers that EMPLOYERS NOTICE AN APPLICANT'S SHOES — but it was very difficult to imagine walking into Brooks Brothers and not feeling like a stooge. While I was resigned to working all day for a large corporation, and a thirty-minute commute on public transportation each way, somehow wearing a different outfit than I'd normally wear, that struck me as just too much.

According to the logic of *Dress for Success,* the 1975 bible of ambitious wardrobe, what I'd done with the $14.99 jacket was "precondition" the company environment to reject me. Prejudices based on clothing choices were widespread, the author John T. Molloy stated, and most people were pretty comfortable with having them. Molloy first started thinking about wardrobe considerations in the late 1950s, when he was a bored English teacher at a Connecticut prep school. One day he noticed something so ordinary that he'd never thought to think twice about it before—namely, that men's raincoats came in two standard colors, black and beige. Before long he concocted a theory: the color of a man's raincoat was an indicator of his class status. Beige coats meant upper-middle-class, while black raincoats typically signaled lower-middle-class. Molloy decided to submit this idea to experiment. First, he went to fancy Fifth Avenue stores in New York and counted the coats on the racks—four to one in favor of beige. In more low-budget stores downtown he found the reverse distribution, far more black than beige. For phase two of his clinical studies, he sent interns out on rainy days to stand at subway entrances in different neighborhoods and note coat colors (an experiment he later repeated in Chicago, Los Angeles, Dallas, and Atlanta). Still later, he showed 1,362 test subjects two photos of a clean-cut, expensively but not extravagantly dressed man. The photos were identical in every way except for the color of the man's raincoat. Molloy asked each test subject to choose which man looked more successful. Eighty-two percent picked the man in beige.

Then Molloy's attention turned to the necktie. While working the counter at one of those fancy Fifth Avenue stores one day (he'd left his teaching job to focus on menswear), he was the victim of an armed robbery. Down at the precinct station, the cops handed him the book of mug shots, and Molloy couldn't help but notice that in thousands of photos—not a single tie. His first thought was that thugs might want to start wearing them because cops clearly weren't accustomed to arresting men in ties. His second thought was that ties might speak as loudly as raincoats did, so he took to the streets again. At both Grand Central Terminal and the Port Authority bus station, he stood around in the middle of evening rush-hour foot traffic and tried to appear anxious. Then he went up to people and said he'd forgotten his wallet and could they spare seventy-five cents to help him get home? For the first hour, he wore no tie; for the second hour, he did. During hour one, he was given $7.23; during hour two, the hour of the tie, he pulled in an even $26.00. The average American's reaction to clothes, he decided, was like Pavlov's dogs to the ring of a bell.* Beige raincoats rang better bells than black ones, and neckties made a cha-ching noise, like a cash register.

After compiling his research — he claimed *Dress for Success* encompassed "the opinions and subconscious reactions" of over fifteen thousand business people — Molloy felt confident in saying he could engineer a wardrobe to "elicit just about any desired effect." The smart man would let hard research, not the dictates of fashion or personal taste, choose his clothing. Some social groups preferred navy blue solids, others responded better to gray and stripes, and depending on whom you wanted to cozy up to, you'd simply pick one over another. Molloy desperately wanted people to understand that the correct way to think about clothes was as a means to a socioeconomic end only, and beyond that, fashion wasn't worth thinking much about. By far the best choice for anyone who hoped to do well financially was to dress upper-middle-class. "I will never ask you to concede that it is fair or just or moral for a man's success or failure to depend, to a large extent, on how he dresses," he wrote in his introduction. "But that is very much the way the money-oriented sectors of our culture work; and it is my contention that in matters of individual striving, it is far more rewarding to let reality be your guide, to use the system rather than ignore or flout it."

By "money-oriented sectors" I don't think he meant banking exclusively, but any arena outside academia. The thrust of

---

* The budding social scientist might object that his study had fatal design flaws. It's possible, after all, that people who stayed at the office a little later were habitually more generous, or else more gullible, than those who skipped out earlier.

Molloy's argument, as well as that of other midcentury minds obsessed with the same questions, was that there were things clothes did well, and things clothes didn't do well at all. While everyone else wrung their hands about how bad, how very sad, it was that all America was *conforming,* these thinkers started toying with the notion that blending in actually has its advantages. Indeed, it has a kind of subversive power. It seemed very relevant the other day when I overheard a gruff man, leaning in close over the café table to say to his lunch partner, "I've come to talk serious. You understand me? I've come to talk serious." He probably wouldn't have to say that, I thought, if he weren't wearing a Charlie Brown T-shirt.

All discussion of dressing for business starts with the suit. Horatio Alger's street urchins often received suits as gifts, because a suit was a gift that kept on giving. Once suited up, these poor boys could stride safely into glittering hotel lobbies and banks and other places they would have been kicked out of before. When the titular heroine of Theodore Dreiser's *Sister Carrie,* destitute and new to Chicago, gets two, soft ten-dollar bills pressed into her hand, it's clear what she needs to do—she needs to buy "a nice new jacket." F. Scott Fitzgerald used a man's lack of a suit as shorthand for his failures as a provider, even as a lover. Says *The Great Gatsby*'s Myrtle Wilson of her cuckolded husband: "The only *crazy* I was was when I married him. I knew right away I made a mistake. He borrowed somebody's best suit to get married in, and never even told me about it."

By the mid-1940s, or after World War II, one school of thought maintained that the best way to get a job was to look like you didn't need one. The perfect interview outfit would have you looking neither too underdressed (like you'd recently left the breadlines) nor too overdressed (which also made you look desperate, just in a different way). When the hero of Frederic Wakeman's 1946 novel *The Hucksters* gets dressed for an interview at an advertising agency, he goes through this thought process: "white unhollywood-looking shirt, of course"; then a plain black tie (nothing too loud); "and finally the shoes he'd bought in London. Those shoes were the goddamnedest sincerest looking shoes in all of New York." That was key — business-like, upper-crust, almost insistently earnest.

Brooks Brothers was the most popular purveyor of the goddamned sincere look, having been around since before the Civil War.* They opened for business when all suits were custom-made, but had been pioneers in off-the-rack, which brought business attire to a wider but still largely well-to-do clientele. "Many grown men would feel uncouth if they ever had to appear in public without their Brooks Brothers suit," the pop sociologist Vance Packard wrote in 1959's *The Status Seekers,* noting a thriving business in secondhand "snob-label" clothing — Brooks Brothers, Burberry, and J. Press — for those men who couldn't afford to buy new every time. Mary McCarthy's 1942 short story "The Man in the Brooks Brothers Shirt" played with the idea that the Brooks Brothers monogram signified someone with feet firmly on the ladder, at or nearing the top. The man of the title was a steel company exec; he meets an antsy young woman in a Pullman car. She's got bohemian socialist leanings and assumes he's a neutered, conformist fool, but, several whiskies later, ends up sleeping with him anyway. A few years after this story was published, Brooks Brothers decided to ride McCarthy's wave and "The Man in the Brooks Brothers Suit" ad campaign was born — cementing the look of the quintessential American success story (professional and maybe even sexual) in the popular imagination.†

---

* Lincoln wore a custom-made black Brooks Brothers coat to his second inauguration. He was also wearing it the night he was assassinated.

† The winning entry in an August 2004 competition for aspiring marketers only perpetuated the Brooks Brothers mythology. Dan Limbach of Oak Park, Illinois, suggested that Brooks Brothers should capitalize on their long-standing association with upward mobility. "Brooks Brothers attire looks at the corner office and says 'That's going to be mine some day,'" he wrote. As FedEx sought to be thought of whenever a package was needed "overnight" and Volvo would be for-

Surrendering yourself to Brooks Brothers today is for some such a reminder of everything they hate about their country-club fathers that they're tempted to say "Screw it" and wear a T-shirt with a marijuana leaf on it to work. Greg, a journalist, noticed a new intern in his office doing just that. "In fact, he wore it every day, the same shirt," Greg said. How did it go over? "The boss figured that unless he was the next H. L. Mencken, he wasn't getting a job." Automatic disqualification, in other words, though it's rarely stated so openly. "Entry-level, it's harder, because the job doesn't require you to dress up," said Ben, who worked at an Internet start-up in the late 1990s and remembers young staffers coming to work in shorts and Reeboks. He realized this made for a less than ideal picture in more ways than one, and yet, barring pressure to do otherwise, it seemed harmless enough. For the young and underpaid, being able to wear whatever you want is a welcome compensation for the more onerous aspects of the job. (This is especially true among undergraduate Marxists forced into capitalism out of economic necessity—"The job I don't like, but it's pretty laid-back, so at least . . .")

In the late 1960s, the Hollywood costume designer Edith Head made a foray into success literature with *How to Dress for Success,* in which she argued that this amounted to infantile narcissism, essentially. You thought you were special, and needed to communicate that uniqueness, but who were *you* really? She addresses herself to young single women in particular:

> The *you* we're talking about is not alone. She is manufactured by the dozens, the hundreds, the thousands, in all sizes and shapes of women, all after success—in many cases, the same success you seek. And in this competitive race, it is frequently the best "packaging" that makes the difference between those who are left on the shelf and those who are

---

ever associated with "safety," Brooks Brothers could reasonably lay claim to "ambitious," Limbach concluded.

sought after and snapped up fast in the well-stocked super-
market of modern life.

Head had won seven Academy Awards (out of thirty nomina-
tions), and her name would have been instantly recognizable to
the young American women accustomed to sewing their own
clothes—which was most of them. And though she was considered an artist in some circles, she was primarily interested in ad-
vancing a completely pragmatic, totally unfanciful understanding of fashion. What you wore had a certain power, sure, and
you'd be foolish not to exploit it, but any girl smart enough to
exploit that power also had to understand that her goals in life
should come first. (And on this score she's decidedly dis-inspira-
tional: "There must be something you want more than anything
else. Is it something that is possible for you to get? If not, get it
off your mind and start again." This is hardly *you can be anything you set your mind to!* rhetoric.) The difference between
a young woman and a can of beans, Head claimed, is that the
beans were going one place only. "You are going many places,"
but even that was contingent on your ability to get over yourself, to be very clear on what your talents were and were not,
and to put on some simple skirt suits and tailored dresses.

It's precisely this blend-into-the-woodwork, lost-in-the-su-
permarket sensibility that many beginning office workers seek
to avoid, though it's often at their own peril. Mikhail, who works
in corporate law in Seattle, used to draw on his entire wardrobe
of vintage cowboy shirts when getting dressed for work. "I had a
. . . well, let's say my hair was different, too," he said. (I've seen
pictures—it was very curly and very high.) "I figured they'd let
it go because I was European." He knew his look stood out, and
would occasionally suffer subtle hints from colleagues that he
might want to tone it down a little, but otherwise didn't think
much about it. Then, after a long holiday weekend, when half the
office had clearly been at the beach and the other half had gone
shopping, he joined the gaggle by the water cooler and compli-
mented his neighbor on his new pants. "Thanks," the neighbor

said, "but y'know, they're not nearly as nice as your *turquoise pants.*" At which point Mikhail had to accept that his more buttoned-down colleagues were driven to distraction by the way he dressed — they could not, would not, let it go. He then also had to come to terms with the fact that he was surrounded by people for whom "Oh, you're so creative!" was not, in fact, a compliment. They meant it as: *I kinda see what you're trying to do here, but I don't quite understand it, and I'm not sure I like it because it seems like there might be some implicit judgment of me* [and my more conventional ways] *in there.*

Edith Head, for all her grumpiness, foresaw these situations and tried to tie the idea of dressing appropriately for work to a new development in film costuming. In years past, she said, movie stars wanted to look glamorous all the time, and might turn down a role if the script didn't contain enough costume changes or incorporate enough clothing that communicated "movie star." So a director would cast Carole Lombard as a poor secretary, and she'd be filmed coming to work in a sable and pearls. But now the studios, having figured out that "fitness for the occasion" made an actor's performance more believable, were demanding greater authenticity in costume design. Head apparently believed this was a foreign enough concept because she tells a story to illustrate: When asked to outfit Natalie Wood for a role as a sales clerk in Macy's pet department, Head and her staff actually decided *to go to Macy's* and have a look around. Then they sewed up a smock for Wood that was very similar to the smocks Macy's pet department employees wore in real life. This was exciting, Head said, and was becoming all the rage, because it helped cement what she called the "acceptance look."

Head said she had no problem with a girl "taking the chance of being classed with the weird ones, including the town drunk and the village idiot," as some committed nonconformists did. But one couldn't do this and then object when the more conventional ones took you up on the offer. Until you proved your worth to the company, you weren't free to dress as you pleased. If you were content to remain "a carefree little file clerk whom nobody sees," she continued, by all means wear whatever you wanted—just know that the company would probably relegate you and your wardrobe to supporting roles. If you wanted to be out front calling the shots, you'd wear clothes that sent signals that you expected—indeed demanded—to be taken seriously.

Unfortunately, this meant no off-days. You could not, as a friend of mine once did, operate on the assumption that a pair of sweatpants two days a week would be canceled out by his blazers and ties the other three days of the week. (He's now a freelancer.) Or that you could only bother to look sharp on days you had a big meeting, or knew you'd be bumping into someone you needed to impress. For one thing, it ignored the power of gossip. If you had a widespread reputation for rayon, or for putting your makeup on in the elevator, the first thing a new person introduced to you might think—that is, on that rare occasion you didn't show up at the office with wet hair—is not "Wow, she looks great," but "You know, she doesn't look that skanky after all."

In the summer of 2005, a company-wide memo sent out by higher-ups at Fairchild Publications, the publisher of *Women's Wear Daily* and *Beauty Biz Report,* was leaked to the Internet. The memo was a "friendly reminder" about their business-casual dress code, and was addressed to the magazine empire's youngest members:

> As an intern embarking on your professional career it is important to remember that your dress speaks volumes about you. Fairchild understands you want to express your fashionista style; however, showing up in a strappy tank top, short blue jean skirt and flip flops is not going to express that you are a smart professional looking to succeed in the magazine industry. Business casual is crisp, neat and should look appropriate even for a chance meeting with a CEO. It should not look like cocktail or picnic attire.

It went on to specify that skirts should cover one's thighs while seated, that slits facilitate walking, not a view of one's legs, and that cleavage was "not appropriate to business and job search occasions."

Assuming those descriptions were drawn from life, the memo gives credence to Molloy's idea that what kept people from dressing properly was not lack of funds (as he suspected when he started his research), but bad ideas. Earlier, Orison Swett Marden nodded in agreement with a young reporter who remarked: "If a man did not look prosperous, people would think he did not have the right ambition or the ability to succeed; *that there must be something the matter with him or he would dress better* and make a better appearance." (Emphasis mine, because it reminds me of the $14.99 jacket decision.)

The reason the suit was so powerful—so fit to the occasion, as Head would have put it—was that it both revealed and obscured. It gave off the correct signals of affluence, but otherwise didn't tell you a lot about the person wearing it. And that kind of reticence and mystery, some felt, was integral to finagling your upward mobility. To a significant extent, a suit still operates much like it always has, as anyone who's attended a meeting wearing a well-fitting dark suit can tell you. You can contribute very little and still get full credit.

Even hopelessly "creative" types have recognized the uselessness of dress rebellions. The midcentury writer and poet Delmore Schwartz in particular was no friend to the Beats and other proud nonconformists. They might pose as if they were "fighting the conformism of the organization man, the advertising executive, the man in the grey flannel suit, or the man in the Brooks Brothers suit," Schwartz wrote, but in fact these young people had no idea what they were talking about. He felt their rebellion was toothless because it ignored some fundamental realities about power, and making a living. In *Growing Up Absurd,* Paul Goodman examined the work attitudes amongst the disaffected youth of his day. This is how they reconciled themselves to work, he said: They'd get a job that paid the bills, just barely, just as long as they got to preserve their style. Goodman offered the example of a young man who got a gig dressing windows at Macy's. He wasn't really in the Rat Race, this young man would say to himself, because he was just doing it for "bread" and would quit whenever. So, say the boss asked him to shave off his beard. He'd do it; he'd pretend to conform because he had to in order to keep the job. It didn't mean anything because he was just playing a role anyhow, he'd say. What the Macy's window dresser failed to understand, Goodman concluded, "is that playing roles and being hip in this way is nearly the same as being an Organization Man, for *he* doesn't mean it either."

Said Schwartz of the man with the corporate acceptance look: "His conformism is limited to the office day and business hours: in private life—and at heart—he is as Bohemian as anyone else. And it is often true that the purpose of the job which requires conformism is solely to support his personal idiosyncrasies, tastes, and inclinations." The Brooks Brothers man might even let his employer believe he was more committed to the job than he really was—so long as it benefited him personally to do so. But all the while, he'd keep what was private—what was his alone—private. Far from stifling his creativity, willingness to button down sartorially gave him greater freedom of movement on a far grander scale.*

It was all pretty easy when you got right down to it, said *The Hucksters'* adman: ". . . a man's got to look bright, act like a Racquet Club member even if he isn't, have two to three simple but good ideas a year, learn how to say yes sir all the time, and no sir once in a while, and every so often have guts enough to pound a

---

* The truth of this statement is confirmed every time you hear about the suited-up Wall Streeter who conforms for five years, then cashes in his chips, takes a year off to travel, and then breaks out the flannel shirts and grows a beard while he fills out applications for a master's program in landscape architecture. I've met at least two of them in person, and everyone hates them. (Not really—what they're experiencing is envy.)

client's desk and tell him that's the way it's gotta be . . . That's all there is to it." It took a little costuming, a little play-acting, and not fooling yourself into thinking that hard work alone would be rewarded. "Many men believe that men receive promotions in business due to their efficiency, reliability and hard work, but this is not always true, not even for the boss's son," Molloy wrote cynically. "More often than not, it is the *semblance* of these qualities that helps success along, rather than the reality of them. To create the look of these qualities, you, your desk and your office must be as neat and precise as possible."

The reason for this was fairly simple: those who held the reins of power—those who'd been wearing Brooks Brothers since prep school—weren't all that likely to hand the reins over to anyone who openly challenged their wool-suited conventions. If they didn't have direct heirs, they still wouldn't relinquish the family firm to some guy with long hair who smelled of patchouli oil, regardless how talented. Blandly WASPy had more destabilizing potential in the long run. In fact, John Molloy claimed, he could honestly say he had no dog in this fight—he was the consumer's man, only and ever interested in helping people succeed. He realized he'd be accused of having "snobbish, conservative, bland and conformist" tastes, but defied anyone to prove this wasn't the best uniform for class warfare. For the lower and middle classes, dressing up like old money made sense from a penny-pinching perspective as well because old-money style—such as it is—did not change with the wind. With minor variations, it was essentially the same, year in and year out.

Head was also adamant that her prescriptions favored the ambitious woman with a limited budget. It meant you wouldn't have to buy a new wardrobe every season just to keep up with trends. Classic clothing may cost more up front, she admitted, but when you got down to the nitty-gritty, it was far friendlier to the outsider with little cash in hand.

Insider or outsider, committed or not to your corporate life, here are the guidelines both scientific research and the midcentury poet might lay down for you:

Do polish your shoes. Unobservant characters are at a distinct disadvantage here, not least because they tend to assume that their own failure to notice—or care about—scruffy shoes means nobody else will either.

Do own at least one white, button-up collared shirt. Seriously. This is the only clothing item that has consistently been above reproach for the last century. Fashion magazines "rediscover" it with eerie regularity. As became corporate legend, IBM once *required* its employees to wear white shirts each and every day. Mary McCarthy's Man in the Brooks Brothers Shirt, we're told, always ordered a dozen at a time. The white shirt was the subject of another of Molloy's twin tests, but this time he asked questions that would assign "moral values" to the shirt, not just socioeconomic ones. Which man would be late to work more often—the one in the white shirt or the other one? Which man was more likely to cheat on his expense account? More than 80 percent of respondents, Molloy claimed, gave the benefit of the doubt to the man in the white shirt. Presumably, women derive the same benefits.

Do realize your desk is your wardrobe. Some superiors want not just tailored shirts, but crisp and clean lines everywhere they look. Letting your desk's inbox overflow, thinking it will impress upon people how busy, vital, creative, and complicated a person you are, is not a sound idea. An overflowing inbox can just as easily be read as incompetence. (As a colleague remarked in another context, "There's punk, and then there's punk like the toilets don't work." That is to say, what might suggest only freewheeling genius to you will suggest freewheeling genius plus self-righteous, ineffectual laziness to others.) The following exchange, from an interview with *Rolling Stone* publisher Jann Wenner, was published in the *Wall Street Journal*.

WSJ: You have a reputation for being intently focused on neatness—so much so that your employees get memos on the subject. But creative
people often thrive in chaos. Why are you so
interested in the condition of a staffer's desk?

WENNER: Well, I'm a neat freak. . . . It seems to me that
an orderly desk is reflective of an orderly and
organized mind, you know? And ██re's a level
of immaturity to people who just c██ clean up
after themselves. And I don't think i██ anything to do with creativity.

An overflowing inbox can lead to being micromanaged. If
you're working for someone who relies on your organizational
skills and who wants, at a glance, reassurance that you're on top
of things, clutter sends the opposite message. Your life then becomes more difficult.

Do wait. Underlings have to wear the expected for a while.
"When you reach the top rung it's a different story," assured
Head. "The eccentricities of the genius who is top man (or
woman) on the totem pole of tycoonery are not only condoned
but admired. What you wear when you sit in the president's
chair is entirely up to you." Winston Churchill, everyone knew,
directed Britain's war effort in red pajamas half the time. Albert
Einstein could disregard protocol and show up at a formal wedding in a stocking cap, echoed Grace and Fred Hechinger in the
anti-anticonformity *Teen-Age Tyranny* (1962), not because Einstein had been encouraged to do whatever he liked "but because
his knowledge and achievements had lifted him to the rare level
at which men can fix their own standards in behavior."

**Do, if you're inclined to break the code, know what the costs are and whether
you're willing to pay them.** If you're going to deviate, deviate with
real flair. The most inspired rejections of norms are carefully
planned out *and* tempered by meticulous boringness in other

arenas—picture the flamboyantly dressed journalist who turns in clean, workmanlike prose. Successful rebellions are rarely carried out on a whim, and never without taking into consideration the people who'll be doing the buying, hiring, or selling. My friend Stephanie, for instance, regularly turned up for work looking like a cross between Pippi Longstocking and an overmedicated 1970s housewife. She sported dreadlocks for a while. But she was usually at her immaculately clean desk by 8:30 A.M., and stayed long after most of her colleagues had left for the day. All this to suggest that if you're going to break code, it's best to do so spectacularly.

>>

The Brooks Brothers Man would be trotted out again in the 1970s, this time to poke fun at hippies. Gerald Nierenberg and Henry Calero's *How to Read a Person Like a Book*—one of the first books to systematically examine how people revealed themselves through body language—claimed that despite jokes to the contrary, hippies "preen as much as, if not more than, a young executive decked out in a Brooks Brothers suit." This was because hippies typically had more hair to contend with, the authors continued, so they were often seen brushing it away from their faces.

The sociologist Edward T. Hall—active in the 1950s and '60s—once remarked that people who lived in cultures in which the rules of social interaction were heavily prescribed were often a little more relaxed: "There is never any doubt in anybody's mind that, as long as he does what is expected, he knows what to expect from others." And this provides some relief, he said. It's not as bad as it sounds. It's certainly true that if somebody or something (like scientific research) decides what you should wear, you've saved some mental resources to throw behind other problems. The author of *The Power of Positive Thinking* (another midcentury hit) claimed that successful men had realized many decisions were simply not worth the time it took to make them, so they subtracted as many decisions from their daily routine as possible—decisions like what to wear.

Meanwhile, rest assured that if you're a genuine freak, it will show. You won't be able to hide it. Take a pair of trousers, white shirt, navy blue blazer, and put it on a granola-eating bird-watcher, then put the very same outfit on someone who meets all his dates at AA meetings and got three hours of sleep the night before, and trust me, you'll be able to tell who's who.

7

When It's Just
Not About You

Helen Gurley Brown on Having One's
Underwear Forcibly Removed

> "Stuck" is a relative concept.
>
> —ROSABETH MOSS KANTER,
> *Men and Women of the Corporation*

A FEW YEARS AGO, longtime *Cosmopolitan* editor in chief Helen Gurley Brown described a game that was played at one of her first jobs. Still a high school student, the eighteen-year-old Helen Gurley was working at radio station KHJ in Hollywood, California. The game was called Scuttle, and it began when all the men in the office with time to kill would select a female coworker and set upon her as a group. They would chase her down the halls, up through the music library, and back around to the announcing booths. Once she'd been caught, they would hold her down and remove her underwear. End of game. Everyone would disperse and get back to work. "De-pantying was the sole object," Gurley Brown recalled in a *Wall Street Journal* op-ed. No complaint was ever filed, and no Scuttle player was ever reported to the director's office. Some women chose to cope with the practice by wearing their nicest underwear to work.

Well, that's neat, I thought upon first reading this. It's amazing what people will do to kill time, it's incredible what some people will put up with, and it's good to be reminded that there are some workplaces so dysfunctional, so deeply and systemically off-kilter, that no matter what you do, you're going to end up feeling had. Perhaps humiliated, perhaps anxious, but definitely vulnerable. Only at the time you won't be able to say quite why. You'll just find yourself wondering whether you should start wearing better panties to work or preemptively kicking people in the shins whenever they get too close.

I had the first twinge of awareness that I might be in this kind of sticky, no-win situation a couple of years into a job I loved. All my early progress had sputtered slowly to a halt. The momentum I enjoyed during my rosy-cheeked, eager-beaver first months was completely lost. The details aren't especially interesting, but the trajectory—for everyone—goes something like this: Year one you're on the fast track. Year two you're still on track, or so you think, but there just doesn't seem to be as much enthusiasm in the air for you. So you consider a haircut. You rearrange the piles on your desk, go to the supply closet for more pushpins, and stick up some different pictures in your cubicle. At the beginning of year three, there's still no measurable change in your status, though your efforts still seem to be appreciated. That is, to the extent you can determine, because no one in the office is telling you much. Meanwhile, people are hired from the outside while the ones inside stay unpromoted. You start to wonder if you'll ever make it to the next rung.

The immediate effect of this game of existential Scuttle is that you'll start dabbling in routine bouts of self-flagellation. You speculate wildly but without conviction, knowing only that you seem to be failing. A former colleague of mine, after working five years for a woman I knew to be a cold, cold fish, with no promotion in sight, tentatively ventured that perhaps—he wasn't sure, "It could just be me"—that his boss enjoyed humiliating people. Seeing as how this very same woman had repeatedly made me feel like a slatternly chambermaid who couldn't be trusted to keep her apron on straight, I gently suggested that, um, yeah, maybe he was onto something.

When you're stuck in the shame spiral—not getting better projects, more recognition, more money, more love—you rarely pause to consider that your powerlessness, and the fact that it looms indefinitely into the future, might just *have nothing to do with you.* Sometimes the problem is bad management, or an asthmatic corporate culture, or some other rot that set in long before you darkened the company doorstep and will continue long after you leave the place behind. This idea can be very hard to grasp. Abdicating responsibility is at odds with the whole self-reliant, make-it-happen strain in American success literature to this point. When in reality, the whole idea of a meritocracy ruins many a striver's Sunday night.* Even in pay-your-dues industries, where people are supposed to start at the bottom, there are always some higher-ups who employ deliberate amnesia, forgetting their own mad scramble to the top, and go on blithely assuming that everyone's potential is commensurate with their current station. In other words, if you're still working near the bottom, you must be a bottom feeder. After prolonged exposure to these people, you start to wonder whether they might be right.

---

* The British Labour Party minister Michael Young, who first coined the term *meritocracy* in 1958, warned that this might happen. He wrote a book, *The Rise of the Meritocracy,* that surveyed, Aldous Huxley–style, a hypothetical England after decades of pure meritocracy as government policy. It was a bleak portrait. In the days of dimwitted crown princes and blatant prejudice based on sex, creed, or skin color, or back when many believed God himself preordained status, those at the bottom of the ladder had factors beyond their control to blame. But if, in both theory and practice, all those in power were there because they were the *best,* what did that imply for those below? That they deserved their poverty and powerlessness because they were just not that bright? Young claimed he intended *The Rise of the Meritocracy* as both argument and counterargument. Perfectly realized, it was always going to be tinged with sadness: the upper classes wouldn't feel obligated to help out the lower classes, and while those at the top would be brilliant (a good thing), once they mated with each other and passed on the smart genes to their kids, membership in the elite would become hereditary again. In short, the downside to meritocracy is that those born on third base think they hit a triple, and everyone else is subject to self-loathing.

Looking your powerlessness squarely in the face, however, can actually be pretty liberating. Which brings us back to Helen Gurley Brown. Gurley Brown was writing for a generation of young women who had to consider the possible forcible removal of their underwear when getting dressed for work every day. It was a time when offices still employed gal Fridays—glorified gofers even more lowly and underpaid than secretaries. It was when a secretary emptied her boss's ashtray. When her time was considered his to waste. The bit of pop culture that really put this era in perspective for me is the musical *How to Succeed in Business Without Really Trying*, which premiered on Broadway in 1961. One scene has a highly competent female secretary—been with the company for years—cooing at a young man trying to break into business. "You have the cool clear eyes of a seeker of wisdom and truth," she trills. "Yet there's that upturned chin and the grin of impetuous youth. Oh, I believe in you. I believe in *you*." The young man—a window washer just the week before—is promoted to junior executive after only three days on the job. No mention is ever made of her potential.

Helen Gurley Brown herself had seventeen secretarial jobs before landing the ad agency stint that led to the copy-writing job that finally led to professional recognition—sometime around age thirty. She couldn't have believed in meritocracy if she tried. And she has some interesting things to say about feeling—and being—stuck.

Gurley Brown's route to the editor in chief's spot at *Cosmopolitan*, which she landed in 1966, was a long and circuitous one, and she got it largely because she'd written a bestseller called *Sex and the Single Girl*. The book was everything the title suggested. "I think marriage is insurance for the worst years of your life," she wrote. "During your best years you don't need a husband. You do need a man of course every step of the way, and they are often cheaper emotionally and a lot more fun by the dozen." In the year 1962 this was enough to afford her instant notoriety.

(Betty Friedan's *The Feminine Mystique,* a very different but no less galvanizing book, was still a year away.)

Kicky title aside, fostering a sexual revolution was not foremost on Gurley Brown's agenda, and what's most remarkable about her work today is the number of paragraphs she devotes to "Squirming, Worming, Inching, and Pinching Your Way to the Top." While men of her generation were beginning to find the whole business of being businessmen stifling, for her it was terrifically exciting. *Sex and the Single Girl* was followed by *Sex and the Office* two years later. By that time, Gurley Brown had found that many young women were uncomfortable with the idea of ascending the ranks; they would rather sit in the stenographic pool unnoticed by any coworker who wouldn't eventually be proposing marriage. Other women worried that professional success would cost them the other good things in life — husbands, children, comfortable homes. And some were very concerned about the unsettling effect of having single girls regularly parading around the office.* But Gurley Brown was out to win hearts and minds: the office could and *should* be a veritable pleasure cruise for young women. Why? Because "being great at a terrific job is sexy." Because "when you start having a rather terrific success in your job, it's like little firecrackers going off inside you . . . pop, pop, pop. Sometimes it's a few days between pops, but the sensation is a bit like the sweet, glow-y

---

* The effect on married male colleagues and their families, that is. The 1960 edition of Emily Post's *Etiquette* addressed this issue head-on, as secretaries traditionally accompanied their bosses on business trips (someone had to take dictation, after all). It was a setup ripe for exploitation and other shenanigans, and Post gave a rather cryptic warning to the secretaries: "Certain jobs — particularly those of responsibility leading to the heights of success — carry with them the paradoxical responsibility of upholding a moral code of unassailable integrity while smashing to bits many of the long-established rules of propriety." The onus was on *them* to set firm parameters (and to request a room on a separate floor of the hotel). Other onlookers got even hotter under the collar. In 1959, *Esquire* published a pulp paperback called *Sex Vice and Business* and stocked it with dozens of lurid stories about easy women, prostitutes, and other "favors" routinely enjoyed by the middle-class dad on a sales trip.

feeling at the beginning of a love affair." With all the fun to be had, sex itself was almost beside the point. Unless a young woman was, in her words, a Bona Fide Nester, and content to spend her days at home washing windows, she really ought to be working. The repetition of "sex" in her titles just obscured the fact that Gurley Brown was really most concerned with the mechanics of upward mobility, clothes on.

Gurley Brown's underlying message was that nothing prepared you for power like having to wait for it—and the single girl would do well to use this period of relative powerlessness to study its ways, means, and perversities. That included developing a clear understanding of what factors you *could* control and which ones you couldn't. Gurley Brown had a rare gift for removing her ego from the equation—even in the most intimate of circumstances, even when sex and work mingled just like the calamity howlers insisted it would. In a later memoir, she would confess that for a spell in the late 1940s she'd been a kept woman: she'd spend the day typing and filing, and then she and her boss would knock off around 4:00 P.M., have a few drinks in his office—tossing back Harveys Bristol Cream Sherry like it was Coca-Cola—then retire to the studio apartment he provided for her. Even in these circumstances, she suffered no delusions that her boss wanted her for her interoffice talents. No, he was merely attracted to her because she emitted "waves of waifdom and vulnerability like a civet cat throwing off musk."

That clearheaded diagnosis is probably hindsight at work—the seasoned wisdom of an experienced older woman. I imagine things were more confusing at the time. They certainly were for me, as they are for most everybody who feels their abilities are going unrecognized. So that leaves us with the question: Other than the unmistakable sign of seeing your underwear on the floor, how can you tell when your organizational powerlessness is structural, not personal? How do you know when it's not about *you?*

The first sign is a certain opacity about procedure. Stephen, now in adult education, worked at a magazine right after college. He remembers being mystified by the office dynamics; the editors were secretive in ways that baffled him. They would never go out of their way to explain how things were done, even to the entry-level staff, and there was something furtive in their step as they raced by certain cubicles. It was not that they wouldn't be forthcoming when posed a direct question—about a bit of magazine business, say—but their responses were usually preceded by a silence long enough to imply that they were making calculations about just what to share. He couldn't figure out how a junior person got an article in the magazine. After months of wondering what he was doing wrong—if anything—Stephen came up with a theory: The editors felt that only once you knew how things were done could you start asking for things. If you started asking for things (like, say, the chance to write a piece) then they—not liking to think of themselves as entirely unreasonable creatures—would eventually have to say yes. But that could mean they'd get dragged into supervising more of your work, or if you turned out to be good, that they'd have more competition to contend with, and ultimately it was just easier and simpler if no young eager beavers made any moves. (Other than getting up to make more coffee.)

He may have been slightly paranoid, but it's true that some organizations—and from everything I've heard, this includes the blue chips of any industry: Goldman Sachs, Microsoft, Google, Alfred A. Knopf, HBO, and the like—think you should be grateful just to be swiveling in their chairs. The second sign you may be mired in corporate dysfunction is when you can't—despite your best, sincerest efforts—discern *any* straightforward relationship between the amount and quality of the work someone puts in and the extent and degree of their influence. In every office there is at least one high-ranked individual whose prestige and pay package irritate the larger, lower-ranked half of the organization. According to *Sex and the Office,* this is partly a function of available stock. There simply aren't enough secure, well-adjusted people in the general population to populate the ranks of management. Any given floor of any given office will shelter a couple of charismatic, highly effective individuals—and a whole lot more average sorts. Inevitably some of the average ones will bubble up to the higher echelons, and ultimately decision-making power will be held by a loose conglomeration of lackluster characters. This process is always, Gurley Brown said, facilitated by managerial neuroses. "A very insecure or confused boss will surround himself with idiots while perfectly capable people are either fired or left unused," she noted.

Her goal in pointing this out was to smooth the foreheads of frustrated climbers, but the idea that mediocrity ruled the day, and that substandard employees were never demoted, was already gaining cultural traction. A few years after *Sex and the Single Girl,* Dr. Laurence J. Peter, an associate professor of education at the University of Southern California, would vault himself out of academic obscurity with *The Peter Principle,* a book that asked why advanced societies were floundering in inefficiency. *The Peter Principle* (cowritten by Raymond Hull) was the yin to Gurley Brown's yang, and its message was less than reassuring. Car manufacturers installed gas tanks where they were vulnerable to rear impact; the school system consistently churned out graduates who couldn't read; and going to see a play too often resulted in a really boring night out. "This incompetence would be annoying enough if it were confined to public works, politics, space travel and such vast, remote fields of human endeavor," Hull wrote. "But it is not. It is close at hand—an ever-present, pestiferous nuisance." Stupid things kept on happening, Dr. Peter explained, because people were promoted from positions in which they were completely competent into positions that were beyond their abilities—he called this their "level of incompetence." Yet The System required regular promotions. If no one could be shown to have forged ahead through dutiful service to the company, then The System would start to break down.

Peter's principle was simple: "In a Hierarchy Every Employee Tends to Rise to His Level of Incompetence," and everyone's experience of work—unless you were a freak of nature or a solitary genius—was controlled by the Peter Principle. Some employees would reach their incompetence level very early in their careers and never get promoted. But even exceptionally smart people weren't immune, as they'd just move from areas of competence to greater competence until, over time, demonstrating they could handle the requirements of each new post qualified them for another promotion. The cream of the crop rose until they soured, and the only real work that got done was done by those who had not yet reached their level of incompetence.

Which brings us to the third sign that it's not about you. Gurley Brown's recollections of her early career are filled with anecdotes that illustrate what Peter and Hull termed "the disruptive power of achievement"—the idea that there are times and places where being good at your job, where doing everything you think is right, proves disastrous. If she didn't initially understand this, her experiences after escaping from the secretarial pool made it more than clear. Gurley Brown's first big break was a promotion from secretary to copywriter—she became one of three "girl" copywriters at the Foote, Cone & Belding ad agency in Los Angeles.* Of this bunch, says Gurley Brown, the most creative was fired. (The fired girl then found a job at another agency where she became "the darling" and started working on multimillion-dollar campaigns.) Back at Foote, Cone & Belding, the second girl copywriter got fed up and eventually left. Gurley Brown, the last one standing, kept herself busy by writing the Max Factor advice column in *Seventeen* magazine. She thought she was in management's good graces. But every month, five to seven guys swooped in to rewrite every inch of column she churned out, and eventually the assignment was taken away from her. She kept doing busywork but slowly caught on to the fact that management wanted nothing from her beyond the basic, menial

---

* Girls, young women, women in midlife, and old women are all "girls" in the Helen Gurley Brown universe.

requirements of her job. Being the last girl standing made her a lingering reminder of earlier bad decisions.

It gets confusing. When mired in the lower ranks, you naturally assume that a new assignment means an uptick in status. But it doesn't. Melissa, an event planner, was finally given a plum client by her boss, which she took as license to say, "Hey, do you think we could let up on the photocopying and other stuff?" He said, "Uh, no. No, keep doing what you're doing." So he was being petty, but she was essentially *asking permission* to slack. (Who would do the photocopying then?) Only the most Zen bosses will agree to this and mean it.

Much of Gurley Brown's advice to young women on the job is thus implicitly tied to the Peter Principle's bedrock rule of organizational life: The hierarchy must be preserved. Which is not to say a girl—or, nowadays, any stymied employee—couldn't or shouldn't be plotting her own revolution. It meant she had to perform acts of deference to keep things humming—the hierarchy had to *look* like it was being preserved even if it wasn't. A junior employee had to be efficient and always on top of things, to be sure, but if one's goal was a "sexy office life with marvelous things happening to you," it made strategic sense not to act like you were gunning for the top all the time. No boss enjoys the sensation of someone snapping at his heels. Better to act —better to *be*—wholly emotionally invested in whatever minutiae they toss into your lap. A girl started to get professional traction not by demanding to be taken more seriously, but by being acutely sensitive to every interaction's psychological undercurrents. For Gurley Brown, the hierarchical was always emotional. And once you understood it wasn't *all* about you, you had to act as if *nothing* was about you. As she explained in *Sex in the Office:*

> You're going to hit me with an iced mackerel, but I have to tell you that the way you *get* the most out of your job is to *give* the most. You should feel empathy in your bosom—it doesn't tickle or anything—if you are to get better and bet-

ter jobs and go on to where the money and deep-piled fun
are. When you're trying to get a number for your boss and
it's busy, busy, busy, you're as vexed as he is. When you help
another girl type some reports, you *care* that she has a deadline. When the company gets a new client, you're thrilled.

She suggested the acting—the performance—is what counted.
You didn't have to *feel* sympathy at your core in order to behave
sympathetically. Sometimes the feelings fall in line behind the
actions.

At this point, it may help to remember how many hoops
prominent women of the time jumped through to make their
power palatable for mass consumption. When Ida Rosenthal,
founder and president of Maidenform Bras, was sent in 1959
as the only female member of a U.S. trade delegation to Russia, she prepared some interesting remarks for the occasion: "If
[Russian women] wore bras they would be happier and pret-
tier. The men would be happier. Consequently, the whole country would be more contented and I think Russia's relations with
the U.S. and the world might improve." In all fairness, this is
how she was quoted by a United Press Syndicate reporter. It's
possible she said something less silly, and she certainly did right
by her company with that plug. Still, you can't help but sense an
impulse to downplay her savvy.

Couching one's ambition in enthusiasm and endless resourcefulness was also better, Gurley Brown continued, than
making sure you were never exploited along the way. So when
asked to do just about anything, she suggested you try this approach:

> Of *course* it can be done and yes, of *course* you'll help.
> "Look, you take this end of the desk and lift and I'll scotch
> the rug under" is far better dialogue than, "I'm not strain-
> ing my back—the stupid building ought to tack the carpets
> down."

And then you also play nursemaid. ("Of *course* you are a little
mother to *all* the growing boys around the place. You dispense

Band-Aids and smiles to anyone who is wounded in the job, as-
pirin and Bromo to those who got the wounds the night before.")
And then flirt. ("You compliment them when they do well. You
are charmed by them much as you would be by a date. What's
so difficult about that?") When stuck, you ingratiate yourself
by appealing to sentiment as much as, if not more than, intellect.

What's so difficult about that? Well, if you're as angst-rid-
den as I was as an underling, and if you feel like an outsider
amongst insiders, as I did, being extra superduper helpful to colleagues farther along in their careers than you are is very difficult indeed. And what if your superiors have reached their level
of incompetence, and you're already overworked and underpaid? Extending yourself any further seems senseless. *Rooms
with No View,* a book about women's experiences in publishing
in the early seventies, suggested that if workplace sexism—or
class privilege, or whatever—started to feel a bit thick, it was
helpful to keep perspective. One editor commented that at her
progressive office the "women need have no fear of being pa-
tronized for their ideas or initiatives—they are given the same
support as men's. This may, of course, mean no support at all."
It's not *you* that's dysfunctional, it's the entire industry. Which is
reassuring, for a few minutes.

Should you find yourself stymied for no apparent reason, what
do you do? Before you start hatching a plan, or distributing
blame on others for your failure to get anywhere, Gurley Brown
advised that you honestly assess the amount of volunteer work
you're doing: "Was the last time you worked overtime without
pay when you put up prom decorations in the high school gym?
Do you manage to be frantically busy (writing a letter to your
cousin) when a co-worker is stuck with a mimeograph assembly
job?" Gurley Brown's books are filled with epithets to describe
the "whiner-shirker-pill" underlings who just didn't get this.
Just as the Eskimos have fourteen words for *snow,* so the go-
getting girls of Gurley Brown's universe push forward past girls

she terms *slobs, drones, drips, turnips, squirrelly little pests,* and *scaredy-cats. Slugs* was her preferred term for the go-nowhere girls, and they were much like *pills* in that they vocally protested they were always really busy and put upon, and used that as an excuse to act selfishly.*

The worst thing to do when you're stuck is to make the mistake of thinking that a powerful boss is also an empowering one. People can have power over you—and very little power over their own dark thoughts and fears, and therefore don't have it in them to help anyone else in any meaningful way. *Sex and the Single Girl's* approach to these bad bosses was withering. "Usually you have to work your way through some toads. Shiny bright junior executives are the worst," Gurley Brown writes. "They're afraid to send you to the accounting department to cash their expense check for fear you'll pick flowers on the way." If a girl found herself with the wrong sort of boss early in her career, that was to be expected (because most junior people don't work for the firm's top brass). At a certain point, however, a girl should be able to find herself a boss she liked—"a rich, successful, beautiful, kind, wonderful, lovable employer with fabulous friends." These criteria automatically eliminated most bosses younger than thirty-five, she ventured in *Sex and the Office,* as most were so neurotic and scared that it was hard just getting along with them. Gurley Brown wanted girls who found themselves working for loser bosses to fire *them*—in other words, quit. (Judging from her track record of seventeen secretarial jobs in thirteen years, we can assume she adhered to this philosophy with some vigor.) If a boss was too unsure of his own power to be benevolent, a girl was wasting her time waiting for him to change. These bosses only directed their energies upwards, so that *their* bosses would see them keeping the lights on late into the night,

---

* While she doesn't spend much time teasing out philosophies (the ladies, perhaps, being more pragmatic about these things), Gurley Brown traces a direct line from being selfish to being marginalized. She saw a straightforward cause-and-effect relationship between the two.

and wouldn't spend any effort advocating for powerless people below them.*

This was Gurley Brown's gloss, essentially, on the Dale Carnegie self-absorption standard. Bad bosses thought about themselves — and about you, perhaps, only in the moments when you were gulping down Harveys Bristol Cream Sherry with them. This type of bartering — I'll do this if you do that — is not just about sex. It colors *all* exchanges with insecure bosses: you get approval only when you make them look good. *The Peter Principle* framed the problem this way: If your superior was competent, he or she would evaluate you based on your *output*. If your superior had reached his or her level of incompetence, things looked very different. What mattered then was how well you laid low and didn't upset anyone or draw attention to problems.

It's this dilemma — being at the mercy of a boss who's clearly in over his head, but on whom you, as a junior employee, are dependent for a promotion — that is toughest to handle. Gurley Brown suggested all kinds of private rebellions to help take the immediate psychic pressure off. Remembering a young woman who would seat herself at the conference table with a "little red alligator notebook" in which she'd take "smashing little red alligator notes," Gurley Brown recommended you bring similar props to meetings, because then you could tend to your own business while also picking up points for style and diligence. She also suggested that girls who got antsy in meetings (because no one cared what they had to say) do Kegel exercises. Her larger point being that one shouldn't just sit, stare, and nod dully at the appropriate intervals, or doodle, but that it's possible to use their time for one's own ends.

---

* An influential *Harvard Business Review* article would go over these very same themes in 1969. "Pygmalion in Management" posited that unskilled bosses had a devastating effect on the careers of entry-level employees. "Rarely do new graduates work closely with experienced middle managers or upper-level executives," wrote the author J. Sterling Livingston. "Normally they are bossed by first-line managers who tend to be the least experienced and least effective in the organization," a recipe that amounted to "the worst possible circumstances" for the young upstarts.

Whatever strategy you employed to help you cope, stomping one's feet was a no-no—because it was pretty much guaranteed not to work. For instance, a friend of mine once went to her boss with the hope of convincing him to take her more seriously—"as a colleague, not just a little helper." She did this stoically, she thought, and with heroic restraint (she was really very angry by this point); she simply told her boss she couldn't keep doing what she'd been doing for two years already, she was bored, she was ready for more. She hoped this would force a reevaluation of her abilities. It had no effect, at least none that was encouraging. His response? "You know, maybe we should have lunch sometime. Maybe next month, after my vacation?"

"There's a way in which you can perform a task for someone that lets them know that you are really the master and they the slave," a former colleague once told me. When I asked him to give an example, he just smirked. But he (in his midforties, and boss to dozens of people) was hinting at something interesting, and it's not far removed from what Gurley Brown was saying about acts of deference. Let's say your boss, Miranda Priestly, asks you to get her daughters the new Harry Potter book so they can read it on the train en route to grandmother's house tomorrow. The book is not available for sale anywhere because it hasn't yet been printed. But you wriggle and plead and miraculously manage to wrestle a copy of the manuscript away from the publisher. When Miranda comes in the next morning and sees the rubber-banded manuscript on her desk, she hides her surprise that you actually pulled this off and demands to know why the manuscript's just sitting there, why it hasn't already been sent out. You inform her that you already made two copies, one for each daughter, and had them neatly bound and shipped off earlier this morning. The manuscript on her desk is the original, just for safekeeping. You stand straight and smile brightly. You ask, "Will there be anything else?"

Gurley Brown's disdain for slugs who fail to grasp this dynamic makes sense when seen in the light of her hardscrabble background. The eager-beaver helpfulness she prescribed undoubtedly came easier to someone who hadn't been raised to feel mundane tasks were beneath her. (She also seemed to understand that shiny, chirpy femininity, when coupled with *über*-competence and Swiss-Miss efficiency, can come across as more powerful than most tough girl posturing.) She was born in Green Forest, Arkansas, and when her father died young, leaving very little insurance money, she and her mother and sister Mary moved to Los Angeles to a house—literally—next to the tracks. Then Mary's polio set in, before foundations like the March of Dimes were around to help. Later in life Gurley Brown would say that "Needing to Make Up for Things" drove her constantly, like a possessed taskmaster at her lissome, Pucci-clad back.

All that and a perverse pleasure in wrestling with garden-variety jerks. Gurley Brown's patience and willingness to indulge creeps—at least for as long as it served her needs—is fairly rare. But it's worth emulating, if only for the sake of not letting the shame spiral further erode your self-esteem. The following are some of the better ways to channel your resentment over professional scuttling:

Do change the way you think of your job. If you begin to think of yourself as a self-employed person, and define your current employment as Making Your Boss Look Good while gathering up whatever wisdom you can in the meantime, it may alleviate some self-inflicted distress.

Don't tell everyone about it. Be selective about whom you confide in. Conferring with colleagues can help you see your situation more clearly, but if more than two other people in the company hear that you're really very annoyed, you may be compromising your position. You'll go from a contented-but-eager-to-go-places junior to someone who is officially "frustrated"—a death mark in most offices. Two is the critical number; once three or more people know, everybody knows. (I've seen this happen several times.) What happens next is something over which you have absolutely no control.

Do use "I feel" phrasing. This sounds like marriage counseling, but it works in the office. When describing an unsatisfactory work situation, don't ascribe motives to anyone but yourself. Don't claim (publicly) that a senior employee means you harm, or is deliberately trying to stall your advance. Best to demonstrate that you realize the limitations of an unhappy arrangement, aren't too soured by the thought of it, and that you look forward to the next stage.

When it comes to venting in writing, type as many bilious, angry sentences as you like, then save them in a drafts folder overnight, then reconsider, cut half, cut another half, reconsider again, and then—maybe—send them to their intended audience. No one has ever regretted not sending an angry e-mail. Variations on this theme appear in nearly every success book ever published.

Do learn to recognize signs that your boss may not be completely comfortable in his or her own skin. Taking too long to make a decision is one big hint that your boss may have reached his level of incompetence. Dragging out meetings with excessive chitchat is another. So too is leaning heavily on procedure, or insisting that "well, that's the status quo, that's just the way things are done around here," without taking the time to give you a more compelling explanation.

Don't sink so deep that you make an issue out of a box of raisins. Gurley Brown offered this story after she'd occupied the corner office at *Cosmopolitan* for some time. Working late one night, she got hungry. Ravenous, as she put it. So she went to the kitchen, rifled through the fridge—nothing. She started going through her employees' desks. This was pathetic, she realized, but hunger was hunger. Her search turned up the remnants of a box of raisins—twenty-six raisins in all—in the desk of a girl named Lydia. Gurley Brown snatched the box and made a note to herself to replace it the next morning.

She forgot. Lydia, frantically searching for her 11:00 A.M. snack the next day, was not impressed when the editor in chief informed her that she'd eaten it. Lydia made it clear she was annoyed. Gurley Brown was less than impressed in turn. What the girl should have done, she said, is made a joke of it. Lydia now shared this secret with Gurley Brown, her boss's boss, one that involved Gurley Brown having done something bizarre and uncouth, and Lydia could have used that secret knowledge to cement a friendship with her. Instead Lydia turned into a scolding kindergarten teacher. In Gurley Brown's next book, she gets quickly dismissed with the phrase "we simply can't be stuffy, snippy, selfish, snapping-turtle little bitches and succeed."

Gurley Brown was probably part of the last generation of American girls weaned on the idea that personal dignity was a matter of knowing when to make allowances for the lack of same in others. As Agnes Morton (an Emily Post bandwagoner) asserted in her *Etiquette: Good Manners for All People; Especially for Those Who Dwell Within the Broad Zone of the Average:* "Only clear and unmistakable evidence of *intention* should lead one to infer a slight. It is not only more *polite,* but more *self-respecting,* to 'take offense' *slowly.*"

Do freeload. The manuscript for *Sex and the Single Girl* was typed on paper lifted from the L.A. advertising firm that Gurley Brown was convinced was going to fire her. She was further adamant that you accept all offers of free food and drink when you're a financially strapped underling. And that you find out who's in charge of the supply closet, and become that person's friend. "I never did anything *but* freeload as a young person and can't fault anybody else for taking advantage of older people willing to be exploited." In the modern workplace, other potential buffets include the postage meter, catered-lunch leftovers, and the expense account (if available). Companies should understand that, short of embezzlement, these compensations are simply the cost of doing business. After all, there's no meritocracy if only those born rich can afford to work for a pittance.

Do be charming. You may not be going anywhere interesting career-wise for a while, but that's no reason to let yourself go. Dysfunctional organizations offer good training grounds for refining your skills because, weirdly, insecure and anxious people often react most strongly to charm. Which is not to say they'll like it, or that it will prompt them to open professional doors for you, only that their *reactions* to you will be clear. Turn on the charm in front of toady junior executives—male or female—and pay close attention to their faces. You can always apply the things you learn at your next job.

And for all its cutesiness, *Sex and the Single Girl* includes the most intriguing definition of personal allure I've come across:

> If you can sum up what charm is, I think it's *total awareness*. A charmer has her antenna up and valves open at all times. With sensitive radar she detects what the other person wants to hear and says it. And she senses what he doesn't want to hear and refrains from saying *it*. Charming people, either men or women, are usually warm-blooded, affectionate and compassionate, but they are also *thinking ahead all the time*.

Then Gurley Brown offers an example. It's worth reprinting in full:

> I had lunch the other day with a charmer, accompanied by her mother. Two of the girls in the party had babbled ten minutes or so about their new office manager whom the mother didn't know. Presently the charmer said, "You know, Mother, he's kind of like Joe Winslow at the bank . . . sort of Prussian." Mother was back in the conversation. This particular charmer, so accomplished she should package it, puts everything in terms of *you*. "You would have loved it." "You

would have fainted." In describing a gown she saw at the opera she says it was a little deeper than your red velvet coat. She remembers what you told her last time and asks questions *this* time. It's appalling the things people can forget you told them ... and never ask you about in subsequent conversations.

It seems Gurley Brown got the hang of it. Here's how the novelist and freelance writer Nancy Weber, who wrote for Gurley Brown at *Cosmopolitan* (even though she found the magazine "mostly unreadable"), described her editor's brand of charm:

> She is a maddening woman, all the more so because it's impossible not to like her. Back in the days when I was writing for *Cosmo* with some frequency, Helen called to ask me to do a piece on Why Lying Is More Elegant Than Telling the Truth—4,000 words, and could I turn it in by 10 o'clock the next morning? You're the Only Person in the World Who Can Do It, she said, and I unmade plans for dinner, and did it. The next morning she had decided that Truth Was More Elegant, and because I hadn't used an agent, or my head, I didn't even get a kill fee. I no longer write for *Cosmopolitan,* but if Helen called me right now and put on her Iron-Butterfly act and told me I was the Only Person who could do a piece about why anthologies on writing are dangerous, I would probably pull this piece out of the typewriter to accommodate her by ten o'clock tomorrow morning.

Do remain aware, nonetheless, that someone will always hate you. The hating can't be avoided, especially if you're finally going places. ("A little turnip who spends most of her time backcombing her hair will feel outraged because you have the job she feels she deserved.") Understanding how prevalent resentment is, and how some people might *enjoy* disliking you, and how little you can do about it sometimes, gets you halfway toward not letting the hatred keep you awake at night.

»»

A slow start might be better than rocketing to the top, all things considered. Gurley Brown once told a story of a colleague who used to make her feel totally inadequate. They worked together at a radio station—probably KHJ in Hollywood—when they were both really young. The day after the attack on Pearl Harbor, this girl was busy establishing herself as the next Martha Gellhorn, out on the roof of the station trying to spot bomber planes and filing reports. She worked through that entire night, while Helen wanted to crawl under her desk in embarrassment for being so relatively ordinary. Helen didn't see this girl again for years, and then bumped into her one day—at the Laundromat, where the former crackerjack was now working. For Gurley Brown, it led to a strange, self-consciously petty feeling of triumph. *Like little firecrackers going off inside you . . . pop, pop, pop.*

It's probably worth mentioning that I recently ran into the guy who said maybe his boss enjoyed humiliating people, a few weeks after he had found a new job at a different company. "I feel like a different person," he said. He looked it, too.

Interlude

Why Most Everything from the 1970s Doesn't Help

THERE'S NO GOOD office politics advice from the 1970s because everything written then presumed that people were dumb.* Not just dumb, but slobbering bundles of infantile need. The psychotherapist Eric Berne can be blamed for starting the trend in the mid-1960s by publicizing a concept he called "transactional analysis," which held that people were forever walking around seeking "strokes." Strokes, he said, were "the fundamental unit of human interaction," and just as infants needed physical touch in order to survive and thrive, so too adults were hooked on getting stroked, though in a more metaphorical, psychological way. Unless you were unusually well adjusted, or had spent years in therapy, you'd always be unconsciously scanning the room for someone to tangle with.

Once you got a reaction—exchanged strokes with someone, in other words—you had a transaction on your hands, and if that transaction followed a recognizable pattern, and neither party to the transaction was really clear about his or her true

---

* John T. Molloy's *Dress for Success* a notable exception.

motives, then you had a game on your hands. Once a game was in play, you could analyze, categorize, and identify it (because the same games kept cropping up), and this, Berne argued in his 1964 bestseller *Games People Play,* was the key to more productive relations with your fellow man. The names Berne gave to the most common games tell you a lot about his worldview: Now I've Got You, You Son of a Bitch, was one. Then there was See What You Made Me Do; Alcoholic; Kick Me; Look How Hard I've Tried; Frigid Woman; Blemish; and I'm Only Trying to Help You, among many others. The roles were more basic: people acted as Parent, Adult, or Child.

It wasn't long before Berne's ideas got taken to work. In 1973, *Everybody Wins: Transactional Analysis Applied to Organizations* appeared. Its author, Dorothy Jongeward, was a transactional analysis disciple who believed that people used company time "to reinforce negative self/other concepts," and that this might be a drain on company resources. Being able to call the games was both more efficient (less 9-to-5 time spent tangling with people's personality issues) and, she felt, more in tune with the Age of Aquarius. Being liberated, and feeling good vibes, was important. Strange, then, that she spent so much time dissecting games with undercurrents of shame and self-loathing —games like Kick Me and Poor Me. There were many variations, Jongeward wrote, but most people playing these games were starting from positions like this:

"I'm stupid."
"I don't deserve to live."
"I can't do anything right."
"I'm handicapped."
"I'm ugly and clumsy."
"I can't help myself."
"I feel sorry for myself."
"It's not my fault."

So you'd be sitting at your desk, trying to get some work done, and before you knew it a broken, unhappy coworker would be trying to goad you into helping him feel better about himself. *Or,* feel even worse about himself, depending on his particular neuroses. People stuck on a negative self-concept just couldn't help themselves.

With the benefit of advanced neuroscience, we now know that one of the fundamental assumptions of transactional analysis—that, as Thomas A. Harris put it in his hit *I'm OK—You're OK,* "the brain functions as a high-fidelity tape recorder"—is incorrect. Humans tend to be selective, even creative, when recalling their own past experiences. The 1970s, however, was in thrall to the inner child.

Here's how Jongeward described the game Schlemiel. Similar to Kick Me, Poor Me, or even Stupid, people played Schlemiel to get reassurance that they weren't screwups or otherwise unworthy. The Schlemiel player just wanted to be loved, and tried to get proof of that love by first doing something klutzy. Here's how Jongeward describes such a scene:

> One young man was transporting a new piece of equipment from one tabletop to another. In the process he dropped it. After he dropped it, he went into a long performance about how dumb it was of him to do such a thing. "Here is a new piece of equipment worth several hundred dollars. No one has had a chance even to use it, and I am so clumsy that I dropped it and broke some of the important parts on it. How could I do such a dumb thing? I don't know how people can stand to have me around here."

Then she begins her analysis:

> This young man's pitch was not to evoke a kick or a scolding. He was asking for something else. He was asking for forgiveness. His expectation was that if he put on a pitiful enough act, that if he could come on remorseful enough, someone's nurturing Parent would eventually say to him, "Don't worry about it, George, it is only a piece of machinery and no one was hurt." Next week he may spill the ink on the freshly mimeographed programs.

Faced with such a situation, Jongeward suggested it was best to withhold the "forgiveness stroke" because being sympathetic would just keep the Schlemiel game going, and she couldn't advise enabling people to repeat the same silly patterns. Then she offers the example of a visiting sales rep who left a cigarette burn on your nice Formica-topped desk. That cigarette burn might look like an accident, but it *wasn't,* not really. The sales rep would probably put on a big show about feeling bad about it and you'd tell him not to worry, that it wasn't worth getting too upset over. And that, according to Jongeward, was playing right into that man's hands.

The "est" movement went one further. Not only were people clumsy, and clumsy on purpose because life was just too disappointing, but they were assholes too. est — it was always lowercase — was started by a former car salesman who left his family, changed his name from Jack Rosenberg to Werner Erhard (because he thought it sounded more exotic, more powerful), and decided to start a movement and make some money while he was at it. (He was inspired by L. Ron Hubbard's success with *Dianetics.*) The plan worked — for a while — and he became a sought-after pseudoguru. est stood for "Erhard Seminars Training." Or, as writer James Kettle put it in his short book on est, you could also think of it this way: est stood for *est*, a form of the Latin verb "to be," and the training was all about, you know, just learning to be. "est is NOW. You're what you are, and that's how it peels."

Erhard said he wanted to help people get over anxieties, insecurities, anything that hobbled their effectiveness. While the goal sounded softball enough, the actual training was anything but. A typical est session involved sitting in a gray metal folding chair in a stuffy hotel conference hall for two days. There'd be two hundred fifty souls lined up in tight rows, sitting knee to knee, forbidden to use the facilities or eat or drink or smoke except at designated intervals designed with participants' maximum physical discomfort in mind. People came away from est weekends with reports of sobbing, vomiting, fainting from exhaustion, and begging to use the bathroom and being denied. The lecture was usually delivered by one of Erhard's disciples, and the standard script included phrases like this, delivered loudly into a microphone: "You people are cruds! You don't have the sense to dry off. A fart in a windstorm has more intelligence; at least it lets it happen!" And: "How the hell are you ever going to be a winner if you're always picking the wrong horse? You're an asshole. You're all of you assholes!" And: "There's not a one of you doesn't think he's God Almighty and who isn't lower than whale shit!"*

They paid good money for this—a few hundred dollars for your first seminar—and many people who felt it worked came back for more. Just how being likened to a fart in a windstorm proved beneficial is not entirely clear, but Erhard's revelation was basically that people tried too hard to change the world, or themselves, or other people, and they should stop. Kettle tried to sum up the est philosophy by acknowledging that it was a mishmash of ideas stolen from other sources—"Zen, Gestalt, Yoga, Dale Carnegie, et cetera," maybe with some guided meditation thrown in, "a bit of body awareness and relaxation, along with variations of exercises and ideas, some imagination, some fantasy, too," and all of this "folded in with Eric Berne's *Games People Play.*" But say at the end of day two of the seminar, you hadn't yet grasped what you were supposed to be getting out of est, so you spoke up and told the instructor that you weren't quite getting it. The scripted response to that was, "Then you're getting that you don't get it."

est had little to say to people who didn't see their lives transformed. "Sure, there are some who are dissatisfied," Kettle wrote. "So it didn't work, but that, too, is the *way it is.* Get it? You are what you are. Accept it. Stop being, as the est people have colorfully put it, an asshole."

---

* All from Kettle's firsthand accounts.

So what we have from the 1970s so far is: Don't extend sympathy or forgiveness to people who screw up, and Don't be an asshole. Not only is it very difficult to reconcile those two pieces of wisdom, or do both at the same time, but it's very hard to think along either line without becoming ugly and bitter. How can you think your coworkers are childish, manipulative slobs and still look forward to work in the morning? (That is, unless you *are* an asshole?) How is encouraging people to go with whatever mood they're in, not worrying about anyone or anything else long-term, not just a recipe for *more* obnoxiousness and head-butting? By the time *Winning Through Intimidation* rolled out onto store shelves, the success rhetoric had taken a real *Revenge of the Nerds* turn. The book begins with the author Robert J. Ringer congratulating himself on his choice of title: "When I tagged my book with the label of *Winning Through Intimidation,* I knew that it would evoke a conditioned-response reaction from many, that the goody-two-shoes disciples of unreality would be offended," but, because he was so fierce and uncompromising, he bravely forged ahead.

Ringer, who would go on to write *Looking Out for No. 1,* then described how his education in real life—life as it was really lived, you know, not as described in namby-pamby self-help books—started out during his undergraduate days, when he was ostracized by the smarter, taller, more sexually successful students. What he learned at "Screw U," he wrote, was that there were basically three types of people in the world. Some would announce their intention to leapfrog over you and let you choke on their dust, and then they'd do just that. Others might tell you that they weren't really interested in cutting corners, leapfrogging over you, or reaching for your stash of poker chips, and would proceed to do it anyhow. The third type would give you every assurance that they weren't going to do it, and sincerely meant you no harm, didn't really want to have to, but through happenstance and "extreme rationalizing," they'd end up reaching for your stash too. In short, nice guys always lost, so you better watch it, and listen close. Now that he'd learned a thing or two, Ringer wanted his readers to consider themselves warned. "That sound you hear behind you is me," he concluded, "breathing down your neck."

And that's the fundamental problem with all of the above. Where all the 1970s success-lit authors went wrong is in taking their systems one step too far.* There's a line between an ability to notice patterns in people's behavior and congratulating yourself—even getting high on—your ability to "see right through them." These writers went crashing right through it. Once you start seeing your day as a series of petty, predictable interpersonal games, people become pawns—chumps whose hopes and fears do not need to be taken seriously. Being so quick to categorize gets you Dilbert coffee-mug wisdom on one end of the spectrum, Sudanese warlord wisdom on the other. Neither is appropriate for the office.

Do be determined to see coworkers as endlessly fascinating, multifaceted individuals, regardless of how reliably they work your nerves. I was recently on the subway without the crossword or an iPod, staring up at the ads that run the length of the car near the ceiling. Most were for ESL classes, podiatrists, and attorneys specializing in lead-paint-poisoning claims. One was for a new book that promised to teach you how to get rid of the irritating people who were ruining your workday. Two things immediately struck me as wrong. One, if your day is being "ruined" by annoying colleagues, perhaps you have deeper emotional issues you may want to look into first. Two, the day you rid yourself of that last irritating person is probably the day before a brand-new one steps off the elevator onto your floor.

---

* I'll leave aside all the other ways Werner Erhard is a troubling figure. But that's worth looking into, if you've got the time and the inclination.

8

Self-Deprecation

The Art of Humble Beginnings Stories

> The trick of the successful ingratiatory is to let modesty
> reflect the secure acceptance of a few weaknesses that
> are obviously trivial in the context of one's strengths.
>
> —EDWARD E. JONES

ONE OF THE MORE INTERESTING aspects of corporate life is communing with people who remember their SAT scores. You've conveniently forgotten yours. Their fathers supervised clinical trials in pediatric oncology. Your father teaches phys ed. They got red, hand-me-down Audis for their sixteenth birthdays. You got $100 and a beige cable-knit sweater. They interned on Capitol Hill. You kept busy painting houses that same summer.

These disparities don't have to cause much trouble. For one, "it's easy to gain advantages that have nothing to do with money," says Lane, a former lawyer turned freelance writer. "In college"—he went to Harvard—"a group would be standing around talking plans, and someone would casually mention they were off to Paris for a long weekend. Now, you'd never say, 'Gee, I could never afford that.' Instead you'd respond with how much you were absolutely loving some obscure eight-hundred-page novel, and were looking forward to holing up in your dorm room all weekend. And reading." This way, Lane and the Paris-bound could pretend they've simply made different life-style choices, and no one had to be self-conscious about money or lack thereof.

Once careers and salaries enter the mix, this technique does not cut it. In the aggregate, college is the great equalizer (it greases the wheels of upward mobility, and pumps more people into the knowledge economy), but in smaller, more personal in-teractions, it can become a divider. Some went to colleges that impress people, others attended schools that don't impress, and when individuals from these two factions meet, assumptions about respective intellectual capacities tend to get made. In some circles, where one attended college comes up during cock-tail conversation long, long after graduation. (If you had told me as a twenty-year-old University of Minnesota student that this would be the case, I would have snorted in disbelief.) You can always see this particular line of inquiry coming, however—the chin lifts, the throat's cleared, and the delivery is remarkably consistent: "So. Where did you go to school?"

This tension explains why debates about where to find the best pizza in New Haven can be so irritating. A University of Texas grad had to endure one of these discussions during a conference-room celebration of her twenty-third birthday. She was working at a Washington, D.C., newspaper at the time. As plates of dry chocolate cake got passed around, and she sat there chewing silently—"why was everyone talking about this? why so animated?"—it slowly dawned on her that this conver-sation was actually designed to advertise that all of its partic-ipants had gone to, or were somehow extraordinarily familiar with, Yale. Maybe referring to Yale without actually saying the word "Yale" had been the whole point—or else she'd underes-timated how strongly these adults felt about New Haven restau-rant culture. She tried to swallow, choked on her cake, and got a friendly slap on the back.

Given how much Americans love to toss people from vastly

different backgrounds into the same room together, you might think there'd be more popular wisdom on how to handle these situations—situations in which your list of accomplishments is, by conventional meritocratic standards, inferior. There should at least be some cliché as tried and true as "Have a firm handshake," but there isn't. Flailing about trying to find something to brag about that might even the score, as some people choose to do in these moments, rarely works out well. You can't, for example, start explaining how amazing Austin barbecues are because your point gets tangled in the subtext: Do you actually want to talk about homecookin', or are you just too dense to realize that regional cuisine is not, in fact, what they are talking about?

The only way to stumble through these conversations, I've come to believe, is to slyly, very slyly suggest that any soft spots in your résumé are beside the point. Your overall prowess, in fact, is such that not only can you not be reduced to a particular educational institution, but any mistake, unfortunate incident, or humble circumstance in your past only testifies to your superior skill overall. And biographies of executives and industry leaders suggest that the best way to announce your greatness —and emerge from best-pizza-in-New-Haven discussions unscathed—is not to talk about how big and strong you are. Quite the opposite. Read magazine profiles dating back to the robber baron era, or former General Electric CEO Jack Welch's *Straight from the Gut,* any variety of capitalist memoir (if you will), and you'll find self-deprecation is the way to go. But the humiliating experiences of more than a few of my friends, not to mention my own, suggest that successful self-deprecation is a delicate art. Do it wrong and you risk looking like the nonentity those born smarter, richer, or luckier may already think you are. Do it slightly wrong and you sound resentful. Do it correctly and you spin those historical liabilities into gold.

Self-deprecation as career tactic first took the form of the "humble beginnings" stories of the late nineteenth-century industrial magnates. When the novelist William Dean Howells published

The Rise of Silas Lapham in 1884, he had the self-made man of the title living in chichi Boston but still picking the Vermont hayseed out of his teeth. The book opens with Silas Lapham, mineral paint tycoon, being interviewed for the local paper. "Any barefoot business?" his interviewer asks. "Early deprivations of any kind, that would encourage the youthful reader to go and do likewise?" The reporter thinks it all rather ridiculous, but Lapham is more than happy to regale how his frail, saintly mother worked her fingers to the bone, how much he learned from *Poor Richard's Almanack,* and how the beginnings of his now globe-spanning empire—outlets in South America, Australia, India, China, and the Cape of Good Hope—could be traced to an accidentally discovered paint mine on the edge of the old family farm.

Horatio Alger also dabbled in the barefoot business. His 1881 biography of James Garfield opens on the future U.S. president, age four, stumbling shoeless and "earnestly" from a small, crudely constructed log cabin into the surrounding forest. So too Dale Carnegie, who managed to pack the suggestions that he lacked shoes, received an inferior education, and enjoyed only childhood's simplest pleasures into a single sentence: "Years ago when I was a barefoot boy walking through the woods to a country school out in northwest Missouri . . ." opens a chapter of *How to Win Friends and Influence People.* For his part, Napoleon Hill once described the backwater he grew up in as a place dominated by "feuds, moonshine, and stupidity" (no great business leader himself, he knew this gambit well). As the years went on, variations on the childhood-was-rough theme grew more varied. In his bestselling 1984 autobiography *Iacocca,* the former Chrysler chairman reminisced at length about the Great Depression, and how school kids had called him a tomato-pie-eating dago "wop."* Jack Welch has remarked that while his parents weren't exactly poor, they were poorer than he *wanted* them to be. He also mentions that he stuttered as a child, and

---

* Wop = an anti-Italian slur. It was short for "without papers," as many Italian immigrants were suspected of being in the U.S. illegally.

was a bit of a momma's boy. And Bill Gates, though born into money, has made no attempt to suppress publication of a 1977 mug shot that shows him to be a grinning, decidedly geeky twenty-two-year-old.

There's been some theorizing about why VIPs flaunt their less than glitzy beginnings. In his studies on high-status people (and how they finagled their way into people's hearts), Edward E. Jones claimed that self-deprecation made them more approachable. Being at the top of the heap, they needed to command respect and authority, but they also needed to be seen as regular folks in order to enjoy unmolested success. If they were too aloof, too distant, they were more likely to be attacked by disgruntled employees—or by anyone they outranked. But if they made self-denigrating remarks now and then, or stressed how, at the core, they were painfully plain people, they would be less vulnerable.* They would also, Jones believed, be associating themselves with characteristics Americans prized, like modesty and honesty. Most important was the simple fact that they delivered these humble beginnings stories from the very top of their professions. *That* provided the punch line: they'd scrambled up from nowhere special, sometimes from somewhere very crummy indeed, and so were clearly made of the right stuff. It made their success even greater. (Getting a book deal, so you can explain all this at length, never hurts.)

Self-deprecation is obviously trickier when you're low on the totem pole—you have no status, and maybe for good reason. You can't exercise your humility too much because there's no roaring success to serve as juxtaposition (and make the larger point of your brilliance for you). Here's one example of how an attempt at self-deprecation can go terribly wrong: During an informal job interview at a small retail-design firm, I was asked about my first real out-of-college job, which, it so happens, was assistant manager of the Fifty-seventh Street Rizzoli Bookstore in New York. My first day on the job—I was twenty-

---

* Nowadays, *US Weekly* features such as "Stars! They're Just like Us!" help celebrities do this. It invariably catches them pumping gas or leaving Starbucks.

two—I was given a set of keys. Three days a week, I opened the store—switched on the lights, booted up the computers, opened the basement safe, counted the cash and put the cash drawers in the cash registers, and made sure all three floors of the store and everyone on them were ready for business. Then I ran around for eight hours. Three nights a week I closed the store—tallied the day's receipts, counted the cash, closed the safe, shut off the lights, and locked the doors behind me.

Ten years later, this is how I described that job to my interviewer: "Pretty much everything. I ordered the toilet paper." I realized my mistake when he, sitting across the café table, repeated this phrase back to me: "You ordered the toilet paper." He said it flatly, declaratively, without affect, as if he were accusing me of an unhealthy fixation on bathroom humor. I was counting on the chance to expand, to explain how in fact the job was much more than that, but he quickly changed the subject.

Clearly my attempt at self-deprecation fell flat. (I'd just come off five years in a corporate setting, and didn't want to appear to be above retail work. But he evidently thought my qualifications plenty humble.) There's some comfort in knowing this mistake is a fairly common one: people will trumpet their humility and unimpressiveness to convey that they're really down-to-earth when, in fact, everyone thinks of them as quite earthbound already. "There was this girl in our office who boasted about the dismal small town where she went to high school," said Jill. "You know, one of those 'Population: 817' towns, as if she wanted to say, 'Hey, look at me now!' but the thing is, she was a mess. So for me it became more like, oh, that explains why you saunter in at 10:30 with your hair unbrushed."*

But a humble beginning is too great a potential asset to

---

* My sister—a do-gooder in the nonprofit sector—came up with a term for this: "the stupid chills." She got the stupid chills whenever the liability a person *thought* they were exposing wasn't the one they were actually exposing, and it wasn't a pleasant sensation. (Like goose bumps, only tinged with despair.) Anyone can get the stupid chills watching Jerry Springer, or following any scene where the person at the center of attention is somehow not in on the joke. I guess you could define the stupid chills as a form of empathetic embarrassment.

waste, regardless of your position on the totem pole. In *Secrets of a Corporate Headhunter,* from 1980, the author and executive recruiter John Wareham claimed that a little bad start went a long way. He said that he always looked for "a slight abrasiveness" in the people he recommended for million-dollar leadership positions. These men and women needed to have a kernel of resentment somewhere inside—like "the grit an oyster needs to produce a pearl, or the rich manure that feeds a luxuriant rose"—in order to be truly effective. Coupled with complementary character traits like tenacity, an inferiority complex could be very useful in an executive (as it meant he would always be "proving something to the demons in his head").

Wareham's book wasn't alone among books that ushered in the business-mad 1980s in highlighting the appeal of a less than spectacular past—as long as resentment didn't take over. In his book *The Over-Achievers,* the former Helena Rubinstein executive Peter Engel ventured that the key component in an executive mindset was not being spectacularly smart (excess intelligence being "a very sly asset" in his opinion), or in any way pedigreed, but that you were above all "emotionally glamorous." Every important businessman, he claimed, knew how to turn liabilities into assets, and this required complete objectivity, even when considering personal matters. Being emotionally glamorous, then, meant being able to assess one's own strengths and weaknesses as critically and dispassionately as if they were someone else's. Overachievers knew better than anyone else what was wrong with them—and they weren't afraid to have their faults, flaws, or shortcomings aired.*

---

* Engel's motivations for writing *The Over-Achievers*—subtitled *The Ultimate Businessmen: How to Find Them, Use Them, Be Them*—are interesting. He wrote it, he said, because he was tired of attending cocktail parties and hearing bejeweled society matrons decry "being dominated by big business" while snapping their fingers for more canapés. It had become quite fashionable, he'd noticed, to say things like this. He figured the only way out of this public relations doldrums was to educate people about the new breed of businessman occupying executive suites—not the starched bureaucrats of yesteryear, but energetic nonconformists

Figuring out where the chinks in your personal armor were could be difficult, and so it was important to undergo regular and ruthless self-inventories. "Don't kid yourself," advised Crawley A. Parris, author of *Mastering Executive Arts and Skills.* "Essential to successful self-development is the ability to see yourself as you really are." Easier said than done, of course, which is why so much of the success canon stresses listening over talking—if you weren't really listening and observing other people "aggressively" (as Mark McCormack advocated in his 1984 *What They Don't Teach You at Harvard Business School*), you wouldn't be aware of how other people were reacting to you, and if you weren't aware of how other people were reacting to you, you'd be much more prone to self-delusion. Therefore much of the work of becoming emotionally glamorous took place off the clock, at home alone, while you stared into the bathroom mirror and pondered the events of the day.

In practice, on the clock, demonstrating emotional glamour meant mastering a jaunty, "Well, that sure blew, but what do I care about it now? Life is good!" way of describing the past. All humble beginnings stories needed to sound matter-of-fact, to minimize real suffering and conveniently skip over any emotional fallout. Some people do this very well. They recall stupid incidents from their past and deliver them with a laugh.

This is how my colleague Jenny describes her first job out of college. She wasn't keen on going back home to Wisconsin after graduating from Cornell; instead, she wanted to explore more of the East Coast, and eventually found a job at Harvard's career counseling office. She found it somewhat awkward dispensing advice on how to get jobs, given that this was her very first one. But it was good work, and she calculated that being able to add Harvard to her résumé couldn't hurt either. Still, the students Jenny was asked to counsel were only two years younger,

---

driven by desires deep under the skin. He anticipated the Richard Branson template, in other words.

and she always felt a little self-conscious about that. She decided to use her own inexperience as a plus, a way to relate to them better. "I just graduated from Cornell," she'd say. Then, as she tells it now, she often received the following response: "Oh, but that's a good school!" These students were taking her "just" to mean not "recently," but "only"—that is, they were assuming she probably felt a little inferior. Jenny, who now works in fundraising, clearly enjoys telling this story. Every time she delves into it (I've heard it three times now), her eyes—big and brown—sparkle.*

As Parris insisted in *Mastering Executive Arts and Skills,* griping was a definite no-no for any middle-management guy who aspired to higher levels. Griping had a decidedly "unexecutive look" to it. One also needed to avoid any sort of hangdog, woe-is-me posture. This too is critical to the effective self-deprecating remark: it has to focus, if not directly then with a sideways glance and a wink, people's attention on a slate of positive, ready-for-prime-time qualities. And this is where most people go wrong. In his work on ingratiation, Edward E. Jones floated the idea that a lot of low-status people tend to deprecate important qualities and play up insignificant ones. In other words, they think they are testifying to their grit, when in fact they are making themselves look like the guy who's going to careen off the edge in a haze of self-destructive tendencies and unresolved seventeen-year-old rage. Or they want to show off a sense of humor, when their basic integrity hasn't yet been established. This is a costly mistake.

The wrong type of self-deprecation always has an element of self-mortification to it—and it generally follows the same pattern. Coworker drapes herself over the top of your cubicle, leans in, rests her head on her hand, and sleepily drawls out a story of stupidly agreeing to that one last drink, or of getting

---

* Not least, I think, because it's amusing to imagine moving in circles where a degree from Cornell is seen as a potential drawback.

lost and arriving late and stepping in a huge puddle, of losing a wallet in the back of a cab, or of making a mistake that elicited a spectacularly scathing fax from a major client. She tells you how her college Italian professor had requested that she please drop the class because she was clearly never going to learn, or how her roommate blamed her for the new dead-animal smell in their fifth-floor walkup apartment.

Caroline—who admits this now with admirable candor—prided herself on telling these stories, which nearly always got a laugh. Then she noticed some other reactions, reactions like, "You poor thing. That *would* only happen to you." Caroline was tempted to ignore the first person who resisted her charms because this other woman generally limited her interoffice chitchat to things like her last visit to London, and how funny it was that she went to the British Museum looking for the Rosetta stone and walked right past it—*twice*—before she finally asked a security guard and he informed her—*stupid*, right?—that she was standing only six feet away from it. Or how that novel she edited, the one that became such a sleeper hit, well, the fact that she even discovered its author was a *fluke*. Caroline was aware that she sounded very different from her colleague, whose style —which she found weirdly brittle and hollow—was one she did not want for herself ("I think not admitting to weakness is itself a sign of weakness"). Then one morning a more soft-spoken colleague, a friend, left a long pause after one of her puddle stories before saying: "You always have stories like this."

Which suggests that in addition to boring people, her stab at emotional glamour was not making the correct larger point. She was always the unwitting victim of circumstance; that is, when she wasn't laying down and rolling around in it. While growing up in some backwater town or receiving an inferior education can be overcome, the same can't be said for a bad work ethic, chronic lateness, or sloppiness—so if your audience already has misgivings about your ability to compete, best not to encourage those doubts. Caroline was also making the rookie mistake of volunteering information no one needed to know. As the run-down in *The Over-Achievers* suggests, the smart self-deprecator would have figured out what flaws people had already picked up on, or what exactly about her habits, looks, or résumé any given person might find tacky or objectionable. And then she'd bring these things up herself, essentially saying out loud what she guessed her audience was thinking already.

This preemptive self-deprecation works, I believe, because most of us—perversely, sometimes meanly—enjoy locating the chinks in someone else's armor. If you can point out where your own chinks are first, you take away someone else's fun—and disrupt whatever play for dominance he or she might be attempting. It's undoubtedly why a writer I know often says, "Oh, I went to a stupid school . . ." before going on to say that he attended the University of Michigan.* An aspiring Hollywood player who has never sold a screenplay but who regularly gets enthusiastic commendations from producers and agents says he is "the Dan Marino of Screenwriters" (and then relates how a studio exec once called him that to his face, only he didn't know who Dan Marino was, and then the studio exec had to explain that Dan Marino is widely considered the greatest quarterback who never won a Super Bowl). This preemptive self-deprecation disposition is on every page of *Bridget Jones's Diary.* With Ms. Jones admitting that she "smoke[d] self into disgusted frenzy" on a regular basis, Helen Fielding has her character flagellate herself before anyone else does, making her less pathetic, more endearing.†

It's a more nuanced strategy than it seems at first hearing. "The Million-dollar Executive"—Wareham's term for the new high-rolling head honcho—was very aware that he might be called on his bluff someday (that alone was reason for trotting out that humble beginning story). So he had to develop some-

---

* The University of Michigan, I should add, is not a stupid school.
† Witness also David Sedaris's entire career.

thing close to clairvoyance. Which is to say that F. Scott Fitzgerald made a strange choice when he had Jay Gatsby going around telling people he was educated at Oxford, and boasting of having spent subsequent years "like a young rajah in all the capitals of Europe—Paris, Venice, Rome—collecting jewels." Surely Gatsby would have already figured out it was better to let folks know he'd brushed the dust of North Dakota off his jacket before coming to Long Island.

The successful self-deprecating remark also has a particular inflection—it ends with a falling intonation (not the "uptalk" that suggests a question, or implies you have no idea what you're talking about). It's delivered snappily, and sometimes veers into the cinematic. Wareham's own version reads like the opening scene of a black-and-white movie: "sixteen years ago, clutching the proceeds of a $1,000 IOU scrawled upon the back of an envelope, I took my first office and hung my first shingle outside a 200-square-foot walk-up office suite. It boasted rat holes and the solid vista of a decaying brick wall." The most perfect one-line example I've heard was delivered by a D.C. congressional aide, who summed up her background by stating simply—and factually—that her high school's mascot was a cotton-picker. The same rule of delivery applies to mistakes or professional miscalculations. The screenwriter William Goldman claims that one of the best pieces of film dialogue ever, the one that makes the lead character come across as personable, fallible, honest, tough, and generally sympathetic all at the same time, is when *Casablanca*'s Rick, after being asked what had brought him to Casablanca, responds, "The waters." What waters? his questioner wants to know—Casablanca was in the desert. Says Rick: "I was misinformed."

In order to demonstrate how high-status people emphasize their positive character traits in important areas, it's worth returning to Helen Gurley Brown. One version of her many humble beginnings stories goes something like this: at eighteen—"flat-chested, pale, acne-skinned, terrified"—she gets her first job,

sorting mail for Mr. Wilson, the emcee of a radio breakfast show
called *Rise and Shine*. A big part of his show was announcing
listeners' birthdays, anniversaries, and so on, and it was Helen's
job to distill the pertinent information from listener letters and
type it up on index cards. Wilson would take these cards into the
studio and pretend to read, pausing and hemming as if he were
perusing the actual letters. "Well, well! . . . Little Deborah Jean
Dallyrumple over in Gardena is having a fourth birthday! Let's
see. It says here if Deborah Jean will go look out in the garage
in Daddy's tool chest, she'll find something . . ." Gurley Brown
claims she wasn't good at this, often mixing up names and locations, and that she botched a lot of Happy Birthdays for boys
and girls across Southern California.

Now, whether she was really terrible at this job is beside the
point. The story somehow manages to suggest that she was a
dedicated worker (job at eighteen), has a good memory (lots
of details), is honest almost to a fault, that she tried but failed
sometimes, and maybe only failed because she knew how inconsequential her job was (is four-year-old Deborah Jean really
going to remember, later on, that the radio announcer man directed her to the wrong part of the house?). And yet her post
was not *so* inconsequential that her gaffes didn't have far-reach-
ing effect (it's possible she made Deborah Jean, and hundreds
like her, cry).

The successful self-deprecator always places herself not just
at the center of her narratives, but as the character performing
the pivotal action. Not only is she no victim of circumstance, but
things happen because of her. She sets things in motion. This
is perhaps the big-money, bedrock reason for self-deprecation's
effectiveness. One of the stories told about Jack Welch is of a
GE management training class held sometime in the mid-1980s.
It's late in the evening, and in the conference room are ten new
hires, mostly young guys, who've been at it all day. At the end
of the table is a flip chart, on which are scribbled two proposi-
tions for debate: (1) *Jack Welch is an asshole*, and (2) *Jack Welch*

is the greatest CEO GE has ever had. This exercise was done with Welch's full blessing—it may even have been his idea. It struck me as particularly shrewd, for several reasons. Holding yourself up for criticism when you're on the top of the heap, even instructing your minions to do it, is smart. But Welch also sketched out the very terms by which they could do it. No dabbling in gray areas for him, none of the shadowy regions inhabited by more lackluster personas. Either Welch was a jerk or he was *the best man that company had ever seen.* (Or both. The categories aren't mutually exclusive.) But any way you sliced it, he was an archetype, one for the ages.

I can understand if you'd prefer a slightly different tack. Some take a more Dada approach. At social events, where she's surrounded by Ivy Leaguers, a former colleague of mine throws off comments like "I just assume everyone went to Yale unless they tell me otherwise" whenever the conversation allows. She herself did not attend Yale, and has never pretended to. But the phrase—it makes no sense, honestly—somehow neutralizes the air. If hearing "So where did you . . ." still causes your spine to stiffen, here are a few more suggestions for how to handle a legacy of state schools and cashiering jobs:

Do highlight diligence rather than libertinism. The best self-deprecating remarks suggest nerdiness, anxiety, or a near-OCD level of desire to get things just right and just so. It's always better to admit dedication to something that, doggone it, just didn't work out for you in the end, than to toss off a "sorry, I'm still drunk from yesterday" type of remark. This is also why a time lag helps. If your self-deprecating stories are mainly about troubles experienced very recently, there's not enough of a critical distance separating you, the narrator, from the projectile vomiter you were thirteen hours ago.

That said, regularly claiming to be "super, super busy" is rarely a good idea. People notice when you say this a lot, and it's usually regarded as boastful, and mildly annoying.

Do keep it simple. Long-winded stories can draw more condescension than you faced initially. Quick and pithy is better—especially when your self-deprecating comment comes on the heels of a compliment. Say someone tells you he likes your outfit; you say thanks and "Target. Juniors section." This is preferable to going on about how, gosh, you haven't been able to afford new clothes in so long, and you can't wait for your mom to come visit in September so she can take you shopping. Quick also adds a slight veneer of mystery—if you're generally a person who doesn't lack for words, the shortest truth about the plainest of accomplishments can sound fairy-dusted.

Of course, any deviation from the absolute truth should be so clearly false that no one would believe you anyhow. If it could be true (but just isn't in your case), it's best to avoid it. In other words, joking, "Yeah, cut it myself" when someone compliments your new hairstyle *could* be true. (I can personally attest to this.) Similarly, when someone expresses admiration or envy at the fact that you attended Brown, don't say, "Yeah, I got in because Dad paid for a new dorm." *Could* be true.

Do say it with hands on hips, literally or metaphorically. In *How to Read a Person Like a Book,* the authors Nierenberg and Calero claimed that after reviewing thousands of hours of videotaped negotiating sessions, they could say with scientific certainty that people who were more conscious of their body's subtle movements could—as long as they didn't succumb to crippling self-consciousness—wield more influence over others than those who just flopped about, unaware of what their legs and arms were doing. "Think for a moment about someone you know well who normally assumes the hands-on-hips position," they counseled. "Is that person by definition goal-oriented? Does he enjoy competition? For several years we have kept a record of executives who have attended our seminars. Approximately 75 percent of them will, when asking a question during the first hour of the seminar, assume a hands-on-hips position with their coats off or unbuttoned." Striking this pose, you could state as many down-home proclivities as you'd like, express a preference for Kraft Singles over aged Gouda, or admit "I just don't know," and still suggest that you've arrived at a higher level of sophistication and reason than someone slouching with hands in pockets.

Do it only when the attention is already on you, not when someone else is the subject of conversation and you just happen to have a similar story. You're at a party or a bagel breakfast or some such company function, and someone's regaling everyone with a funny humble beginnings story, and you experienced the exact same thing, just a little differently, only your story doesn't end as well, or that impressively, and isn't funny. Maybe don't mention it. Smile, nod in recognition, mention you can sympathize, but do not spin your whole unpracticed yarn. Save it for another time, after you've rehearsed.

In a similar vein: **Don't offer up your humble beginnings story as a rebuttal.** I was once in a situation where an older colleague, licking her finger and flicking through résumés, said it was not worth considering anyone who hadn't gone to the right schools. Either she didn't know I didn't go to the right schools, or she didn't mind bugging me. (The small satisfaction of having correctly predicted that she was a closet snob wore off in about eight minutes.) In any event, I didn't volunteer the information ("Hey, guess what? I went to . . ."), but just smiled and excused myself (". . . have to get back to my desk!"). It's a delicate calibration, but I've found that when people betray certain prejudices—confident they're in a group where everyone shares the same background and views—and unwittingly disparage you as a result, they don't always take it well when confronted with that fact. Regardless of how politely or charmingly they're informed. They'll either be really embarrassed (if they're soft at heart), or just riled (if they're total egotists).

But still, whenever self-mythologizing: **Do avoid folksy nonsense.** Silas Lapham nearly loses the sympathies of his interviewer when he's asked to describe the process by which his plant manufactures industrial-strength mineral paint. This is how he responds: "When folks come in, and kind of smell round, and ask me what I mix it with, I always say, 'Well, in the first place, I mix it with *Faith,* and after that I grind it up with the best quality of boiled linseed oil that money will buy.'" Needless to say, adding anything objectively false to one's résumé is also not smart. Anyone who tells you that *everyone* lies a little on these things is — duh — a liar.

»»

Quentin Crisp, a writer and latter-day Oscar Wilde who spent much of his life around and sometimes under the poverty line, had some interesting insights for those who, despite their best efforts, were still embarrassed by humble circumstances. He was a master at making do, and once claimed that if you could survive on cocktail-hour peanuts and champagne, and knew where the good parties were, you'd have no need for a day job. But even the poorest of the poor had nothing to fear from noxious socialites, Crisp claimed, because which conversation is going to be more interesting: the one that starts, "An amusing thing happened as I was driving down the Champs Élysées the other day ..." or the one that begins, "An amusing thing happened as I was sleeping in the bus station last night ..."?

Which suggests to me that if fortune didn't hand you the material for bus station stories, you may want to go get yourself some. Go fail at something, if you can do it without hurting anyone. Then read the next chapter to help you recover.

9

On Defense

The Dark Heart of *The 7 Habits*
of Highly Effective People

> If you're going to bow, bow low.
>
> — A piece of "Eastern wisdom"
> as per Stephen Covey

O N A TUESDAY MORNING in June, Paul's boss stops by his desk and asks, "Do you have a minute? In my office?" And so Paul gets up, reflexively wipes his hands on his pants, and follows his boss into her office. Seated, she folds her arms, leans in, and proceeds to accuse him of flouting the policy on freelance work—and to explain that she suspects this was deliberate, because the two of them had discussed this policy in April. Paul hadn't seen this talk coming, and doesn't feel his boss's stance is at all justified. "So I tell her that actually, when we renegotiated my contract back in April, she gave me blanket permission to freelance as long as I kept up with my obligations here, and it was my understanding that I wouldn't need approval for every individual project. So . . . I felt I had operated well within the bounds of that agreement, and, furthermore, we had discussed this *particular* freelance piece two weeks earlier—I had brought it up then *precisely* because I saw how she might think it'd be an issue. But basically I said that whatever it looked like, subterfuge or lack of respect for her policies, I could assure her that that was just not the case."

Did it work? "No." What happened? "She exploded."

Advice from the success-lit canon is pretty thin when it comes to defending yourself. A lot of books talk about recovering from Failure, capital *F*, or what to do when you lose your warehouse in the Great Chicago Fire (rebuild it), or when you've made the umpteenth electric light bulb and it still doesn't work (try again). But not much has been written about those moments when you've done something dumb—or just pushed your luck, or made a mistake—and get called on it. The New Thought people didn't discuss mistakes much, presumably because they believed that dwelling on them was a recipe for making more.*
Dale Carnegie's line on blunders was to "talk about your mistakes first," but that was only in the context of calling someone else on theirs. In all the strivers' literature, you find an impatience with setbacks that borders on physical revulsion—Budd Schulberg put it best in *What Makes Sammy Run?* when he wrote that Sammy Glick "always made you feel that any confession of failure was on a level with admitting that you had a yen for nothing but female dogs and ten-year-old corpses."

Novels about zealous professional climbers often include a scene that shows how ingeniously they cover their mistakes. This is a solid narrative device; the scramble to avoid detection has more comedy (picture a *The Secret of My Success*–style madcap, rapid change of clothes in the elevator, don't let the boss know you slept with his wife scene) and it also holds more dramatic tension than other narrative structures (the entire, tangled plot of *The Bonfire of the Vanities* rests on "Master of the Universe" Sherman McCoy's unwillingness to fess up to a hit-and-run). Then there are those sitcom scenes where the blundering, stam-

---

* Case in point: Hugh MacNaghton opened his book on Émile "every day in every way, I'm getting better and better" Coué by writing: "It is always difficult to know how best to begin. No sooner had I written these words than I realized that I could hardly have made a more disastrous start; to talk of difficulty (ask M. Coué) is to court failure, but my blunder is so instructive an example of what we should avoid that I will let it stand."

mering, aw-shucks corporate underling gets called to the mat
and is yanked from the brink of disaster by some unforeseen
twist—usually some bigger blunder happening offscreen. All of
which leads you to the notion that if you're really smart, you
should be able to talk your way out of anything.

Imagine my disappointment when I discovered that the best
advice for dealing with the inevitable screwup comes from Stephen Covey's *The 7 Habits of Highly Effective People*. My dis-
taste for Stephen Covey runs deep; coming of age white, middle
class, and midwestern in the 1990s meant having a copy of *The
7 Habits* somewhere in your house, and being ashamed of it. My
senior year of college I worked at a Barnes and Noble bookstore in St. Paul, Minnesota, where this book was never, ever allowed to go out of stock. Wander into any garage sale and you'd
find at least one dog-eared copy. (It was never far from a copy of
M. Scott Peck's *The Road Less Traveled* and Robert Fulghum's
All I Really Need to Know I Learned in Kindergarten. Together
they formed a nice stack.) To me, wanting to be "highly effective" seemed as ambitious and interesting as shopping for a
good deal on car insurance, or getting your teeth professionally
cleaned every six months, or looking forward to next week's episode of *ER*.

Say the words "The 7 Habits of Highly Effective People" today and most people under forty giggle. But pretending Covey
never happened just isn't possible—or, it turns out, wise. His
ideas were adopted by multiple Fortune 500 companies that
have a deep reach into the American living room, he has advised
U.S. presidents and sold millions of books, and though walking
to the register with his book in hand made me physically uneasy,
it seemed flat-out intellectually dishonest not to do so. As I discovered, Covey addresses himself specifically to the lost souls
in the office park, the men and women comfortable with using
terms like "team building" and "facilitating long-term client relationships." When Covey tries to describe what he is up to, he
explains the benefits of his principles this way:

In harmony with the natural laws of growth, they provide an incremental, sequential, highly integrated approach to the development of personal and interpersonal effectiveness. They move us progressively on a Maturity Continuum from dependence to independence to interdependence.

And a bit later:

They become the basis of a person's character, creating an empowering center of correct maps from which an individual can effectively solve problems, maximize opportunities, and continually learn and integrate other principles in an upward spiral of growth.

The kind of writing, in other words, that drives kids to crystal meth. (Not even the Man in the Grey Flannel Suit talked like this.) But Covey's first big idea—and the substance of the first habit—can be stated much more succinctly: Highly effective people react differently than regular folks. They don't follow the usual stimulus-response schema, and they never say so-and-so or this-or-that "made me do it." They never imagine that any situation compels them to react any particular way, but instead believe they always have a choice as to how they're going to react. From this point on, if you read *The 7 Habits* closely, you'll find an implicit endorsement of saying, essentially, the hell with all the "you should always stand up for yourself" advice. Most of the wisdom of the last fifty-odd years, Covey claimed, was shallow and misleading. What's your best defense? Maybe none at all. What's the best way to justify your course of action? Maybe don't even bother, he says. How and why not bothering to explain yourself works to your advantage is the secret, dark heart of *The 7 Habits*—and what lifts it to a higher plane of uncomplicated genius.

Our first instinct when confronted with trouble is to make sure we don't get blamed for it. Being wrong is something that happens to C students—and hardly anyone is a C student anymore.

Then there's the understandable fear that you won't get far if someone's unhappy with you or your work. "Your ability to focus seems delayed for a second," said Tom, a branding consultant, "and you can almost *feel* the sentences move around in your head, shuffling like a deck of cards, rearranging themselves so you'll be ready to spew forth a good excuse." This, of course, is on those happy occasions where you realize your mistake before someone else does. More often you're caught out simply by running out of time. Confrontations over missed deadlines are the stock footage of corporate American drudgery—a tall, bespectacled man in a tie, brandishing a manila folder, strides purposefully into the frame yelling, "Ferguson, that report I asked you about Friday!"* These occasions generally include presentation of the following facts: so-and-so asked you to produce something, you assured them you would do it, and then you didn't. You failed to (a) do it in time, (b) do it correctly, or (c) do it without having it adversely affect your handling of sixteen other tasks.

It might be useful at this point to mention some of the ways people express their disappointment—because without extensive experience, it can be hard to ascertain what's normal. Sometimes there's simply a sincere expression of dismay—sadness, really, that the world is not what it could be. Sometimes the moment takes an unexpected turn, as when Mary had to answer to an older colleague for delivering a report riddled with typos. "I said no, I didn't have dyslexia. And she said, 'Well, I think you might.' And recommended I get tested." I was once asked, by someone very red in the face and standing two feet in front of me, if it was physically possible for the basic guidelines concerning elementary office procedure to penetrate the thickness of my skull, his hand hitting his own forehead to demonstrate how it might be accomplished. (I can't even remember what I'd

---

* When the "report" became the key signifier for lost autonomy I don't know, but hopefully some young academic is writing a paper on it somewhere.

done—or more likely, neglected to do—to bring this on, but I do recall it was about 9:15 in the morning, and there was an audience.) Sometimes objects, including but not limited to coffee mugs, manila file folders, and staplers, are thrown. Yelling is very common but even more so is a stiff, silent formality that communicates they're having a hard time sharing physical space with you at that moment. "I don't understand what's so difficult about this" is another popular phrase with frustrated superiors. It can come in a slow staccato (I. Don't. UnDer. Sta-and. What's. So. Diffi. Cult), or rattled off quickly (though with so many hard consonants in rapid succession, that gets spitty).

So Stephen Covey, Habit One: "Be Proactive." Proactive people realize that their response cannot be dictated to them by someone else's accusations or meltdown.* On pages 90–91, where the index instructs us to look for wisdom on mistakes, we find this: "The proactive approach to a mistake is to acknowledge it instantly, correct and learn from it. This literally turns a failure into a success. 'Success,' said IBM founder T. J. Watson, 'is on the far side of failure.'"

This is undoubtedly why some snicker when Stephen Covey comes up. It's simply difficult to imagine that acknowledging your mistake "instantly" is sufficient to answer the bundle of insinuations in a phrase like "Am I the *only* one who does *any* goddamned work around here?" as Anthony—and all of his colleagues— used to hear from his boss. Many people cope with such situations by reaching back to the tricks they learned as high school debaters: "You explain what happened, stress any mediating circumstances, and correct any misinformation that spilled out in the course of their accusation." (This was explained to me by an actual high school debate-team champion.)

---

* "I did retail for a day," Heidi Montag from the television show *The Hills* once remarked. "It was really incredibly boring. You just sit there for hours and hours. I'm very proactive." Covey did a lot to knead the word *proactive* into the American vocabulary, but he can't fairly be blamed for how it gets misused in this way. Proactive never meant "in favor of activity."

The logic of this approach is sound: They are unhappy with the state of affairs, so you inform them everything is not what it might seem, and figure this will calm tempers and set things right. "You just go down the list and pick off their objections one by one, like you're at a shooting gallery."

Bringing up "the list" is telling, because increasingly people discover their blunders over e-mail. Conveying their displeasure in writing allows accusers to both avoid face-to-face confrontations *and* get wordy. (Anger always encourages eloquence.) With no constraints on time, or the need to pause for a response the way one would in regular spoken conversation, there's no need to limit oneself to a single primary grievance. Here's a typical example of the confrontational e-mail, sent by an author when he discovered that a prepublication book mailing hadn't gone off without a hitch:

> Hey xxxxx,
>
> xxx just called and said he never got the book. I wasn't going to say anything last week because I wanted to give you the benefit of the doubt (and you've been so diligent in the past). But xx, xxxx, and xxxxxx—all people who are crucial to this book really getting off the ground—also haven't received theirs. Now xxxxxx is off to Buenos Aires for a couple weeks, so turns out he won't be needing it after all. In the future, please tell me if you plan on not using my entire list, despite assuring me otherwise beforehand, so I can anticipate these embarrassments and prepare for them. It is just ridiculous and profoundly insulting that I have to micromanage this process. Also, I'm still owed $47 for the cab to O'Hare. Thanks.
>
> PS. Saw xxxxxxxxx at lunch. He said he liked the book. That was nice.

It doesn't take mastery of nuance to appreciate that there are a lot of what Suzette Haden Elgin, in *The Gentle Art of Verbal Self-Defense,* would call "relevant presuppositions" in this e-mail. The e-mailed grievance often contains layer upon layer of trouble and innuendo. Whatever the length, the formula for angry e-mail writers is: Mention the precipitating problem (you did this), then a second (you also did this), then highlight a factor that compounds the difficulty (*while* you were supposed to be bearing *that* in mind), another factor (that too), and stress the efforts made to compensate for the problem you created (meanwhile, *I'm* doing all this), and how your failure to foresee what might result from your blunder just makes it all the more upsetting (*now I wonder if you're as competent as I thought you were* is always the implication).

It's clear from this how every mistake holds the potential for a more prolonged disagreement. Covey is quite astute on how discord inspires palpable unease—and how in large swaths of the population, agreeing to disagree is practically unheard of. "When other people disagree with us, we immediately think something is wrong with them," he writes in *The 7 Habits*. And proactivity, he knew, wasn't a big or bracing enough concept to deter people from launching into lengthy explanations or rebuttals. Or so one might assume from the fact that Covey brings in two separate schemas—one involving "Emotional Bank Accounts" and another involving "a goose that lays golden eggs"—to try to convince people that taking it on the chin sometimes may be the best thing for them.

I'll repeat that. Covey uses Emotional Bank Accounts and a goose that lays golden eggs to suggest that sometimes you should just accept blame for a mistake. This next part needs to be read slowly. Confrontations, according to Covey, start when someone is expecting to get something—could be $47, could be affection, validation, that report, whatever—and doesn't get it. This constitutes a withdrawal from the Emotional Bank Account at the center of the relationship. If it's you who didn't deliver, it is you who made the withdrawal. Now, if the relationship is strong, and built on a healthy amount of trust and goodwill, it won't be damaged by the occasional small withdrawal. (You arrive late, but

nineteen times out of twenty you're on time, so it'
given.) But over time, making withdrawals from the ⌐
Bank Account without making an equivalent amount of de⌐
its threatens the integrity of the relationship. A mistake might
constitute a withdrawal, but an earnest apology upon making
that withdrawal was a deposit.

The golden eggs illustrate a concept Covey called the P/PC
balance. The golden eggs are what you enjoy, the effect you
desire, the end result—P, for production. The goose that lays
these eggs is PC, for production capability. You might not relish
spending time on this goose, but if you didn't feed it, tend to it,
stroke it, then its ability to lay golden eggs would be seriously
compromised. In time it might stop producing golden eggs altogether. So one shouldn't, Covey suggested, get so distracted
by the sheen on those eggs that one neglects the goose. If you
understood the eggs to be "the effectiveness, the wonderful synergy, the results created by open communication and positive
interaction," and the goose to be the relationship at the heart of
that wonderful synergy, then your decision about how to handle any given conflict becomes clearer. You have to tend to the
relationship first. Here's the point, at last: Having to be right
and correct and good all the time makes feeding the relationship
much, much more difficult.

In other words, sometimes the boss just wants an apology
and that's it. When I read this, I thought I'd seen this advice
somewhere before, so I was curious if Covey's approach was really as fresh as he claimed it was. And there it is, in Mark Mc-
Cormack's 1984 *What They Don't Teach You at Harvard Business School,* page 80, not on mistakes per se but specifically on
going mano a mano with the boss: "If you win the battle you're
probably going to lose the war. And the more right you are, the
more damage it will probably do in the long run." But even that
didn't smell new to me, and I dimly recalled J. P. Morgan saying something similar. He didn't. What he said was, "A man always has two reasons for the things he does—a good one, and

the real one." Dale Carnegie, on the subject of arguments, para-
phrased Morgan's line this way: "A person usually has two reasons for doing a thing: one that sounds good and a real one."
Whatever the phrasing, it's a good reminder that there's a limit
on how much you gain by arguing certain interpersonal matters.
Even if you start talking up all your good intentions, you've got
about a fifty-fifty chance of being taken at your word.

And now's probably the right time to bring up Jennifer Aniston. In 2005, at an evening of story performances to celebrate
the release of a book called *The Underminer,* the actress Nancy
Balbirer regaled the audience with a story involving "Jane," a
former roommate who was never identified as Aniston but who
was described as a then-struggling actress, daughter of a soap
star, of Greek heritage, graduate of New York's High School for
the Performing Arts, and recipient of a career-making nose job
who then went on to star in an ensemble sitcom about twenty-
somethings living in the West Village. A number of unflattering snippets about "Jane" were relayed that evening (including
her instructing Balbirer to stuff a bra with chicken cutlets), and
a New York gossip columnist described the event in his "Lowdown" column the next day. Balbirer objected to his coverage
—in particular his fingering Aniston as "Jane," and his suggestion that Balbirer was upset over snubs from Aniston and
a rejection from *Friends*—and wrote a letter to the editor in
which she sought to "clarify some inaccuracies." The article, she
claimed, made a series of false allegations. At no point did she
mention Jennifer Aniston by name, and "furthermore, the *Daily
News* article misleadingly puts in quotation marks the Lowdown
spy's summary, which completely misquotes my performance
piece." She'd read a story about a former friend, a friend named
Jane who hurt and betrayed her, and what happened to her "was
sad, not hilarious." The piece was intended as a profound exploration of the compromises people make as they chase fame,
and at no point did she, Balbirer, say that Jane was a pseud-
onym for anyone else. Nor did she claim that the real person
named Jennifer Aniston had at any point had cosmetic surgery.

Nor is she a gossip. "I am an artist ... I use the backdrop of my life experiences to examine larger issues. It's not about airing anybody's dirty laundry." If anyone had any doubts about that, they could consult the "well-known personalities" who were in attendance at the event that night, which, she wanted to mention, was a benefit for a nonprofit organization that taught inner-city schoolchildren to read and write. Oh, and she also had a book coming out.

If *The 7 Habits* can help people avoid huffy train wrecks like this, reading it is nothing to be ashamed of. Balbirer didn't make the case for her Snow White–ness so much as confirm everything the columnist suggested, plus more that wasn't so flattering—about herself. Lengthy explanations always come dangerously close to sounding shrill, and angling for sympathy has the paradoxical effect of making you unsympathetic.*

Back at the office, shrillness weakens the argument because it gives the impression that resentment has been bottled up for a while. And unfortunately, resentment, like beauty, is often in the eye of the beholder. "Ever get into a fight at work?" Julie —one of the most mild-mannered women I know—was once asked during a job interview. No, Julie said, she had good relationships with her coworkers and generally managed not to let misunderstandings escalate. But what if someone attacked her? "Well," she continued, "I'd try to explain what happened, or what I'd done and when and how"—and here Julie made a wavy hand gesture that made an unintentional little thump on the desk—"and hopefully we could come to an understanding."

The interviewer nodded. "Uh-huh. I see. So do you always bang your fist on the table like that when you're mad?"

There's also the possibility that your explanation will give the wrong message entirely. As Jayson Blair, a *New York Times* reporter caught plagiarizing, explained in an interview with

---

* Just as you should never ask a favor right after delivering a compliment, you probably shouldn't defend yourself *and* shill for whatever you're trying to sell at the same time. Unless you're extremely rhetorically gifted, it will always sound delusional.

ondon's the *Observer,* his initial impulse when the wrath came down was to compare himself with Stephen Glass, a similarly precocious reporter for the *New Republic* who was similarly disgraced not long before. "Were our stories treated differently? Sure," remarked Blair. "He got this whiz-kid ride, and I was just dumb and black. The problem with pursuing that argument is that the inevitable conclusion you end up with is: 'Hey, I'm an evil genius too!' And that's not the point you're trying to make."

Or, as Paul the freelancer realized after his careful defense only increased his boss's ire, he must have "sounded like Mr. Rogers. Like, 'Come now, boss, you don't understand the situation. Let me explain to you.' And that ... evidently comes across as a little condescending." Covey also asserted that the time spent concocting exhaustive defenses might be better used trying to figure out the full panoply of reasons for someone's anger. Habit Five: "Seek First to Understand, Then to Be Understood." Most people, he said, most ineffective people, be they bosses or employees, went through their days not really listening. That is, they listened only so far as they needed to come up with a response; when they weren't doing the talking, they were usually just waiting for the other person to finish, so they could start up again. This pseudolistening, Covey claimed, happened at one of four levels: people may actually be ignoring you, they may be pretending to take in what you're saying but not really bothering to let anything sink in, they could be listening selectively, or they may truly be attentive to what you're saying but not really *hearing you* hearing you. If you really sought to understand instead of going through these fruitless motions, there was less chance of conversations devolving into political quagmires.

And at this point it might be useful to mention the situations in which it is always and absolutely counterproductive to try to emerge blameless. Whenever you work in an office that prizes group harmony, is one. (You'll know this about your workplace if you've been paying close attention. Occasionally you encounter a person who will say, out loud, "I'm a company man" or "I'm a company woman," but it's rare. Usually you discover this premium on loyalty indirectly.) You will lose these battles even if you win on points because company men and women don't like it when a lone ranger causes such a ruckus. Grappling directly with the boss is one thing, but a boss that's uncomfortable with confrontation will get fidgety over *any* office battle — not just the ones that directly involve him or her.*

Whenever it's clear that preservation of the hierarchy demands that *someone* get hurt, is another. In some work cultures, any involvement in conflict will land some kind of punishment, regardless of who and what started it. "You could get sucker-punched while saying a rosary and still receive the same punishment as your attacker," remembered *Rivethead* author Ben Hamper of life at a GM Truck and Bus plant. In the stiffer white-collar world, the cc on a confrontational e-mail is usually a strong signal that someone is seeking blood. Cc's are a passive-aggressive person's Christmas miracle, as they can be used (a) to summon backup; (b) to place the menacing suggestion in the recipient's mind that more than one minder is awaiting a response; or (c) to suggest that more than one person is culpable, and as to who takes full responsibility, that doesn't so much matter. If you ever find yourself in any of these situations, you might want to take one for the team, and volunteer to clean up any mess. A willingness to solve a problem you didn't make is a largely risk-free way to generate goodwill, not least because it saves someone the trouble of assigning blame. Barring sadism on the boss's

---

* Covey doesn't pay much attention to body language, but by *fidgety* I mean literally, a fidgetiness you can observe: they rub their eyes, wring their hands, or to reassure themselves, touch their neck, their tie, or the back of the chair before sitting down. Watch Ricky Gervais's characterization of David Brent in the BBC version of *The Office,* and you will see this tie-stroking gesture about once every three minutes.

part, meting out blame and subsequent punishment is a moot point once someone's taken responsibility. Admitting, acknowledging instantly, absorbing the blame—there's a touch of emotional glamour to it as well. "People with little internal security can't do it," said Covey of genuine apologies. "It makes them too vulnerable."

But ultimately, you shouldn't underestimate how much people like it when someone gets nailed. It's exciting. If taking the heat doesn't immediately seem like it could help relations with the boss—or if that relationship is something you're willing to sacrifice—it might be smart to fall on your sword just to show your coworkers a good time. Tom, our branding consultant, described a woman he once worked with who, every few weeks, could be heard tearfully explaining to the department head that she worried she wasn't doing her job as well as she could. It brought him a little blush of joy in the middle of a drab day.

This is schadenfreude, and it's another big lacuna in the American success canon. There's no English word for this phenomenon, which can loosely be defined as the small pleasure we take in someone's pain, bad luck, or costly blunder. Schadenfreude is laughing when someone trips, and feeling strangely elated when an acquaintance is dumped, laid off, or forced to take it on the chin. Covey didn't use the word himself. But *The 7 Habits* comes very close to a sensible explanation for what drives it:

> The Scarcity Mentality is the zero-sum paradigm of life. People with a scarcity mentality have a very difficult time sharing recognition and credit, power or profit—even with those who help in the production. They also have a very hard time being genuinely happy for the successes of other people—even, and sometimes especially, members of their own family or close friends and associates. It's almost as if something is being taken from them when someone else receives special recognition or windfall gain or has remarkable success or achievement. . . . *Often, people with a Scar-*

city Mentality harbor secret hopes that others might suffer
misfortune—not terrible misfortune, but acceptable misfor-
tune that would keep them "in their place" [emphasis mine].
They're always comparing, always competing.

The Scarcity Mentality idea, by the way, is pure Orison Swett
Marden. But it's interesting to think that being the Golden Boy
can constitute a withdrawal from someone else's Emotional
Bank Account, and that you might actually be doing people a
small favor by failing from time to time. If only because it provides them temporary relief from their nagging insecurities.

Covey, of course, would never suggest you exploit anyone's
nagging insecurities in this or any other way. Sometimes not defending yourself just boils down to acknowledging that trouble
will find you, simply because you take up space on this earth.
"You know, that first big mistake, that major blowup . . . I think
it's something you have to go through," said Daniel, an executive
assistant who has weathered his fair share of storms. "Your time
will come. It's almost better just to get it over with." If you're
still waiting for that day, or even if that inaugural smackdown
has come and gone, the following are some good habits—not
Covey's, but inspired by them—to fall into:

Don't start talking particulars if you think the premise is flawed. Arguing the details of an accusation is an implicit endorsement of the
broader indictment. How do you win an argument that you believe is flawed at its foundation?

Do ditch rhetorical questions. Many people begin their exhaustive
defenses with sentences like "What would *you* have done if you
were in my position?" Usually people only phrase a question
this way when they've already determined what the correct answer is and also doubt your ability to come up with it. "What
would *you* have done if you were in my position?" doesn't sound
like one but is, essentially, a rhetorical question if it's followed by

a lengthy justification for the course of action you took. So too a rushed "What *should* I have done?" They both sound argumentative, and ultimately defensive.

While you're at it, you might also excise words like *furthermore* and *moreover* from your vocabulary. They belong on college papers but they only set you up nicely for blowback in any kind of office setting.

Don't say "I'm sorry you're upset." People say this when they're too lazy or insecure to apologize — or don't actually want to accept responsibility but feel they should make some motion in that direction. A popular variation of "I'm sorry you're upset" is to couch the apology in a passive construction, as if no human hands could possibly be implicated in the mishap, and it usually sounds something like this: "I'm sorry it didn't get done," or, more popular still, "I'm sorry this happened," or "I'm sorry if anyone was offended by my . . ." The smarter or angrier the audience, the less chance these nonapology apologies will be effective.

You might also want to be careful about saying, "Oh, I could *never*_____," whenever a vice or tacky habit comes up in conversation. According to Lord Chesterfield, it was the exclusive domain of the pretentious and self-righteous. From my experience, it also invites people to think that perhaps you *often* _____, but feel suitably guilty about it. I once had a literary agent in my office for a meeting. She had requested the meeting, and I was thrilled to have her there because it felt like professional recognition. Five minutes into our conversation, her cell phone rings and she answers. She proceeds to talk on her cell phone for quite a while, sitting directly across from me at my desk (it was a small office), occasionally glancing up to smile while I pretended to check my e-mail. When she finally hung up, she said she was oh so sorry, that as a rule she never does that. But it was an important call, you see, as one of her authors had a new hardcover coming out in two weeks and this author was leaving for Bangkok tomorrow and, would you believe, the jacket art just arrived with the author's name set bigger than the title of the book itself? Funny, wasn't it, how hugely popular this author had become? Anyhow, it was important they discuss all this before Bangkok, but she hoped I didn't mind her taking that call because she, as a rule, never does that.

(This left me less annoyed than weirdly discouraged, because it was a forceful reminder of my low status. If she'd needed my business half as much as I needed hers, she's right — she probably wouldn't have taken that call.)

Don't burst someone's bubble just because you value truth and honesty so much. This one also dates back to Lord Chesterfield, who told his son not to take it upon himself to correct an ugly woman who spoke of herself as if she were beautiful. Most functioning adults rely on small self-delusions to get through the day (this has been confirmed in recent scientific studies on happiness), and as long as their "mistake" makes them more comfortable and remains a victimless crime, it's better — and strategically smarter — for you to just let it be.

Do let your friends do the defending for you. This is a corollary function of the Master Mind. You say nothing about your strong heart and good intentions. Your Master Mind, either by invitation or simply because they care, will go out of their way to sing your praises. Either way, more convincing than going on about your own virtues.

Don't, after the fact, belittle those who called you on your mistakes. In the movie *Bright Lights, Big City,* the head fact checker who fires the main character is depicted as a faintly ridiculous, curt, sour, birdlike old spinster. In Jay McInerney's book of the same name, he does not caricature her so. Perhaps because McInerney knew that having his narrator mock the person who caught him out would make that narrator too much of a brat — and a predictable brat at that.

»»

Early in *The 7 Habits,* Covey describes the many people who feel worn out by the demands of their job: The executive who doesn't know his own kids, the unhappy singleton, the guy who can't keep the weight off, the hard worker so threatened by other people's promotions that he can barely see straight. He hints that they were unhappy because they occupied a fundamentally dependent position; they were dependent on the health of the global economy first and foremost, the fortunes of the company after that, and the whims of their boss most immediately. The tone and texture of their day is determined by other people and larger forces.

And perhaps this is why not bothering to defend yourself is so powerful. Say you're sitting there in your cubicle, and you've messed up, and you know it, and your job is on the line because you've got very little leverage, and your boss is a screamer. And then in the face of this Sturm und Drang, you take a risk. You'll be sitting there, seemingly about to shrink from whatever the overlords have in store, and then from this dependent position you produce behavior that lifts you above it all. You say yes, you did it, it was your fault. You act as if your fortunes are completely independent of the organization, as if you answer to some different, higher calling. Of course you're sorry. Of course. But you don't need all the gold stars anymore—maybe you'll pick and choose which gold stars you're going to go for.

And that's a major step to putting junior-level employment —maybe even corporate life altogether—behind you.

10

The Uses of No

Donald Trump and "You're Fired"

> My number one instinct was not to be a jackass.
> And I think I achieved that.
>
> —KWAME JACKSON

TUCKED SOMEWHERE IN THE middle of *Trump: The Art of the Deal,* Donald Trump describes sitting with his mom and watching the 1953 coronation of Queen Elizabeth II on TV. His mother is enraptured, misty-eyed, proud just to be witness to the spectacle, even from the vantage point of a family room couch in Queens, New York. Then his father, Fred, enters the room and says, "For Christ's sake, Mary. Enough is enough, turn it off. They're all a bunch of con artists." This explained a lot, Trump wrote in 1987, about how he himself saw the world. His father was turned on only by efficiency and competition, while his mother was moved to tears by opulence and pageantry. The Donald had grown into the perfect synthesis.

When *The Apprentice* started drawing huge Nielsen ratings in early 2004—number one among total viewers *and* number one among adults ages eighteen to forty-nine specifically—a number of theories were floated as to why the show was such a hit. Producer Mark Burnett had already proved his mettle with *Survivor,* but that didn't explain why a bunch of unknowns sitting in a cramped wood-paneled conference room comparing returns on initial investment was drawing 20.7 million viewers every week. Trump was famous, but you couldn't say he was terrifically well liked. The formula for *The Apprentice* didn't deviate much from standard reality TV fare: sixteen type A's camping out in tight sleeping quarters, pretty women wearing less clothing than is normal, rivalries, sexual tension, and emotional meltdowns.

When asked to explain the show's success, Trump gave credit to the good care of Jeff Zucker, president of NBC. (In *Trump: Think Like a Billionaire,* the book published on the heels of this ratings triumph, Trump gives a shout-out to the "brilliant" Zucker and his team no fewer than eleven times.) Zucker in turn told the press that the show worked because of Trump's personal charisma. That answer didn't really satisfy anyone either. In a 2005 interview with the business writer Robert Slater, Trump came closer to a definitive answer. During the taping of the first *Apprentice* episode, he remembered, in the final boardroom scene, the words just came tumbling out of his mouth. "David, you're fired," he'd said. It wasn't planned or scripted, but it worked. He liked the sound of it, and so did everyone else on set. "Those two words are very beautiful. They're very definite. You can't come back and say, 'Well, let's talk it over.' It's, like, over," he explained. "You know, I'm not even so sure that the show would have been a huge success had we not done that."

Honestly, it seems cosmically dumb to elevate Trump to the status of Dale Carnegie or even Stephen Covey. Before all this, Trump was regarded by many as a lightweight — more showman than business philosopher. He's no Bill Gates, and hardly Warren Buffett, whose investment approach earned him the admiring nickname "the Sage of Omaha." Still, Trump had been a man of letters for some time — along with the bestseller *The Art of the Deal* and the billionaire book, there's *Trump: The Art of the Comeback, Trump: The Art of Survival, Trump: How to*

Get Rich, and a few more that don't have his name in the title. Trump has also tried at various times to paint himself as a hardscrabble climber who defied the odds, a task made more difficult by the fact that his father, Fred, was a millionaire several times over.* Everyone expected *The Apprentice* to be just another stab at self-mythologizing. While Burnett said he actually considered the show educational programming—it was going to show people how making it in America was done—hardly anyone expected Trump to deliver much in the way of wisdom.

He didn't, really—at least not quite as intended. What Trump and his wannabes did best was serve as object lessons in how to lose jobs. "You're fired" nicely illustrates a principle that is rarely displayed quite so baldly, which is that people who are able to stay perched somewhere near the top for any amount of time—in addition to posing right and working hard and observing carefully and being resilient and optimistic and owning up to their mistakes—have a sophisticated understanding of rejection. They say no easily, convincingly, without unnecessary apologies. And when told no themselves, they don't crawl under the duvet with a copy of *The Bell Jar.*

It's worth spending some time with Trump because losing jobs is important. It's important because there comes a time, after you've been introduced to the broom, and endured the humiliations, and watched enough marginally competent egomaniacs do what they do best, and with any luck, watched enough talented people do what *they* do best, and you've stayed way too long at the Christmas party two years in a row, when you look around and realize that you've nothing left to learn in your current position. You need to be promoted or exit the building.

---

* Not surprisingly, Trump arrived at a novel formulation to allow himself to claim humble beginnings anyhow. He stresses that Fred was a real estate developer in *Brooklyn* and *Queens,* unfashionable outer boroughs, and that he, the son, had to hustle like mad to get accepted as a player in *Manhattan,* just across the river. (". . . family money didn't get my first Manhattan projects built. I had to raise tens of millions from investors for those jobs.")

Learning how to lose a job is also important because job security is a relic of the past, and yet many people fear being without a salaried position for any length of time. ("Don't ever quit until you've got something else lined up," they'll tell you.) In fact, anecdotal evidence suggests walking out can be a wise move, not least because there's a(nother) law of diminishing returns at work: the longer you stay put at a job that doesn't satisfy, the less likely it is to evolve into something satisfying—either for you or your employer. I've seen employees lauded for their loyalty, but I've seen an equal number—if not more—tacitly deemed dead wood.

My friend Sam has a four-year rule: every four years he must jump ship. For me, the decisive moment came when I was waiting in line to pay for my breakfast, to-go, at a deli on Twenty-eighth Street, just around the corner from my office. Nice, well-lit place, friendly staff, fresh bagels; and as I stared distractedly at the counter lady, all I could think was, "No more Bagel 'N Schmear. I don't want this in my life anymore. That's it. I'm done here." Smart people, I now realize, start laying the groundwork for this moment long in advance. They slowly, subtly start firing themselves. It's a process that means paving the way for their replacement, not doing their job, and judicious deployment of *no*. Before going any further, I should add: This is a good time.

Firing people is fun, or at least beneficial—that was the wisdom percolating when Trump was just a puppy on the real estate development scene in the late 1970s and early '80s. In *Secrets of a Corporate Headhunter,* John Wareham suggested that humans tended to make heroes out of ruthless people because at the end of the day, in our unguarded private selves, we all "enjoy the smell of blood on the floor." He told company executives that while they shouldn't act capriciously, or start firing people willy-nilly, they nevertheless shouldn't be afraid to use rejection to fluff up a bigger cloud of mystique around themselves. "The capacity to take ruthless action is admired because most people

have no such ability," he wrote. "Ruthlessness appeals to the
darker side of our nature. We feel that we should not admire it,
but secretly we do. . . . Firing doesn't damage an enterprise at
all: it is good for morale, inspiring of loyalty and awe, and exciting to everyone—not least, the person fired."

It was a sentiment you might not expect to last beyond the
American Psycho cultural moment, but it proved to have legs.
The forced ranking system that many Fortune 500 companies
championed meant that every year the bottom 10 percent of
all employees were systematically cycled out. The standards
for judging performance were called "the 4 E's": "high Energy
level, the ability to Energize others around common goals, the
Edge to make tough yes/no decisions, and the ability to consistently Execute and deliver on promises." It was gooey busi-
nessese for what became a galvanizing policy. "That was very
controversial," Jack Welch admitted to *Fortune* in 2006. "Weed
out the weakest. It's been portrayed as a cruel system. It isn't.
The cruel system is the one that doesn't tell anybody where they
stand." In 2001's *Good to Great,* the author and strategy consultant Jim Collins made the distinction between ruthless and rigorous. When firings couldn't be avoided, he said, to delay them
any longer than strictly necessary was far from compassionate.
"To let people languish in uncertainty for months or years, stealing precious time in their lives that they could use to move on
to something else, when in the end they aren't going to make it
anyway—*that* would be ruthless." But to deal with those people
"right up front" and allow them to start making other plans, that
was *rigorous,* and it was the hallmark of a healthy company.

By the time *The Apprentice* rolled around, American workers had become surprisingly comfortable with layoffs en masse.
(*Who Moved My Cheese?* was basically written to talk people
down from the ledge after being downsized.) Here was the
chance to see firing on a more intimate scale. There was techni-
cally no job for the *Apprentice* candidates to be fired from—as
was repeated many times, it was just a thirteen-week-long job in-

terview. But the phrase picked up momentum every time Trump said it. In episode two: "This is a tough one—you're fired." Episode three: "It's over, don't you think it's over?" Episode five, Trump adds that it's too late for the firee to appeal. Episode six: "I didn't like what she was doing, and it was repulsive to me. But worse, was the way you took it. . . . And I have to say, you're fired." Trump claims that within weeks strangers started yelling, "You're fired!" after him as he walked down Fifth Avenue. He'd hear it out of the mouths of children, from tourists at Trump Tower, and from the African street vendors that sell knockoff Gucci handbags on midtown Manhattan sidewalks. Some commentators mused that it was odd that displaying such cutthroat behavior seemed to make Trump more, not less, approachable.

What Trump recognized, though, is that being agreeable doesn't *necessarily* make a person more likable. There are a number of obstacles getting in the way of employees saying no and it's worth dispensing with them right away. Many good employees don't actually believe that you can say no to anything a colleague or boss asks you to do without said colleague or boss automatically resenting you. It also means changing established patterns, because when you're trying to gain recognition in the beginning, saying no is completely counterproductive. You can't prove you're capable of doing something by not doing it. Saying no is also an uncomfortable stretch for all former good students in the office—it feels like defying the teacher, or not turning in your homework. For still others, saying no arouses vague dread that it amounts to tempting fate—"what if I say no, and no one else asks me to the prom ever again?" is the unspoken fear. For most people I talked to, the reluctance to say no came down to not wanting to be seen as *not nice*. "I have trouble with saying no," admitted Cynthia. "And it's not even that I have an articulate position on the subject. I suppose I like being helpful. And I suppose I'd prefer if everyone acted more like me, at least in this regard."

Here's where saying yes all the time turns from sweetness

and light into something else. Every office has one person who if you just say to him, "Hey, can you help me with this?" will drop whatever he's doing and give you his time—a can't-say-no person. Send him an e-mail asking for a quick favor, or even a complicated one, and you'll get an answer within the hour. And so with a steady trickle of requests he soon gets overwhelmed—and sometimes, ends up doing his colleagues' work for them. Looking back on her time as an editorial assistant, Cynthia recalled being at the office past 9:00 P.M., working on an editing job that a senior colleague had asked her to tackle. He had his own assistant, but for whatever reason—Cynthia wasn't sure, and never asked—the assistant wasn't tackling this assignment for him.* Cynthia reasoned that her pitching in would be rewarded. It wasn't. ("Instead, it became more like, 'Oh, Cynthia will do it,' whenever something onerous came up.") Before long, an office's most accommodating types get the sense that not only have they lost control of their day, but they've lost some of their colleagues' respect as well.

Trump has left a considerable paper trail documenting the many ways he keeps his days to himself. He incorporates daily diaries into his books (a typical entry: "4:00 P.M. I call back Judith Krantz"), and stresses how much he hates it when minutes get frittered away. This means no computer on his desk. No e-mail ("E-mail is for wimps"). No intercom (extraneous technology and button-pushing—he hollers instead). He does not drink alcohol, and never has. He skips parties ("I rarely go out, because mostly, it's a waste of time"). When Trump recognized he was sufficiently established that people would come to see him, he began saying no to leaving the office. All his meetings now take place at Trump Tower.

A lot of people see this and think, well, OK, that's fine, but still can't do it. Because they're perfectionists. Perfectionism helps immensely at the outset of a job ("She's marvelous. She

---

* This is one of those times when asking a question might have come in handy.

catches all my typos") and then starts to get in the way. ("She's great with the details," any superior reluctant to promote you can then say. "But, you know, I'm not sure she gets the big picture.") Perfectionism becomes corrosive when it means you don't budge from your seat until you get everything just so. When you'd rather contribute zilch than create a product that's not flawless from every angle. Or when it means you won't delegate because you suspect no one else can do it as well as you. In the 1972 *Instant Secretary's Handbook,* a sensible woman named Martha Luck pointed out that acting this way—she called it wanting to be indispensable—was maybe just a neurotic tic. She was referring specifically to how some secretaries got a private thrill out of not sharing information, like where certain files were stored, so that things wouldn't go smoothly on their days off. The neurotic secretaries reasoned that this would impress upon people how necessary they were to the vital functions of the office. It was a way of securing their jobs, and it followed a sound logic: If they couldn't be replaced, they wouldn't be let go. But they failed to consider that if they couldn't be replaced, they wouldn't necessarily get promoted either.

Even those who'd mastered the broom, Andrew Carnegie said in his 1885 janitor speech, needed to get a little uppity at some point. "Faithful and conscientious discharge of duties assigned you is all very well," he said, "but the verdict in such cases generally is that you perform your present duties so well, that you would better continue performing them. Now, this will not do."

No, indeed, it won't do. Once you've decided you're ready to move up or on, control of your day is important because you need to be spending less time on small tasks and more time on significant tasks—like updating your résumé. Thanks to the aforementioned mass layoffs, most offices these days are very thinly staffed, so there is no end to the time-consuming administrative chores that get dumped on those lowest in rank. You think you'll get caught up someday, but you won't. So you say no in order to keep your desk reasonably free. But there's also something to be said for saying no just for the sake of saying no. It has the strange effect of plumping up some personal mystique. If you've been consistently agreeable up to this point (and you should have been), it will plant the suggestion in people's minds that you've got ambitions beyond helping them realize theirs.

The first thing you'll notice when you start saying no is that people react to you differently. It can mean you find yourself in sticky situations where you're expected to nod in agreement but you suggest an alternative instead. Or that awkward moment when you decline happy-hour drinks for the third time in a row, while in the past you were always game, and the colleague who invited you lingers by your desk, absentmindedly running his index finger back and forth across the top of your cubicle, waiting for a lengthier explanation that never comes. However subtle these rejections, they put people on notice that you're "going through some changes." Maybe you're *not* a team player after all. You might get funny looks, as if you just made an inappropriate joke but no one dares ask you to repeat it. For the former yes person in the office, like Cynthia, the strain is often the greatest because her new stance means big changes for her colleagues as well. But as Cynthia eventually realized, people were not necessarily thinking unkind thoughts about her in these moments. They were simply mildly put out that now they'd have to do the work themselves — and adjusting to a new reality wherein she wasn't quite so pliant.

Finding a right way and a right time to start incorporating strategic *no*'s into your day is difficult. A number of the *Apprentice* candidates apparently knew enough of Trump's plain-spoken "no thanks" posturing to try it for themselves. Omarosa Manigault-Stallworth refused to pitch in on the episode seven apartment cleanup, insisting that being clunked on the head by a piece of falling plaster gave her dispensation to sit things out. She also thought she'd be wise to say no to sharing in the camaraderie. "I made a conscious decision not to establish relationships with [my fellow contestants] during the taping . . . because I thought it would cloud my judgment," she later told an interviewer.* The result was that she got branded group villain. Then there was Tammy Lee, who thought that Trump's opinion of her was the only one that mattered; she too said no to cozying up to her fellow contestants, and ended up fired for being "disloyal" to her team. And when Nick Warnock didn't like the let's-pretend-Kwame-Jackson-is-an-NBA-star stunt at Planet Hollywood, he refused to participate, saying he thought it was unethical and in bad taste. No one, including Trump, seemed charmed by his stance.

Clearly, all these people were aiming for a particular effect and airballed. Nick ended up looking petulant rather than principled, as if he were simply saying no because it was someone else's idea. Petulant is not what you want. Petulant is not "high Energy." So phrasing is important.

Heidi Bressler's experience suggests that the effective *no* is also a question of leverage. Near the end of episode five, when Heidi thought she was going to be taken to the Trump Tower boardroom for the "You're Fired" showdown, she made sure everybody in the candidates' suite knew she felt it was undeserved and that she was very upset. She ranted in a vocal fit—some of it bleeped out—that dragged on far past the point of everyone's comfort. (Which is to say that her phrasing did not impress either.) She boasted later on that this was typical of her, as she was "an upfront person," but her fellow candidates stared at her whirling-dervish-in-three-inch-heels act with mild concern. (In a rare moment of droll analysis, Omarosa commented, "Well, Heidi speaks her mind, but what's on her mind isn't always that appealing.") The problem with this performance was that the performer had no leverage. It didn't matter if Heidi disapproved

---

* "The Omarosa Experiment," by Keith Hollihan. From *The Morning News,* an online magazine.

or was saying no, this really isn't working for me, because—after only five weeks in a highly competitive setting—she hadn't yet proven her value. And if you make a show about being unhappy when no one within earshot cares enough to try to return you to happiness, you've not so much raised people's estimation of you as made a big problem for yourself. What you've got is loud and spastic. What you want is *rigorous.*

An example of how the pros do it comes from Slater's account of Trump's visit to one of his new building sites. As the two men approached the site, Trump noticed something screwy with the curb. He called the site manager over and within minutes everyone had heard how Trump felt about the lousy workmanship—he was furious. Not much else about the curb incident was said at the time; Slater and Trump left the building and moved on to other business. Later in the day, Trump felt compelled to explain his outburst. "That's the way I get things done," he said. It was mostly an act, he admitted, "but I *did* feel that way. It was a terrible job." Trump's philosophy was that painstaking attention to high standards was essential to his bottom line; if one small corner of the brass empire looked shoddy, the entire brand would suffer. So he was always looking out for chipped paint and upholstery stains, he said, for burned-out light bulbs and droopy flower arrangements. And he knew that when he withheld his approval, somebody would scurry around until everything was fixed. His perfectionism was a form of multitasking—it got stuff done, and it got it done by other people, which was a bonus. But it also burnished his image as a man who had an agenda, standards, and an ability to set things in motion.

How would this work in real life? First of all, Trump's example should reassure you that if you abandon perfectionism at some point in your career, perhaps at this very crucial point right now, you can—and will probably want to—pick it up again later. In order to start saying no, this isn't working for me, and get the desired response, you have to have lived through chapters 1–10 of this book. You can't start saying no too soon, because then you don't have the necessary leverage. If you haven't asked enough questions, you might not know enough about your colleagues to anticipate their reactions. Your *no* will also have zero effect if you've historically been seen as a slacker.* But when you're quite convinced the moment is right, you start firing yourself by sloughing small tasks first. "You don't even have to say no, you're not going to do something. You just don't do it," Teresa, an assistant to an overbearing man, claimed. "When I realized that he didn't actually read the reports he was asking me to prepare all the time — overnight — I decided to have 'forgotten' to do it one morning." Her boss got the point, and now she's only asked to prepare them when he really needs them, taking care to tell her why he needs them and precisely how urgent they are. (She's in the same job, but enjoying it much more.)

You also start selectively turning down some of those requests for little favors, and sitting on replies for a while. "I began waiting longer between e-mails," said Cynthia. "Whereas I used to respond with the 'No, stay strong. That Weight Watchers angle is really going to change people's lives' e-mail within hours of receiving a client's panicky message, now I wait a full day — at least — before I send reassurance."

You gradually reduce your visibility. Whereas before you'd stay late, time-stamping e-mails at 10:30 P.M., now you don't, and you let people see you walk out the door with everyone else, or even earlier. You stop showing up for the meeting five minutes ahead of schedule, as you used to, but get there right on the dot at 3:00, maybe even 3:01, subtly implying that you've got better things to do than wait for proceedings to begin. (While I'm on the subject, I'm willing to wager it was no accident that Trump entered the *Apprentice* boardroom after everyone was already seated. And also, that he would have said he was "really busy today" upon entering — as he did notably in episode one — even

---

* There may, in fact, be no better practical argument for volunteering a lot, as Helen Gurley Brown suggested you do, than the leverage it provides you at this moment.

if he'd just been standing in the wings picking his cuticles for the past half hour.) Firing yourself is a slow weaning process, in other words. You're not preparing yourself to move on so much as preparing *other people* for your moving on.

At the same time, you start praising junior colleagues to the skies. Because the first question on everyone's mind will be, If *you're* not going to be doing all this work, then who will? Which brings us back to Martha Luck's neurotic secretaries: Your boss is less likely to promote you if he doesn't already have someone on staff who can do your job as well as you can. Your boss is also less likely to get testy when you give notice if he has someone on staff who he suspects is as competent, or even more so, than you are. So your primary task becomes convincing your boss that you're *not* indispensable, because those ranked below you are ready, willing — chomping at the bit, really — for more responsibility.

It's a process that might be started by increasing the amount of happy vibes you send out in all directions. Trump's books are full of references to idiots, morons, scoundrels, charlatans, losers, human garbage, and the occasional "total dope." But a closer reading reveals he's equally adept at throwing kisses, and on *The Apprentice,* his willingness to tell people how much he cared was on full display. Advertising executive Donny Deutsch, who lent his name and time to episode two, is "the best there is." Yankees manager George Steinbrenner is "a truly great winner."[*] When Trump tells Broadway impresario George Schoenfeld that he's taking his kids to see *Cats,* he turns down Schoenfeld's offer for free tickets but tells the world about it in *The Art of the Deal* — a book chock-full of thank-yous for services rendered — saying that it was "a nice gesture from a very nice guy." Don Imus is also told he's the greatest. (Trump's exact lines are another marvel of the well-packed message: "I tell Imus he's the

---

[*] Episode five: Trump and Steinbrenner also exchange *I love you*'s in Steinbrenner's Yankee Stadium office.

greatest, and I invite him to be my guest one day next week at the tennis matches at the U.S. Open. I have a courtside box and I used to go myself almost every day. Now I'm so busy I just send my friends.") Judith Krantz is both a nice woman, he tells us, and did you know, author of three number-one best-selling books in a row? The verdict on Cardinal O'Connor is that he's very personable but also "a businessman with great political instincts."*

It may simply be that Trump recognizes you can only get away with calling people morons when you couple that with outsized demonstrations of love for other people—nonmorons, presumably. In your case, proceed more modestly. You start by working in a reference to how capable someone is, or how well he does such-and-such, whenever you're talking with the boss or other company decision makers. You consider using the word *superstar* to describe your cubicle neighbor.† And you start sharing information with your junior colleagues, taking them to lunch, passing on as much insider information to them as you can. Usually, if they too have some ambitions, they'll be thrilled to have additional chances to show off what they can do. And the vague, perhaps even subconscious, suspicion that you'll be getting out of their way soon—also fun for them. Best of all: If before, you feared that saying no made you appear selfish and mean, well, this should take care of that.

In *Think Like a Billionaire,* Trump indulges in the following rumination: "I've been in the same offices at Trump Tower for over

---

* A few pages later, Trump tells us that he put Cardinal O'Connor down as a reference on his application for a Nevada gaming license, so he could buy another Las Vegas casino. Which, depending on your views of the Catholic Church, is either genius or genius.

† Interestingly enough, if you time this gambit right, it might boost your boss's opinion of *your* abilities as well as those of your younger colleagues. Or at least help him see you as hovering slightly above and apart from the undifferentiated lump of underlings. This was one of Edward E. Jones's *Ingratiation* insights: Implicit in a compliment is that you put yourself in a position to judge.

twenty years. The location and space work as beautifully today as they did twenty years ago. It's not dumb luck, though. I knew exactly where I would be today twenty years ago." It's a clunky boast, sure, and of questionable veracity, but it nonetheless contains a kernel of truth about Trump and many more people like him. They know exactly what drives them, and they have a clear, distinct picture of what success for them looks like. Sometimes, as in Conrad Hilton and the photograph of the Waldorf slipped under his desktop, this picture is a literal one.

This concrete vision frees them to say no to what doesn't fit the picture very easily. Trump once described how he turned down an offer from a Texas friend to go in on some oil wells together. They were talking on the phone. "Listen," Trump said, "there's something about this that bothers me. Maybe it's that oil is underground, and I can't see it, or maybe it's that there's nothing creative about it. In my case, I just don't want to go in." So he didn't. Several months later, oil went "completely to hell," as Trump put it, and every partner lost every cent they put into the deal. It's a striking anecdote, but not for the fact that Trump's reaction prevented his losing money. It could just as easily have gone the other way and still been a good story. What's striking is that Trump pinpointed, with considerable self-awareness, what didn't work for him: He couldn't see it. The oil was underground, and there wouldn't be any "breathtaking" building involved. So he excused himself without regret.

A few final thoughts that might help get you to that same *I'm going to have to pass on that oil deal, but hey, thanks! So good of you to think of me* place:

Do strive for *no*'s that don't come padded in lengthy explanations. In other words, keep those polite declines brief. Those who say no, but wrap that *no* in bubble wrap and ribbons and lengthy apologias as to why they *have* to say no, are probably in thrall to the same idea that lengthy apologizers are: that excess verbiage makes it go down easier. It doesn't. Too specific rejections are also problematic, as book editors will tell you (being too specific can give the rejected the idea that if she just fixes those one or two little things, then . . .). As long as the tone is gracious, less is more. There are times and places to speak your whole truth, but this is not one of those times. A good basic formula, pared down to the essentials: gratitude for the offer, then a *no* that keeps you as the subject of the sentence. In other words, not "That's a terrible idea, no way," but more "Thank you so much for asking, but I'm going to have to pass."

One corollary: *Maybe* is never a suitable prelude to *no*. A lot of people say maybe when they're too "nice" to let people down right away, so they stall, encourage false hopes, and then, perhaps a week later, say no. It's an old salesman's saying, but worth repeating: The first-best answer is a yes, the second-best answer is a no. Saying maybe is, as Trump would say, a *yuge* waste of time.

Don't stop talking to people. See "Do be completely democratic in outlook," from chapter 5.

Don't have a perfect attendance record. While it's important to be seen, it's also important not to be seen sometimes, if only so people will wonder why you're not there. It could even result in them thinking about you at greater length than if you had shown up. Take days off.

Do understand that a superior's refusal to do something is not necessarily a sign of ineptitude. I was once called to the corner office. The boss was in a bit of a panic. "Do you know anything about printers?" he asked me. He couldn't get his desktop printer to work, his own assistant wasn't there to help, and he had no idea how to begin addressing the problem. As it turned out, the printer wasn't so much broken as it was out of paper. At the time I thought this was really disturbing. I have since realized that this kind of learned helplessness is fairly typical of people occupying the higher ranks. It's not that technology has outstripped their ability to keep up, or that they're incredibly out of touch (they may be out of touch, but that's another matter). Not knowing how to interpret a desktop printer's flashing red error button is a lifestyle choice. Some men and women choose not to worry about it, because they realize they can convince someone to come running to their aid while they contemplate larger, more abstract transactions.

Don't expect to build a career on tending to undotted i's. Your e-mails are straight out of *The Chicago Manual of Style* and your boss's look as if Jessica Simpson typed them up. This is troublesome, because you can't expect people to reward you for something they clearly don't value themselves. Which is not to say that you should lower your standards if your attention to detail is greater than your boss's. It simply means you shouldn't wait for pats on the back, or plan on using your perfectionism as a bargaining chip when angling for a promotion.

Do smile like you mean it. Or don't smile when you don't mean it. A lot has been written lately about the utility of smiling—that just doing it can actually change your mood for the better, that it makes you look more attractive and affluent. (Charles M. Schwab liked to say he owed his million-dollar salary to his megawatt smile.) But distinctions should be made among smiling in order to boost your serotonin levels, smiling because you're happy already, and smiling in the way that got the *Apprentice* candidate Amy Henry branded a Stepford Wife by one of Trump's senior staffers. A lot of people smile because they think the situation calls for it; they smile an obligatory smile, and it's horrifying. (The Pan American smile, in other words.)

Consider, then, how Trump is either scowling or looking constipated in most of his own publicity shots. He is seldom photographed smiling. Given that, as he so often stresses, the details are not lost on him, we can assume this is deliberate. He insists you should always believe in what you're selling—"if you don't really believe it yourself, it'll never work, it'll never sell, it'll never work, and you're going to be miserable." So if you honestly can't find a reason to smile, if you can't sell your mood with conviction, then maybe try another facial expression. Surprise, wide-eyed fascination, amusement—any of these could work. As long as you realize that overestimating your ability to dissemble is always alienating, and never more so than when you're smiling a fake smile.

»»

There's a reason Trump and *The Apprentice* come last in this book—a reason beyond chronology, that is. It only occurred to me when I watched the candidate Ereka Vetrini, who, in episode eight, having just informed Bill Rancic that she planned on taking him to the boardroom showdown with her, which meant she considered him partly responsible for that week's loss, feels compelled to add, "It's not personal." Bill recognized that this comment was not really meant to soften the blow to his ego (and was probably only said to forestall him getting mad at her), so he replied with something like, "Just because you say it's not personal, doesn't mean it isn't."

This rattled around in my head for two reasons. First, Ereka evidently thought she could readily define the situation for Bill, a reasonable adult capable of drawing his own conclusions. Second, she was doing exactly what you need to do at the very beginning of entry-level employment: scrambling really hard to massage reality for people, to steer them toward a durable definition of you and what you're capable of. You spoon-feed your story to whoever will bite. And then, very gradually and then all of a sudden—or so it seems—you have a track record, and your record begins to speak for you. You're ready for the next thing once you're ready to stop spoon-feeding. More important, you're ready for the next thing once you stop *wanting* to manage people's reactions to you. It's a perfect 180-degree turnaround, but I've never encountered an admirable, honest, principled, ethical, ambitious, dare I say successful person who didn't go through it. Such people are less interested in what you think of them because they're more interested in their work—and in you, and how you're doing, and if maybe there's something they can do to help you out. The last thing they want to do is waste anyone's time.

Jessie Connors, who was eliminated in episode six, had a surprising take on her last moments on the show, one that suggested she'd picked up a few things during her short stint in Trump Tower. Her words are goofy, they're sweet, but they also demonstrate a good grasp of getting in, getting out, and closing with a rueful snap. Here's what she said from the back of the booted-off taxi: "I think that this life . . . life, and the universe, revolves around rules. There's just rules to the universe, and it all comes back to people. It all . . . it all comes back. So I'm not worried. I'm happy."

That's it. She was done. On to the next thing.

Epilogue

THE BEST ARGUMENT for reading one hundred–plus years of success literature is that it helps you become re-enchanted with work. It's the best antidote I've found to the cynicism that infects you before you even walk in the door. And it's so effective because, as with any lasting piece of literature, it pulls and pushes you to a vision of your day as part of a grander story. For me, that re-enchantment began with Rivington Street.

Throughout researching and writing this book, I lived in a small apartment on Rivington Street on the Lower East Side of Manhattan. Once the most densely populated area on record anywhere, the Lower East Side is a neighborhood steeped in lore. It even makes an appearance in one of the novels that helped cement the popular image of the venal, backstabbing striver. I could have written an entire chapter on *What Makes Sammy Run?*, but here's all you need to know: The Sammy Glick of the title started his climb as a scrappy, know-nothing copy boy at a New York daily paper. In a few short, action-packed years he's head of a major Hollywood studio, eating rare steaks, and about to walk down the aisle with a rich, beautiful redhead. To get to this place he's cheated, scammed, lied, and basically displayed no scruples, loyalty, or true compassion whatsoever. The question—what makes Sammy run? why does he chase success at all costs?—is one that haunts the book's narrator, a one-time coworker. So he goes snooping around in some old HR files and discovers the answer: Rivington Street. Rivington Street is what made Sammy run. He grew up in such noisy squalor, assaulted on all sides by poverty and anger and rotting-fish smells, that of course he wanted up and out and far, far away, as fast as his skinny legs could carry him.

Sammy Glick's putative address—136 Rivington—is no more. That entire block of tenements was torn down to make way for a terrifically ugly public high school years ago. My building, 210 Rivington, was built in 1900, and for better or worse, still stands proud at six stories and no elevator. The ground-floor façade is covered in a thick, industrial red paint that looks like it was applied by someone with cataracts. The graffiti on the front door almost enhances the place. On floors above and below, families with grown teenagers live in the same cramped layout I share with one roommate. The projects are right across the street. One of the kids who hangs around the building deals pot. He's an extremely amiable guy. He's always instructing his friends and customers to get out of the way when their stoop-sitting blocks my path to the front door, which is every day from 5:00 P.M. onwards, May to October. I also happen to know—though how this ever came up in our brief conversations is anyone's guess—that he coaches a neighborhood girls' softball team.

I bring him up to lend this book some street cred. Actually, I bring him up because I like him so much it pisses me off that he's not more ambitious. Maybe he enjoys being a happy-go-lucky smalltime pot dealer, maybe he likes living with his mom, but it doesn't strike me as a strategy for the long haul. I want more for him, even if he doesn't—yet.

But back inside 210. Once you get inside the front door, the smell—still a big part of Rivington Street life—is always a surprise. Usually it's some unholy blend of bacon, stale tobacco,

and off-brand bleach, though there are subtle, day-to-day variations. The steps to my fourth-floor apartment are often littered
with empty Cheetos bags, and once, a small pile of something I
was relieved to realize was only rice and black beans. An ever-
rotating cast of men bags up our trash and takes it to the curb
twice a week. They're subcontracted on the sly by Juan, our super. When I'm running out the door, and they're there sorting
junk in the entryway, I generally say hello. The most common
response is, understandably, a grunt. Sometime last spring, when
I was nearing a deadline and more harried than usual, I noticed
a new man on the job. He had wire-rimmed glasses. He smiled
at me, which was enough encouragement for me to toss off a
"Hey, how are ya?" as I started my sprint up the stairs.

"I am blessed," he said. His accent suggested Africa, though
the Caribbean may be a better guess. The next week, again, he
smiled and said, "I am blessed." Week three he went with: "I am
blessed, and so are you."

Anyone worried that these were *Chicken Soup for the Soul*
moments for me can go ahead and relax. That a sane adult male
would consider himself blessed to be bagging trash for no thanks
and five dollars, that's something I'll let stand for itself. It's certainly possible that given where he's been and what he's seen,
Rivington Street flows with milk and honey.

But I do think of this man whenever I feel an unseemly
amount of self-pity coming on. And here's why he matters, as
a counterpoint to Sammy Glick and everybody else who might
tell you that striving to be successful is a fundamentally narrow,
selfish undertaking. It's usually taken for granted that the motivations for doing well are materialistic, ego-driven only: houses,
vacations, Vera Wang wedding dresses. But it's important to remember that there are some people striving for someone else's
sake, and they're not always who you'd think, either; I've a
friend who endures a draining job as a corporate lawyer because
his elderly parents back home in Bulgaria rely on the checks he
sends them each month. (Bulgaria's state pension system, as you
might imagine, is hardly going gangbusters.)

There are cynics who'd look at the man bagging up garbage in the entryway and see first and last a reminder of the evils of colonialism and institutionalized racism—or if they stand at the opposite side of the political spectrum, an argument for stricter immigration policies. (They'd probably prefer Juan to return to Puerto Rico too.) But the man in the entryway didn't seem to think along these lines. *Should* he start thinking of his life in terms of other people's moral failures? Would it make the garbage smell less? Should he grab a gun and start armed insurrection? It's always an option. Or does he have a better shot at improving his prospects—and those of his children—if he continues the slow process of swapping a crappy job for a slightly less crappy one? Repeating until he finds satisfaction?

I know where the cynicism comes from, though. A couple of years ago there was a Citibank ad campaign that urged people to "Live Richly." A SURE WAY TO GET RICH QUICK, the bus stop signs proclaimed, is to COUNT YOUR BLESSINGS. I had a hard time taking this advice from one of the globe's largest financial institutions and the very bank that subtracted $1.50 from my balance every time I couldn't locate one of their ATMs. There's something to be said for telling Citibank and their ad copywriters where to stick it when they use that word—*blessings*. But I also think we ought to believe that same sentiment from our man in the entryway. Believe that he truly considered himself blessed, believe that he knew what he was talking about, and that he understood what he was saying when he told me *I* was blessed.

You can imagine my editor urging me to get to the point about the office now. Here's the first one: If you think of your life as happening in separate compartments, as just about every outlet of popular culture tells you to do, then you're in deeper trouble than this man. Magazine articles and television talking heads are constantly blathering on about different "tracks" to fulfillment and the good life, as if we could disassociate ourselves from crushing failure in one area long enough to fully glory in our success in another. This is a "Well, my job sucks, but I'm really happy with my boyfriend right now" kind of mindset. Whenever I hear it I find myself thinking, "Yeah, OK. Good luck with that."

I realize it's supposed to be psychic balm: If you're not happy with your job, you can still enjoy your life. (Jobs don't define you, after all.) The correct response to this, like Citibank exhorting you to "Live Richly," is located somewhere between befuddlement and angry suspicion. You spend more than half your waking hours under that bank of fluorescent lights. You may even eat two meals a day there. If your work is unsatisfying, you might as well go right ahead and let that dissatisfaction seep down into the cracks.

And then let it rest there for a while. Then consider how much truth and beauty lies in compartmentalizing. Then ponder this notion: Your day at the office is not just about you and your life. Suppose you're a white male born on Park Avenue, and your dad got you a job at his old college friend's firm and you cleared $135,000 plus bonus your first year on the job. By reporting for work every day, you uphold both your family's class status and the status quo. Or maybe you're from Oklahoma, and your parents never finished college, or lived anywhere but Tulsa, but you wanted to work at *Rolling Stone,* and somehow you got the gig. Every time they glimpse the cover on the Barnes and Noble magazine rack, everyone who knows you from high school now has a different experience than before, and sometimes just passing that magazine rack makes them think twice about their own lives, and the choices that they made. Or maybe you grew up in a tenement on the Lower East Side, and you've decided to forgo that restaurant job and hang out on the stoop and sell pot instead.

Everyone's work choices have consequences far beyond our ordinary imagining. Then, I think it's necessary to ask yourself: Even if I hate my job, do I consider myself blessed? The wire-rimmed-glasses man stopped coming about a month after he first appeared. I like to think he went on to something better, something that doesn't involve literal garbage.

You will never see yourself as blessed, I believe, if you believe your day at the office is your story and your story alone. I tried that; it doesn't work. But regardless of how many hours you spend at the photocopier, if you see your standing there as part of a grander story, one in which you have historical agency, it's hard to see it as entirely dull. It's even possible to see it as an epic adventure—and yes, adventure in a swashbuckling, click your heels, skip-and-a-jump kind of way. So much is predetermined at birth: height, hair color, the arch of our eyebrows, our ability to carry a tune. We're born at a specific geographic location to specific parents and into a specific position on the socioeconomic ladder. None of the things we're born to may be to our liking. But we can try to change that last one—to trade up—and that's a most intriguing opportunity. If you can't love your work, you can at least fall in love with this process.

There's a passage in Fitzgerald's *This Side of Paradise* in which the protagonist, a privileged white student thinking deep thoughts at Princeton, is getting some advice. His mentor is trying to rouse the boy—he's twenty—to reapply himself to his studies. Of course, the Monsignor says, the boy was too smart to adopt whole theories of life, or of success, but, "If we can do the next thing, and have an hour a day to think in, we can accomplish marvels." Which is the fundamental message of the best success literature. Namely, that moving up means not believing that where you are is where you belong—while still, paradoxically, being grateful you have any place to stand at all. It means accepting that you have to start somewhere, and then you take steps, you do the next thing, then you keep doing the next thing until one day, you're in scoring position, and formerly dim ambitions become the stuff of your everyday life.

This next passage is a good example of the re-enchantment at work. It's sentimental and slight, and the fact that it speaks to me doesn't say much for my taste in poetry. It's Conrad Hilton, again. (Who never intended his great-grandchildren to be heiresses, incidentally. He left his money to religious charities. Long story.) Hilton's describing his first visit to Manhattan. He's thirty years old, and he's with a friend from the army:

> Bill and I took our embarkation leave in New York. This was my second metropolis, but most of the sagebrush had fallen from my ears . . . and New York didn't scare me a bit. It was bigger. It was taller. The people seemed in a greater hurry and there were more of them. While San Francisco had welcomed me, New York was hidden by an impenetrable armor. "I don't think an outsider could crack this town," I observed sagely to Bill as we strode along Broadway. "It has been done," he said, "but would be mighty difficult." This decided, we registered at the Astor and had a beer.

It has been done, and it's worth doing again. We need another hotel chain like we need tuberculosis, but still, plenty of buildings that need building and things that need fixing and stories that need recording in this world. So please get back to work.

Acknowledgments

ON MORE THAN ONE OCCASION I've wondered what I ever did to deserve Amanda Cook. She wields her formidable intellect with such easy grace, and I owe worlds to her optimism and faith in this book. There are also days I wonder if Melissa Flashman could possibly be cloned, and if so, how many of her we could make, and what geopolitical hotspots could use her talents most. And throughout the final days of writing and editing this book, Bryan Curtis lived around the corner from me. A crisper illustration that life is not fair, that sometimes you just get lucky, I have yet to experience.

I owe enduring gratitude also to Julie Doughty, for introducing me to *My Super Sweet 16* and for telling excellent stories with rare humor. To Barbara Richard, for free paperbacks and life-sustaining conversation. Erik Benson, who to this very day, dreams twenty-one-year-old snot-nosed dreams with me. Andrew Bradfield bought dinner and gave lectures on the dialectic. Andrew Semans makes beautiful movies. Alex Tilney provided invaluable encouragement, not to mention a good demonstration of what this "natural elite" business is all about. Thanks also to Paul Craig, for his experiments in socialism. And to Jenny Bent, for greater insight into what it's like to manage young minds.

I have learned a tremendous amount from working with former colleagues Isabelle Bleecker, Stephen Bottum, Jason Brantley, Nicole Caputo, Chris Charlotten, William Frucht, Marty Gosser, Bette Graber, Chris Greenberg, Amber Hoover, Stephen McNabb, John

Sherer, John Siciliano, David Steinberger, Diana Tesdale, Jennifer Thompson, and David Tripp. Ellen Garrison, Adam Pringle, and David Shoemaker were fantastic colleagues and remain better friends. As for former bosses, I am forever indebted to John Deen, who gave me my first job in New York. To Tina Pohlman and Edward Kastenmeier, who gave me my first job in publishing. Dawn Davis and Jenny Minton showed me how things get done. And Elizabeth Maguire pushed tremendous opportunities my way.

Deep gratitude also to friends, interviewees, fellow travelers, and all combinations thereof: Lara Lea Allen, Kevin Arnovitz, Timothy Aubry, Holly Bemiss, Rebecca Berlant, Raoul Bhavnani, Tom Bissell, Meredith Blum, Alicia Butler, Liz Cappelluti, Britt Carlson, Luke Dawson, Greg Dinkin, Ben Ehrenreich, Sarah Fan, Dan Firger, Gary Ford, Kristin Green, Carrie Hammer, Richard L. Harris, Vanessa Hartmann, Will Heinrich, Holly Henderson-Root, Evan Hughes, Andrew Hultkrans, Mikhail Iliev, David Johnson, Maris Kreizman, Jaime Leifer, Alexis Logsdon, Christian Lorentzen, Megan Lynch, Ben Lytal, Lorna Macfarlane, Dinaw Mengestu, Peter Neufeld, Benjamin Nugent, Heather Olander, Jamie Pallot, David Patterson, Amber Qureshi, Adrian Rodriguez, Thomas Scott, Ben Sigelman, Sam Stark, Alex Van Buren, Caspar van Vark, Dean Wareham, Patrick Whalen, Matthew Wilkin, Bunny Wong, and Aaron Zagha. If any portions of this book are remotely amusing, these people are the ones to thank.

Thanks also to Will Vincent, Lisa Glover (for wonderfully enthusiastic production editing), Andy Heidel, Sanj Kharbanda, Lori Glazer, Bridget Marmion, and everyone at Houghton Mifflin.

My parents, Stan and Karen Hustad, possess near inexhaustible reserves of grace and patience, and I'm so grateful for their support. This book would also not have been possible without the New York Public Library. That sounds like a standard-issue acknowledgments line, but it's accurate. I'm more convinced than ever that public libraries are the lifeblood of a sane, civil society, so all rich, successful people reading this: Please give to your local library. Relatively timely completion of this book was also aided by the New York–based staff of UPS, Friend House Asian Bistro, the music of The Replacements, and all the inspiration provided by the rest of the Johnson-Hustad cabal. What beautiful role models, everywhere I look.

Bibliography

Ailes, Roger, with Jon Kraushar. *You Are the Message: Getting What You Want by Being Who You Are.* New York: Currency Doubleday, 1988.

Roger Ailes is the president of Fox News Channel, and for that reason alone many of you will want to avoid this one. Which would be unfortunate, because a good political strategist is a good political strategist. Ailes has some interesting insights into how human alpha dogs assert dominance, and how first impressions reverberate far longer than you might imagine. Includes many stories that try to pinpoint Ronald Reagan's allure to voters, and a fascinating one about visiting Charles Manson in prison.

Aldrich, Nelson, Jr. *Old Money.* New York: Alfred A. Knopf, 1988.

An adult child of privilege, Nelson Aldrich wonders late in life why more Americans weren't rioting in the streets over the fact that he — and others like him — got to lap up luxury all his life just because he was born to filthy rich parents. From his preface: "Inherited wealth puts an egregious wrinkle in the nation's promissory claim to be a land of equal opportunity. One would have thought this might cause comment, if not outrage, but rarely in American history has there been much of either." Also, some theories about the symbiotic relationship between Old and New Money.

Alexander, James W. *The Merchant's Clerk Cheered and Counselled.* New York: Anson D. F. Randolph, 1856.

Part of a series. Before this one, James W. Alexander also wrote *Young Mechanics and Other Working Men* and *Youth in Pursuit of a Liberal Education.*

————, et al. *The Man of Business: Considered in His Various Relations.*
New York: Anson D. F. Randolph, 1857.

> Alexander felt the need to explain what this "business man" was all
> about, and what his growing influence would mean for American
> life. (That those two words hadn't yet been joined in the vernacular
> shows you how novel the concept was.)

Alger, Horatio, Jr. *Ragged Dick.* Edited and with an introduction by Carl
Bode. New York: Penguin Classics, 1986. Originally published by A. K.
Loring in 1868.

> Horatio Alger's first big success, *Ragged Dick* was first serialized in a
> magazine called *Student and Schoolmate.* Alger was a peculiar man
> described by many as mustachioed, "elfin," and asthmatic, who be-
> gan writing after his earlier career as a minister came to an abrupt
> end. He'd attended Harvard Divinity School, was ordained in 1864,
> but asked to leave his post sixteen months later when he was ac-
> cused of having "inappropriate relations" with two boys. Whatever
> the nature of the inappropriateness, Alger did show concerted inter-
> est in the fortunes of young boys. After *Ragged Dick,* he would go
> on to write one hundred more "boy's adventure stories," the bulk of
> which followed essentially the same plot line: Boy starts out sleeping
> in boxes on the street and eking out a meager living shining shoes,
> impresses a kindly benefactor who buys him a suit, then starts to get
> himself an education, saves his pennies, resists the temptations of
> drink and nightlife, and then through some mix of pluck, determi-
> nation, and freakish good luck, gets a job that sets him on the path
> to the middle class. (A sampling of his titles: *Andy Grant's Pluck;
> Ben the Luggage Boy; A Brave Boy's Fight for Fortune; The Errand
> Boy; Helping Himself; Joe the Hotel Boy; Making His Way: Frank
> Courtney's Struggle Upward; Mark the Match Boy; Only an Irish
> Boy: Andy Burke's Fortunes; Struggling Upward, or, Luke Larkin's
> Luck; The Young Bank Messenger; The Young Musician, or, Fight-
> ing His Way; The Young Salesman;* and, not least, *The Young Miner.*)
> While Alger's name has become synonymous with rags-to-riches sto-
> ries, most of his young heroes ended up not as millionaires but mere
> bank managers—comfortable, respectable, but hardly loaded.
>
> Alger was read widely by school kids in the last years of the
> nineteenth century but his popularity started to wane soon after that.
> Here's how John G. Cawelti (see below) described Alger's influence
> after the turn of the century: "Parents began to protest against what
> they considered the false values and unreality of the Alger stories,
> and a number of libraries removed his books from the shelves. They

were republished less often in the second decade of the 20th century, and, after World War I, sales declined rapidly. At the centennial of Alger's birth, in 1932, a survey of New York working children showed that less than twenty percent of the 'juvenile proletariat' had ever heard of Alger; only fourteen percent had read an Alger book; and, even more threatening, a 'large number' dismissed the theory of 'work and win' as 'a lot of bunk.' " By the 1940s, another survey put the number of children who had read an Alger book at about one in one hundred.

Amicus, C.B.C. *Hints on Life: And How to Rise in Society.* London: Longman, Brown, Green, and Longmans, 1845.
　　See chapter 1.

Bakan, Joel. *The Corporation: The Pathological Pursuit of Profit and Power.* New York: The Free Press, 2004.
　　Anyone frustrated with working for The Man should look up Bakan's discussion of corporations as "externalizing machines." The basic idea is that corporations externalize costs wherever possible, which means they let someone else pay the price for their practices. Economist Milton Friedman provided the example of a man whose white shirt gets dirty because a nearby factory hasn't placed proper emissions filters on its smokestacks. The owner of the shirt faces higher cleaning bills, while the factory saves money by not making the necessary plant upgrades that would have prevented the shirt from getting dirty in the first place. An example closer to home might be a company not bothering to change troublesome management practices as long as someone else covers employees' therapy bills.

Bell, Derrick. *Ethical Ambition: Living a Life of Meaning and Worth.* New York: Bloomsbury, 2002.

Berne, Eric. *Games People Play: The Psychology of Human Relationships.* New York: Grove Press, 1973.
　　See the Interlude.

Bolles, Richard N. *What Color Is Your Parachute? A Practical Manual for Job-Hunters and Career-Changers, 2005 edition.* Berkeley: Ten Speed Press, 2005.
　　The "best-selling job-hunting book in the world for more than three decades," according to its publisher. Bolles updates it every year. Not for those who can't take a little Christian-ese with their career counseling.

Borden, Richard C. *Public Speaking—As Listeners Like It!* New York: Harper & Brothers, 1935.

    This book and others—Dale Carnegie's, most notably—convinced me that proficiency in public speaking used to be a major preoccupation for your average American head-of-household. As more and more people have access to microphones, radio call-in shows, and public platforms, one might have expected rhetoric classes to become more, not less, popular—but that doesn't seem to be the case.

Brewster, Eugene V. *Success Secrets.* Brooklyn: The Caldron Publishing Company, (n.d.).

Bronson, Po. *What Should I Do with My Life? The True Story of People Who Answered the Ultimate Question.* New York: Random House, 2002.

Brooks, David. *Bobos in Paradise: The New Upper Class and How They Got There.* New York: Simon and Schuster, 2000.

    Not nearly as good as Barbara Ehrenreich's *Fear of Falling: The Inner Life of the Middle Class,* which you should read as a sophomore in college.

Brown, Helen Gurley. *I'm Wild Again: Snippets from My Life and a Few Brazen Thoughts.* New York: St. Martin's Press, 2000.

    As if someone rifled through Helen Gurley Brown's desk and published whatever slips of paper they happened across. Still, more entertaining than it has any right to be.

———. *Sex and the Office.* New York: Bernard Geis Associates, 1964.
See chapter 7.

———. *Sex and the Single Girl.* New York: Barricade Books, 1962.
See chapter 7.

Bruce, Lenny. *How to Talk Dirty and Influence People.* New York: Playboy Enterprises, 1965.

    In this quasi memoir, Lenny Bruce serves up an interesting lesson about defending yourself and the Master Mind. (Not, to be clear, that he ever references the Master Mind.) When Bruce was arrested on obscenity charges before going on stage at New York's Café Au Go Go in spring 1964, his friend Allen Ginsberg announced the formation of an "Emergency Committee against the Harassment of Lenny Bruce." Over eighty prominent personas—Paul Newman, Bob Dylan, Elizabeth Taylor, Richard Burton, Norman Mailer, Susan Sontag, John Updike, James Baldwin, George Plimpton, Henry Miller, Joseph Heller, Gore Vidal, Woody Allen, et al.—signed a petition in protest of the prosecution. Point is, it's always better to have your friends do the defending for you.

Burns, Joan Simpson. *The Awkward Embrace: The Creative Artist and the Institution in America.* New York: Alfred A. Knopf, 1975.
A fascinating examination of the careers of nine corporate executives, based on extensive interviews and skillfully interwoven with the author's analysis. It includes one of the more harrowing statements I came across in all my research. After posing the question of how much anyone chooses his or her particular role in life, Burns concludes: "My impression is that people usually have more limited choices than they think they do and that it is just as well for them as adolescents not to know this: that we arrive at major turning points only once or twice in our lives and, while there, make crucial decisions blindly, not knowing what prices we will have to pay later on." Her larger point, however, has more to do with how strong individualists can fit into, and manipulate, seemingly unmovable corporate structures.

Bush, David V. *Spunk: How to Lick Fear.* Mehoopany, Pennsylvania: self-published, 1924.
If you can possibly get your hands on this, perhaps at the nearest research library, do so. It's a pamphlet, really short, and fascinating in content and execution.

Bushnell, Candace. *Trading Up.* New York: Hyperion, 2003.

Callahan, David. *The Cheating Culture: Why More Americans Are Doing Wrong to Get Ahead.* New York: Harcourt, Inc., 2004.

Capote, Truman. *Breakfast at Tiffany's: A Short Novel and Three Stories.* New York: Random House, 1958.
It's quite different from the film starring Audrey Hepburn. (Rumor has it Capote initially wanted Marilyn Monroe to star.) Here the outsider angle is ramped up, as Holly Golightly's past is a little more Southern and a little more seedy. Required reading if figuring out how people reinvent themselves has you staring at the ceiling at night.

Carnegie, Andrew. *The Andrew Carnegie Reader.* Edited and with an introduction by Joseph Frazier Wall. Pittsburgh and London: University of Pittsburgh Press, 1992.

Carnegie, Dale. *How to Win Friends and Influence People.* New York: Simon and Schuster, 1936.
  See chapter 4.

Cawelti, John G. *Apostles of the Self-Made Man.* Chicago and London: The University of Chicago Press, 1965.
  An excellent academic (but nearly as dry as the word *academic* might lead you to believe) survey of early American success literature.

Citrin, James M., and Richard A. Smith. *The 5 Patterns of Extraordinary Careers: The Guide for Achieving Success and Satisfaction.* New York: Crown Business, 2003.

Ciulla, Joanne B. *The Working Life: The Promise and Betrayal of Modern Work.* New York: Times Books, 2000.

Cohen, Steve. *Win the Crowd: Unlock the Secrets of Influence, Charisma, and Showmanship.* New York: Harper Resource, 2005.

Collins, Jim. *Good to Great: Why Some Companies Make the Leap . . . and Others Don't.* New York: HarperCollins, 2001.

Corey, Lewis. *The House of Morgan: A Social Biography of the Masters of Money.* New York: AMS Press, 1930.

Covey, Stephen. *The 7 Habits of Highly Effective People: Restoring the Character Ethic.* New York: Simon and Schuster, 1989.
  See chapter 9.

Crisp, Quentin, and Donald Carroll. *Doing It with Style.* New York: Franklin Watts, 1981.

de Botton, Alain. *Status Anxiety.* New York: Pantheon Books, 2004.

Demarais, Ann, and Valerie White. *First Impressions: What You Don't Know About How Others See You.* New York: Bantam Books, 2004.

Dodd, Allen R., Jr. *The Job Hunter: The Diary of a "Lost" Year.* New York: McGraw Hill, 1964.
  A novel about a middle-management man being forced into early retirement. Told in the first person, *The Job Hunter* brims with existential regret: "I can skim over the rest of my career in a few sentences and that in itself may be one clue to the way it all ended," the protagonist muses. "We just put our heads down and started running and if you had asked us where we were heading we would have said,

'Why, up, of course.'" Dodd also vividly describes the anxiety older men face over the younger, slicker whippersnappers ("trained in the techniques") that their firm hires.

Dreiser, Theodore. *Sister Carrie.* New York: Doubleday, Page and Co., 1900.
One of the first American novels to paint the social and professional climber as selfish, amoral, and slutty. Although Carrie is not immoral in any kind of systematic or determined way—she's too thought-less. The early scenes of Carrie wandering the streets of turn-of-the-century Chicago, fresh off the train, looking for work, are the stuff of perfect costume drama.

Dyer, Wayne W. *Your Erroneous Zones.* New York: Funk & Wagnalls, 1976.

Engel, Peter. *The Over-Achievers.* New York: The Dial Press, 1976.
See chapter 8.

Epstein, Joseph. *Snobbery: The American Version.* Boston and New York: Houghton Mifflin Company, 2002.

Esenwein, J. Berg, and Dale Carnagey. *The Art of Public Speaking.* Springfield, Massachusetts: The Home Correspondence School, 1915.
See chapter 4. Dale Carnegie's first book—512 pages on how to give a speech (and live justly, ever aware of your civic responsibilities, at the same time). The book also offered a list of suggested subjects for speeches, including "Loss Is the Mother of Gain," "Helen Keller: Optimist," the "Blunders of Young Fogeyism," and, intriguingly, "The Blessing of Discontent."

Esquire Etiquette: A Guide to Business, Sports, and Social Conduct by the Editors of Esquire Magazine. New York and Philadelphia: J. B. Lippin-cott Company, 1953.
The gentlemen's magazine takes on etiquette. An excellent introduc-tion to office mores in the 1950s, *Esquire Etiquette* spills a lot of ink combating the prejudice that good manners were inherently effemi-nate, a matter of "delicate ladies tsk-tsking over the teacups in their Victorian bowers." On the contrary, *Esquire*'s editors claimed, their book was not about pleasing sexless women but about being more effectively manly. ("[I]t tells you how things *are* done, by practical men who know their way around in these high-pressure days.") The section on business manners stressed awareness of hierarchies and organization charts. They stressed that no organization was without

one, regardless of how democratic and casual it might look to the outside observer, and even if the chart was "only a sometimes thing, unwritten and undeclared."

Fitzgerald, F. Scott. *The Basil and Josephine Stories.* Edited with an introduction by Jackson R. Bryer and John Kuehl. New York: Scribner, 1973. Read the Basil stories if you're curious as to what Fitzgerald was like in high school. (Mostly unpopular, it turns out.)

———. *The Great Gatsby.* New York: Charles Scribner's Sons, 1925.

———. *This Side of Paradise.* New York: Charles Scribner's Sons, 1920.

Frank, Thomas. *The Conquest of Cool: Business Culture, Counterculture, and the Rise of Hip Consumerism.* Chicago: The University of Chicago Press, 1997. To give credit where credit is due: Frank's discussion of "conformity" led me to the Delmore Schwartz article quoted in chapter 6.

Franklin, Benjamin. *The Autobiography & Selections from His Other Writings.* New York: The Modern Library, 1944. Notable for its "Chart of Virtues," with which a young Franklin rated his progress toward becoming a more highly effective person.

Fry, Monroe. *Sex Vice and Business.* New York: Ballantine Books, 1959.

Fussell, Paul. *Class: A Guide Through the American Class System.* New York: Summit Books, 1983. Paul Fussell claims that when he told people he was working on a book about class, most people stared at him as if he'd just said, "I am working on a book urging the beating to death of baby whales using the dead bodies of baby seals." Dated in its observations, but worthwhile for its insights into ongoing American discomfort with the very subject.

———. *Uniforms: Why We Are What We Wear.* Boston and New York: Houghton Mifflin Company, 2002.

Gardiner, William. *Getting a Foothold.* Chicago: William Ruth Publishing Company, 1927.

Goffman, Erving. *The Presentation of Self in Everyday Life.* Garden City, New York: Doubleday, 1959. An important book but not one for the faint of heart. (The text is dense, and the sentences seemingly designed to resist ready comprehension.) Erving Goffman claimed that there were some things we did for no other reason than to make a point about ourselves — a point like I'm so popular/smart/easygoing/gentle/sophisticated. One might, for example, ask the receptionist "I'm sorry, but could you tell me where the restroom is?" not because you had to go or needed to check your makeup, but because you wanted to distinguish yourself from someone who'd just say, "Where's the toilet?" This is a dubious summary of only a small portion of the book, which is rightfully considered a classic.

Goldman, William. *Which Lie Did I Tell? More Adventures in the Screen Trade.* New York: Pantheon Books, 2000.
See chapter 8.

Goode, Kenneth M. *How to Turn People into Gold: A Book for Every Business Man.* New York and London: Harper & Brothers, 1929.
See chapter 4.

Goodman, Paul. *Growing Up Absurd: Problems of Youth in the Organized System.* New York: Random House, 1960.
A proper screed and a good encapsulation of teen angst in midcentury U.S.A.

Greeley, Horace. "An Address on Success in Business — for Students of Packard's Bryant & Stratton, New York Business College." New York: S. S. Packard, Publisher, 1867.

Grigg, John. *The American Chesterfield, or Way to Wealth, Honour, and Distinction; Being Selections from the Letters of Lord Chesterfield to His Son; and Extracts from the Other Eminent Authors, on the Subject of Politeness: with Alterations and Additions, Suited to the Youth of the United States; by a Member of the Philadelphia Bar.* Philadelphia: J. B. Lippincott & Co., 1860.
At one point in time, Lord Chesterfield was a household name in the United States — at least amongst the moneyed and highly educated. He comes up in Emily Post's books (she herself was once dubbed "Lady Chesterfield"), and you find scattered reference to him in advice books through the 1940s or so. Chesterfield's *Letters to His Son* was a posthumously published collection of missives in which an English nobleman, Lord Chesterfield, instructed his boy on how to endear himself to the powers that be. (The boy was apparently quite ham-fisted and awkward, and due to the circumstances of his birth — he was the result of an extramarital affair — couldn't count

on steady patronage like his father had.) The original publication includes a lot of pointers for someone who was going to be rubbing elbows with royalty and assorted hangers-on. *The American Chesterfield* merely retained the passages on all that was necessary to make a person "well received in the world," and its central argument was that poise and grace made every difference in your life chances. It may be hard to imagine now, but this was highly controversial stuff in its day. (Because in Puritan America and beyond, the only thing that was supposed to determine your chances was, of course, your moral standing and the grace of God.)

Haden-Guest, Anthony. *The Paradise Program: Travels Through Muzak, Hilton, Coca-Cola, Texaco, Walt Disney, and other World Empires*. New York: William Morrow, 1973.

Hagberg, Janet O. *Real Power: Stages of Personal Power in Organizations*. Revised edition. Salem, Wisconsin: Sheffield Publishing Company, 1994.

Hamper, Ben. *Rivethead: Tales from the Assembly Line*. New York: Warner Books, 1991.

Harris, Frank. *Latest Contemporary Portraits*. New York: The Macaulay Company, 1927.
     Frank Harris, an Irish journalist of some renown in his day, visits with VIPs and records his impressions.

Harris, Thomas A. *I'm OK—You're OK*. New York: Avon Books, 1973.

Head, Edith, with Joe Hyams. *How to Dress for Success*. New York: Random House, 1967.
     See chapter 6.

Hebdige, Dick. *Subculture: The Meaning of Style*. London: Methuen & Co., 1979.

Hechinger, Grace and Fred M. *Teen-Age Tyranny*. New York: William Morrow and Company, 1962.
     See chapter 6.

Herts, B. Russell. *Depreciations*. New York: Albert & Charles Boni, 1914.
     A strange little book that styled itself as a defense of "Art and Affectation." Herts's main beef was with what he perceived as a fetish for sincerity, or just doing what came "natural," among American youth. No one wanted to sound affected anymore, and Herts considered this an unfortunate development: "We are all in a state of 'be-

coming' and only he who stagnates can be completely consistent or supremely sincere."

Hill, Napoleon. *Napoleon Hill's A Year of Growing Rich: 52 Steps to Achieving Life's Rewards.* Edited by Matthew Sartwell, anthology assembled by Samuel A. Cypert. Foreword by W. Clement Stone. New York: Plume, 1993.
A posthumous collection of Hill-isms.

———. *Success Through a Positive Mental Attitude.* New York: Prentice Hall, Inc., 1960.
A retread of some themes from *Think and Grow Rich.*

———. *Think and Grow Rich,* revised edition. New York: Fawcett World Library, 1960.
See chapter 5. Besides the Master Mind, includes chapters on "The Mystery of Sex Transmutation" (arguing that highly sexed individuals are the most successful, as long as they channel that energy well), and "Imagination" (where he makes an interesting distinction between "creative imagination," where you concoct things from scratch, and "synthetic imagination," which is more about putting disparate thoughts and ideas together). Also well stocked with lists of assorted "Causes of Failure."

Hill, Rosa Lee. *How to Attract Men and Money.* Meriden, Connecticut: The Ralston Society, 1940.
This book could fill a chapter in itself—and the main reason it doesn't, besides the fact that it doesn't offer much good advice, is that it's a singular work of wholly deluded narcissism. It is painful to read. I found it mesmerizing. Rosa Lee Hill was Napoleon Hill's second wife. Napoleon married Rosa Lee—Beeland, was her maiden name—not long after the ink on his divorce papers was dry. (Hill's first wife, Florence, finally walked out on him after years of neglect.) Worried that family and former business associates would come after his assets, a prenuptial agreement was drafted that assigned to Rosa Lee nearly all of the proceeds from his books. Neither Napoleon nor Rosa Lee had much cash to speak of at the time, and during the first months of their marriage they in fact lived with Hill's son Blair and his wife in an apartment in New York's Hell's Kitchen.
When *Think and Grow Rich* became a huge success, Rosa Lee (who'd helped edit *Think and Grow Rich*) was able to secure a publisher for a book of her own. The book she wanted to give the world was *How to Attract Men and Money.* If anyone was curious as to how she, Rosa Lee, had got it all—a happy marriage, a beautiful lakeside

home in Florida, and a career that she loved—this book would tell
them how. The publisher's preface touched on many of the book's
themes, including the author's relationship to her "famous husband
with whom she is perfectly happy at all times," Rosa Lee's unswerv-
ing commitment to serving others, her peerless ability to infuse every waking moment with romance, and her sincere desire to help all
single women find the men of their dreams (and then help those men
to achieve financial success if they didn't enjoy it already). Still, Rosa
Lee was sensitive about possibly being dismissed as a woman simply
riding her husband's coattails. "I have been rewarded by more of
the blessings of life than most women ever enjoy," she wrote, "but
no one should jump at the conclusion that I have been blessed without effort on my part. My blessings are of my own creation." She
had never, she said, trampled upon the rights of anyone, and instead
sought only to help people find happiness.

How to Attract Men and Money was released in 1940, three
years after she and Napoleon were married, and the same year they
filed for divorce. The settlement left her with everything, including
Hill's latest Rolls-Royce.

Hilton, Conrad. *Be My Guest.* New York: Prentice Hall, 1957.
This book—Conrad Hilton's memoir—used to be placed in every
Hilton hotel room nightstand alongside the Gideon Bible.

Hilton, Paris, with Merle Ginsberg. *Confessions of an Heiress: A Tongue-
in-Chic Peek Behind the Pose.* New York: Simon and Schuster, 2004.

Holden, Mark. *The Use & Abuse of Office Politics: How to Survive and
Thrive in the Corporate Jungle.* New South Wales, Australia: Allen & Un-
win, 2003.

Howells, William Dean. *The Rise of Silas Lapham.* Boston and New
York: Houghton Mifflin Company, 1884.
William Dean Howells was the Tom Wolfe of his day. One of the first
major fictional treatments of the self-made American industrialist
(and his daughters, whose need for husbands provides a slender romantic subplot). Many pages are devoted to Boston real estate as well.

Huber, Richard M. *The American Idea of Success.* New York: McGraw-
Hill Book Company, 1971.

Iacocca, Lee, with William Novak. *Iacocca: An Autobiography.* New
York: Bantam Books, 1984.
The number one nonfiction bestseller in 1984 and 1985. Lee Iacocca
worked his way up through the sales department to run the Ford

Motor Company for several years, was spectacularly fired in 1978 by Henry Ford II, and then went on to help resuscitate the ailing Chrysler Corporation. Besides being a diverting account of life at the epicenter of twentieth-century corporate America, *Iacocca* includes the revelation that Iacocca was a huge advocate of Dale Carnegie Training (and sent dozens of Ford engineers there on the company dime), and that "except for periods of real crisis" he never worked on Friday nights or on weekends. The beginning pages feature many homespun odes to Iacocca's Depression-minded father (who at one time ran a hot-dog joint called the Orpheum Wiener House), including this diatribe about bad service: "He was really a bird about performing up to your potential—no matter what you did. If we went out to a restaurant and the waitress was rude, he'd call her over at the end of the meal and give her his standard little speech. 'I'm going to give you a real tip,' he'd say. 'Why are you so unhappy in this job? Is anyone forcing you to be a waitress? When you act surly, you're telling everybody you don't like what you're doing. We're out for a nice time and you're wrecking it. If you really want to be a waitress, then you should work at being the best damn waitress in the world. Otherwise, find yourself another line of work.'"

Johnson, Spencer. *Who Moved My Cheese? An A-Mazing Way to Deal with Change in Your Work and in Your Life.* New York: G. P. Putnam's Sons, 1998.

Jones, Edward E. *Ingratiation: A Social Psychological Analysis.* New York: Irvington Publishers, Inc., 1975.
    Much of *Ingratiation* found its way into chapters 2 and 8.

Jongeward, Dorothy. *Everybody Wins: Transactional Analysis Applied to Organizations.* Reading, Massachusetts: Addison-Wesley Publishing Company, 1973.

Jordan, William George. *The Majesty of Calmness.* New York: Fleming H. Revell Company, 1900.

Josephson, Matthew. *The Robber Barons: The Great American Capitalists, 1861–1901.* New York: Harcourt, Brace and Company, 1934.

Kaczynski, Theodore. "Industrial Society and Its Future." Full text available at http://en.wikisource.org./wiki/Industrial_Society_and_Its_Future. (Website accessed on August 6, 2007.)

Kanter, Rosabeth Moss. *Men and Women of the Corporation.* New York: Basic Books, 1977.

Karabel, Jerome. *The Chosen: The Hidden History of Admission and Exclusion at Harvard, Yale, and Princeton.* Boston and New York: Houghton Mifflin Company, 2005.

Kelly, Kevin H., ed. *Books That Shaped Successful People.* Minneapolis: Fairview Press, 1995.

> I pulled this one off the $1 cart at Strand Bookstore. It was compiled by a young man who, as a sophomore at San Diego State University, found himself wondering why more reading lists weren't being published. He wanted advice on what to read ("I didn't want to just grab any book from the shelf at random"). So he came up with a form letter that he sent around to a long list of people, people who'd established themselves in politics (John McCain, Arlen Specter), entertainment (Woody Harrelson, Mike Meyers, Henry Rollins, Bob Costas), business, and a few random others (Jane Goodall also got a letter). He asked everyone two questions: "What ten books do you feel a well-read, well-educated person should read or simply should have read? Also, what do you feel is the greatest book you have ever read?" *Books That Shaped Successful People* reproduced their responses in their entirety—including the headshots sent back with them. (The effect is like sifting through photocopies someone left on the Xerox.) The top fifteen responses, as Kelly tabulated them, were: The Bible, *Huckleberry Finn,* the works of Shakespeare, *Hamlet, War and Peace, The Iliad, The Odyssey, The Catcher in the Rye, The Sound and the Fury, The Prophet, The Brothers Karamazov, Gone With the Wind, The Grapes of Wrath, A Tale of Two Cities,* and *The Inferno.* Ayn Rand's *The Fountainhead* was a near miss. Richard M. Rosenberg, then chairman and CEO of BankAmerica, displayed refreshing candor when he said everyone should read Plato's *Images of the Cave* but his favorite book was *The Hunt for Red October.*

Kemp, Giles, and Edward Claflin. *Dale Carnegie: The Man Who Influenced Millions.* New York: St. Martin's Press, 1989.

Kepcher, Carolyn, with Stephen Fenichell. *Carolyn 101: Business Lessons from* The Apprentice's *Straight Shooter.* New York: Fireside, 2004.

> See chapter 10.

Kettle, James. *The est Experience.* New York: Kensington Publishing Corp., 1976.

> See the Interlude.

King, Larry, with Bill Gilbert. *How to Talk to Anyone, Anytime, Anywhere: The Secrets of Good Communication.* New York: Crown Publishers, 1994.

> Larry King, much to my surprise, has a pleasantly straightforward list of what he believes all the best talkers have in common: They have unorthodox takes on familiar subjects, a broad range of experiences and knowledge to draw upon, are enthusiastic about their lives and interested in others', "don't talk about themselves all the time," and tend to ask some variation of *why* a lot. Good talkers also, according to King, have the ability to empathize, a sense of humor (preferably self-deprecating), and a distinctive manner of speaking. When describing the ideal guest on his talk show, he also mentions the usefulness of "a chip on the shoulder."

Lang, Adele. *Confessions of a Sociopathic Social Climber.* New York: Thomas Dunne Books, 1998.

Layard, Richard. *Happiness: Lessons from a New Science.* New York: The Penguin Press, 2005.

Levenstein, Aaron. *Why People Work: Changing Incentives in a Troubled World.* New York: The Crowell Collier Press, 1962.

Livingston, J. Sterling. "Pygmalion in Management." *Harvard Business Review* 47 (4), 1969.

Luck, Martha S. *Instant Secretary's Handbook: A Reference Source and Guide for the Professional Secretary.* Mundelein, Illinois: Career Institute, 1972.

Lundberg, Ferdinand. *The Rich and the Super-Rich: A Study in the Power of Money Today.* Secaucus, New Jersey: Lyle Stuart Inc., 1988.

Mackay, Harvey. *Swim with the Sharks Without Being Eaten Alive.* New York: Morrow, 1988.

> The CEO of Mackay Envelope Company explains how he became the largest supplier of paper envelopes in North America. Essentially a more Minnesota version of Mark McCormack's *What They Don't Teach You at Harvard Business School.*

MacNaghton, Hugh. *Émile Coué: The Man and His Work.* New York: Dodd, Mead and Co., 1922.

> See chapter 2. MacNaghton, upon observing a Coué workshop, also

recommended reciting the following mantras for dealing with physical or psychic discomfort: "This Is Doing Me Good," "This Is Doing Me No Harm," and "It Is Passing."

Mager, N. H. and S. K. *A Guide to Better Living.* New York: Affiliated Publishers, 1957.
    One of their more provocative lines: "Liking people is something that grows on you, like a taste for olives or for good music."

Marden, Orison Swett. *Everybody Ahead, Or, Getting the Most Out of Life.* New York: Frank E. Morrison, 1916.
    See chapter 2.

————. *He Can Who Thinks He Can.* New York: Thomas Y. Crowell Company, 1908.

————. *How to Get What You Want.* New York: Thomas Y. Crowell Company, 1917.

————. *Little Visits with Great Americans, Or, Success Ideals and How to Attain Them.* New York: The Success Company, 1905.

————. *The Optimistic Life.* New York: Thomas Y. Crowell Company, 1907.

————. *The Progressive Business Man.* New York: Thomas Y. Crowell Company, 1913.

————. *Prosperity: How to Attract It.* New York: Success Magazine Corporation, 1922.

Mathews, William. *Getting On in the World: Or, Hints on Success in Life.* Chicago: S. C. Griggs and Company, 1874.
    See chapter 1.

McCabe, James D. *Great Fortunes.* New York, 1871.
    Capsule histories of the Astors, Vanderbilts, and other prominent families and bank accounts of the Gilded Age. Considering accusations that some of these fortunes were ill-gained, McCabe concluded that while "trickery and sharp practice" may allow someone to rise to great riches quickly, it was also generally true that such fortune "rarely stays with its possessors for more than a generation, if so long."

McCarthy, Mary. *The Company She Keeps*. New York: Harcourt Brace Jovanovich, Inc., 1942.

See chapter 6.

McCormack, Mark. *What They Don't Teach You at Harvard Business School: Notes from a Street-Smart Executive*. New York: Bantam Books, 1984.

Mark McCormack was essentially the first sports agent. He had a hunch that professional athletes might be able to help companies move product—crazy, I know—and signed a young Arnold Palmer as his first client in the early 1960s, sealing the deal with a simple handshake. It was a gesture that made them both millions. McCormack's small start-up grew into the enormous International Management Group, or IMG.

The key to his success, as he expounded at length in *What They Don't Teach You*, was good people sense. In contrast to rah-rah, swaggering corporate warrior stereotypes, McCormack actually chalked up his prowess in hard-rolling environments to what are traditionally seen as more feminine endowments: willingness to sit back and listen, perception into personality, and tuning in to the subtexts of any given conversation. "Talk less," he counseled up-and-coming MBAs. "Ask questions and then don't begin to answer them yourself." Rather than boast of your own accomplishments, McCormack wrote, it's best to shut up and let other people talk. At least that allowed you to pay closer attention—the essence of every successful negotiation, he felt.

McInerney, Jay. *Bright Lights, Big City*. New York: Random House, 1984.

Millhauser, Steven. *Martin Dressler: The Tale of an American Dreamer*. New York: Crown, 1998.

The up-by-your-bootstraps story meets magical realism.

Mills, C. Wright. *White Collar: The American Middle Classes*. New York: Oxford University Press, 1951.

A classic in the postwar pity-white-bread-professionals-because-they've-sold-their-souls-and-hardly-even-know-it genre. C. Wright Mills was an academic greatly concerned about the growth of bureaucracy in American life, and in particular how it grew in tandem with a new class of well-compensated automatons. They wandered down the hall in a conformist stupor, Mills thought, but they also—and worse—were in danger of losing the capacity for independent thought altogether. He took an oblique swipe at Dale Carnegie and his kind, painting their suggestions primarily as manipulation tools that management used to keep employees in line without having to act overtly authoritative. Employees didn't have to be told what to do anymore—they'd submitted themselves to brainwashing. "The formal aim, implemented by the latest psychological equipment, is to have men internalize what the managerial cadres would have them do, without their knowing their own motives, but nevertheless having them," Mills wrote. It's a stance that irks me, because it assumes a lot about people in certain professions (namely, that they weren't discerning or intelligent enough to act in their own best interest). Less interesting as a description of what these white-collar professionals, and their jobs, were actually like, and more interesting as a prime example of what it is—academic criticism of everyone who doesn't have a job in academia.

Molloy, John T. *Dress for Success.* New York: Peter H. Wyden, 1975. See chapter 6.

Moore, Doris Langley. *The Technique of the Love Affair; by a Gentlewoman.* New York: Simon and Schuster, 1928.

Morton, Agnes H. *Etiquette: Good Manners for All People; Especially for Those Who Dwell Within the Broad Zone of the Average.* Philadelphia: The Penn Publishing Company, 1892.

Nierenberg, Gerald I., and Henry H. Calero. *How to Read a Person Like a Book.* New York: Hawthorn Books, Inc., 1971.
One of the first major works exclusively devoted to the importance of reading body language. *How to Read a Person Like a Book* was derived from painstaking analysis of thousands upon thousands of hours of videotaped seminars and negotiating sessions. (The technology that made this all possible was relatively new and exciting—videocassettes had only been around since the late 1960s.) Gerald I. Nierenberg was a lawyer with a reputation as a master negotiator, and he wanted to help people in business, sure, but also to bring mankind a little closer to world peace. He felt that evaluating body language correctly could stop talks from deteriorating, and what was needed was a careful monitoring of physical gestures and a sincere willingness to try to turn things around if relations got tense.
The key to decoding body language correctly was not to get distracted by *individual* gestures and mannerisms, Nierenberg claimed, but rather to look for "gesture-clusters," or a series of related movements and expressions that together betrayed a person's true, un-

spoken feelings. (Nonverbal clues were always more reliable, he'd found.) Hand-to-face gestures—Rodin's thinker pose was one variation—could mean trouble. See someone pinching the bridge of her nose? She's most likely attempting to solve a difficult problem (so best to keep quiet for a while, and not attempt to nudge her out of her situation). See someone orient his body in the direction of the door? He wants you to stop talking so he can leave. If you find it at a used bookstore, buy it for the illustrations alone.

Overstreet, H. A. *Influencing Human Behavior.* New York: The People's Institute Publishing Company Incorporated, 1925.

A book that profoundly influenced Dale Carnegie's thinking. H. A. Overstreet was a professor and head of the philosophy department at the College of the City of New York, and this book was derived from some of his lectures to what sounds (from his description in the preface) very much like an adult education class held at the New School for Social Research. There are many passages illustrative of his tone and outlook, but I'll limit myself to this one, which is essentially a rousing defense of the whole enterprise suggested by the title: "We are simply trying to come to some manner of understanding . . . Life is many things; it is food-getting, shelter-getting, playing, fighting, aspiring, hoping, sorrowing. But at the centre of it all it is this: it is the process of getting ourselves believed in and accepted. That is what love-making is. To make love to one who will not be persuaded, is a fool's game, albeit much indulged in. That is what trading is. The man who can persuade no one to believe in his goods is a business failure. That is what preaching is. The preacher who is a joke to his pew-holders is either a coxcomb or a fool. . . . To get people to think with us! It is an art—the supreme art."

He continues: "Must this art—the major art of life—be simply hit or miss? Or may we be fairly intelligent about it?" And were people to become intelligent about it? "Not by talking vaguely about goals and ideals; but by finding out quite specifically what methods are to be employed if the individual is to 'get across' to his human fellows, is to capture their attention and win their regard, is to induce them to think and act along with him—whether his human fellows be customers or clients or pupils or children or wife; and whether the regard which he wishes to win is for his goods, or ideas, or artistry, or a great human cause."

Packard, Vance. *The Status Seekers: An Exploration of Class Behavior in America and the Hidden Barriers That Affect You, Your Community, Your Future.* New York: David McKay Company, Inc., 1959.

Long out of print but shouldn't be, because *The Status Seekers* stands up pretty well over time. Vance Packard was a pop sociologist who sold tons of books but never achieved much critical cachet.

Parris, Crawley A. *Mastering Executive Arts and Skills.* West Nyack, New York: Parker Publishing Company, 1969.

Peale, Norman Vincent. *A Guide to Confident Living.* New York: Prentice Hall, 1948.
The warm-up to *The Power of Positive Thinking.*

———. *The Power of Positive Thinking.* New York: Prentice Hall, 1952.
A sensation in its day and a strange, often misunderstood book now. Overall, *The Power of Positive Thinking* is an awkward marriage of New Thought, Dale Carnegie–isms, and "practical Christianity." The title has become a catch phrase, and is usually called up only to dismiss all exhortations to look on the bright side as naive, Pollyanna-ish, laissez-faire drivel. Which misses Peale's central point, I think. (It's a deeply flawed book, but not for those reasons.) Peale does indeed call for eliminating negative thoughts from your mind, but not in the sense that you'd then proceed to accept the world's injustices or ignore your problems in the hope that they'd just go away on their own. On the contrary, Peale, a minister at the Marble Collegiate Church in New York City, essentially proposed positive thinking as a means to an end. He believed that if you felt perpetually defeated by adverse circumstances, you would not be likely to screw up the courage to change those circumstances. You'd give yourself over to cynicism or listless despair. If, however, you believed yourself to have *some* ability to affect circumstances, you'd be more likely to try to do so. Positive thinking was less a sop for the brokenhearted than a course steering you toward greater influence in the world. (It might help to remember that Peale felt the need to be preaching this *long* before the self-esteem movement came along. His readers did not grow up being told they could achieve anything they dreamed of—in fact, Peale refers repeatedly to a prevailing inferiority complex among Americans.) The tone of the book is alternately strident and wistful, and Peale includes some prescriptions completely at odds with the mainstream, both then and now: Fifteen minutes a day of total silence, for one. No talking, no reading, no writing, no radio, no music, no nothing. This, Peale claimed, would allow you to empty your mind of all the inane, self-defeating chatter that usually ran through it.
The Power of Positive Thinking is also a good read if you're looking for Hitchcockian set pieces about the midcentury business

traveler. Most of Peale's illustrative stories take place in airless hotel rooms, packed convention halls, over hurried diner-counter lunches, and feature grim-faced executives, dressed in beige raincoats, all waiting anxiously for their trains.

Percy, Walker. *Lost in the Cosmos: The Last Self-Help Book.* New York: Farrar, Straus and Giroux, 1983.
Read his novel *The Moviegoer* instead.

Peter, Dr. Laurence J., and Raymond Hull. *The Peter Principle: Why Things Always Go Wrong.* New York: William Morrow and Co., 1969.
See chapter 7.

Podhoretz, Norman. *Making It.* New York: Random House, 1967.

Post, Edwin. *Truly Emily Post.* New York: Funk & Wagnalls Company, 1961.
A surprisingly well-told account of Emily Post's childhood, marriage, and career. Unusually clear-sighted, considering it's about the author's mother.

Post, Emily. *Etiquette.* New York: Funk & Wagnalls Company, 1922.
See chapter 3.

———. *Etiquette.* Tenth edition. New York: Funk & Wagnalls Company, 1960.
See chapter 3.

———. *How to Behave — Though a Débutante: Opinions by Muriel; As Overheard by Emily Post.* Garden City, New York: Doubleday, Doran & Company, 1928.
A satire of the Paris Hiltons of her day.

Potter, Stephen. *Lifemanship: Or, The Art of Getting Away with It Without Being an Absolute Plonk.* New York: Henry Holt and Co., 1951.
Stephen Potter was quite well known, on both sides of the Atlantic, in the years immediately following publication of *Lifemanship* and *One-Upmanship.* (The first in his series, *Gamesmanship,* focused exclusively on winning without cheating at sports, so I haven't included it here.) All these titles were sold as satire, but as the *Washington Post* said of *Lifemanship* in particular, they were manuals worth committing to memory because, people tending to the perverse as they do, you might encounter someone who actually thought like the sinister glad-handers that Potter skewers.
All of Potter's humor is derived from the central premise that

some people take it on faith that every human interaction has a winner and a loser. If you weren't one up, you were one down, and being one down was bad, but unless you wanted to be a complete social pariah, you had to be very subtle about your methods for winning. The goal of the committed Lifeman was therefore "intimidation by conversation," and the question before him was always and ever, "how to make the other man feel that something has gone wrong, however slightly." There were several ways to accomplish that nagging feeling in the other man, like taking a long look at your shoes whenever he was talking. Potter also described how you could induce an awkward silence, drop fabricated quotes into a conversation apropos of nothing, and generally make someone feel uncomfortable. If your competition were to tell a funny story, One-Upmanship dictated that you never followed it with a funny story of your own. The best reaction, Potter said, was a stony silence. The businessman committed to One-Upmanship wasn't interested in making any real contribution, but instead worked hard at appearing friendly while actually undermining everyone he could. The "Mona Lisa Ploy," for example, entailed sitting at the conference table doodling, a faint hint of a smile deepening the corners of one's mouth, whenever anyone tried to make a legitimate point.

Potter's milieu was smoke-filled drawing rooms in English countryside mansions—the kind of *Masterpiece Theatre* scenes in which a meaningfully arched eyebrow spelled the end of someone's life as they knew it. But his prose and many of his references—Harvard, Stanford, salesmanship, and a fictitious Office of American Enthusiasm—show he knew his way around American success literature, and for all his joking, Potter touched a nerve. One reviewer couldn't figure out how to characterize his work and came up with "mock-serious."

————. *One-Upmanship: Being Some Account of the Activities and Teaching of the Lifemanship Correspondence College of One-Upness and Gameslifemastery.* New York: Henry Holt, 1952.
See above.

Price, Judith. *Executive Style.* New York: The Linden Press/Simon and Schuster, 1980.
A coffee-table book of photographs of expensively decorated executive office suites. Judith Price believed that success was partly achieved through interior design.

Rancic, Bill, with Daniel Paisner. *You're Hired: How to Succeed in Business and Life.* New York: Harper Business, 2004.
See chapter 10.

Ritt, Michael J., Jr., and Kirk Landers. *A Lifetime of Riches: The Biography of Napoleon Hill.* New York: Dutton, 1995.

Schulberg, Budd. *What Makes Sammy Run?* New York: Random House, 1941.

Sears, F. W. *How to Attract Success.* New York: Centre Publishing Co., 1914.
    More New Thought.

Shinn, Florence Scovel. *Your Word Is Your Wand: A Sequel to The Game of Life and How to Play It.* New York: self-published, 1928.
    More New Thought.

Shipler, David K. *The Working Poor: Invisible in America.* New York: Alfred A. Knopf, 2004.

Sinetar, Marsha. *Do What You Love, the Money Will Follow: Discovering Your Right Livelihood.* New York: Dell Publishing, 1989.

Sittenfeld, Curtis. *Prep.* New York: Random House, 2005.

Slater, Robert. *No Such Thing as Over-Exposure: Inside the Life and Celebrity of Donald Trump.* Upper Saddle River, New Jersey: Prentice Hall, 2005.
    See chapter 10.

Smith, Adam. *The Theory of Moral Sentiments.* London: Richard Griffin and Co., 1854.
    Adam Smith wrote this book before he wrote *The Wealth of Nations,* the bible of capitalism. For an introduction to the ideas Smith plays around with in this book—specifically, the how and why of ambition and keeping up appearances—you might want to consult Erving Goffman's *The Presentation of Everyday Life,* where it's cited extensively.

Stengel, Richard. *You're Too Kind: A Brief History of Flattery.* New York: Simon and Schuster, 2000.

Strainchamps, Ethel, ed. *Rooms with No View: A Woman's Guide to the Man's World of the Media.* New York: Harper & Row, 1974.
    See chapter 7. Nancy Weber's account of working for Helen Gurley Brown at *Cosmopolitan* comes from this anthology.

Tichy, Noel M., and Stratford Sherman. *Control Your Destiny or Someone Else Will: How Jack Welch Is Making General Electric the World's Most Competitive Corporation.* New York: Currency Doubleday, 1993.

Traube, Elizabeth G. *Dreaming Identities: Class, Gender, and Generation in 1980s Hollywood Movies.* Boulder, Colorado: Westview Press, 1992.

Tressler, Irving. *How to Lose Friends and Alienate People: A Burlesque.* New York: Stackpole Sons, 1937.

> The first parody of *How to Win Friends and Influence People,* published within months of its inspiration. Irving Tressler styled himself as the head of the "Institute of Human Relations Up To a Certain Point," and pitched this book as the antidote to the *How to Win Friends* movement. His book would tell you how to speak at length about your physical ailments, deliver jokes, laugh loudly at those jokes, and generally get people to start leaving you alone. (If you want to get the most out of this book, there is one major requirement: "*a deep, driving desire to want to make others dislike you just as much as you dislike them, a vigorous determination to recognize the fact that most people are about as interesting as a semi-annual report of the U.S. Gypsum Co.*") Interestingly, it was dedicated to Adolf Hitler ("a Man Who Doesn't Need to Read It").

Trimble, Vance H. *Sam Walton: The Inside Story of America's Richest Man.* New York: A Dutton Book, 1990.

> The "inside story" here is a biography so admiring it glows. Vance H. Trimble gives Sam Walton—father to Wal-Mart—the humble beginnings treatment by directly comparing Walton to Tom Sawyer (and Walton's childhood best friend and high school sweetheart to Huck Finn and Becky Thatcher, respectively).

Troward, Thomas. *The Edinburgh Lectures on Mental Science.* New York: Dodd, Mead and Company, 1909.

> More New Thought.

Trump, Donald J., with Meredith McIver. *Trump: Think Like a Billionaire.* New York: Random House, 2004.

> See chapter 10.

Trump, Donald J., with Tony Schwartz. *Trump: The Art of the Deal.* New York: Random House, 1987.

> See chapter 10.

Wakeman, Frederic. *The Hucksters.* New York: Rinehart, 1946.

> See chapter 6.

Walters, Barbara. *How to Talk with Practically Anybody About Practically Anything.* New York: Doubleday, 1970.

> See chapter 3.

Wareham, John. *Secrets of a Corporate Headhunter.* New York: Atheneum, 1980.
See chapters 8 and 10.

Warhol, Andy. *The Philosophy of Andy Warhol.* New York: Harcourt Brace Jovanovich, 1975.

Welch, Jack, with John A. Byrne. *Jack: Straight from the Gut.* New York: Warner Books, 2001.

Wharton, Edith. *The Custom of the Country.* New York: Charles Scribner's Sons, 1913.

————. *The House of Mirth.* New York: Charles Scribner's Sons, 1905.

Whistler, James McNeill. *The Gentle Art of Making Enemies.* London: William Heinemann, 1890.

Whitaker, Leslie, and Elizabeth Austin. *The Good Girl's Guide to Negotiating: How to Get What You Want at the Bargaining Table.* New York: Little, Brown, 2001.

Wolfe, Tom. *The Bonfire of the Vanities.* New York: Farrar, Straus and Giroux, 1987.

Wortley, Edward. *Impulses to Success: What the Successful Men of Today Read Yesterday, an Anthology.* New York: Park Row Publishing House, 1957.

Young, Michael. *The Rise of the Meritocracy.* New Brunswick and London: Transaction Publishers, 1994. Originally published by Thames and Hudson in 1958.

Young, Toby. *How to Lose Friends and Alienate People.* Cambridge, Massachusetts: Da Capo Press, 2002.
Not coincidentally, Toby Young is the son of Michael Young (just above).

Index